Brother Mathias

Brother Mathias

FOUNDER OF THE LITTLE BROTHERS OF THE GOOD SHEPHERD

Carol N. Lovato

Our Sunday Visitor Publishing Division
Our Sunday Visitor, Inc.
Huntington, Indiana 46750

International Standard Book Number: 0-87973-485-X
Library of Congress Catalog Card Number: 86-62454

Cover design by James E. McIlrath
Photo by Pam Bauer/EXTENSION Magazine

PRINTED IN THE UNITED STATES OF AMERICA

485

For Ben

PHOTO CREDITS: The photographs appearing on the third through sixth pages of the picture section depicting Brother Mathias Barrett's years in Montreal, Quebec, have been made available by the Archives of the Hospitaller Order of St. John of God, Canada. The remaining photos are from the Archives of the Little Brothers of the Good Shepherd in Albuquerque, New Mexico. The author and publisher are grateful to the Brothers of St. John of God and the Little Brothers of the Good Shepherd for the use of these photographs.

Contents

Acknowledgments 9

Foreword by Timothy Cardinal Manning 11

Introduction by Archbishop Robert Sanchez 12

Prologue 14

Chapter 1 / Irish Childhood 19

Chapter 2 / St. John of God 30

Chapter 3 / Montreal 42

Chapter 4 / Los Angeles 59

Chapter 5 / Boston 75

Chapter 6 / Back in Ireland 93

Chapter 7 / The Good Shepherd 101

Chapter 8 / The First Decade 122

PHOTO SECTION 140

Chapter 9 / Expansion 157

Chapter 10 / Brothers 172

Chapter 11 / Organization 189

Chapter 12 / The 1960s 201

Chapter 13 / Into the Seventies 215

Chapter 14 / Sorrow and Acclaim 231

Appendixes
   • Names and Locations 249
   • Sources 250
   • Chapter Notes 255

Acknowledgments

THIS BOOK WOULD NOT HAVE BEEN POSSIBLE WITHOUT THE AS-
sistance and support of a large number of people. I am indebted to
them for their efforts and for their loyalty to the work.

In particular, I would like to thank my academic advisor, Dr.
Frank Szasz, who edited the manuscript and provided major support
throughout the two years it took to write it. The manuscript crossed
the Atlantic Ocean several times. In spite of his rigorous schedule in
England, Dr. Szasz gave me many hours of his time. His guidance
was an inspiration.

The Brothers of the Hospitaller Order of St. John of God went
above and beyond my hopes to provide me with everything I needed.
They were generous with their time, supported me in my fact-finding
trip to Los Angeles, and edited the final draft of the book.

The Little Brothers of the Good Shepherd followed the progress of
the story of their founder's life with great interest. I am deeply grateful for everything they did to make my job easier.

In addition, the members and past presidents of various organizations (particularly the Albuquerque Ladies' Auxiliary and Men's Advisory Board) and others connected with Brother Mathias Barrett
and his endeavors gave me valuable insights into his life.

In particular, Aldo Vaio, Kathryn Kelly, Noel Martin, Don and
Barbara Brennan, Richard Krannawitter, Thomas Mescall, Monsignor Francis O'Byrne, Celina Raff, and Peter Moughan were of great
help to me.

Special thanks go to the many archivists who were most coopera-
tive and helpful. Monsignor Francis J. Weber of the archdiocese of
Los Angeles gave me an entire day of his time. Sister Loyola Maestas
of the archdiocese of Santa Fe copied several years' accumulation of
material to expedite my research. James M. O'Toole of the archdiocese of Boston sent me copies of letters by Cardinal Richard Cushing
to Brother Mathias. Brother Michael Carlyle, archivist of the Little
Brothers of the Good Shepherd, worked with me an entire week in
Ohio and provided me with enough information to write two books.
Brother Anthony Scully, Hospitaller Order of St. John of God archivist in Ojai, California, took three days from his work to assist me.
Because of my limited time in California, he read documents and
selected the most valuable materials. Jean Fournier, historian-archi-

9

vist of the Hospitaller Order of St. John of God in Canada, sent copies of several hundred documents. These were of tremendous value in reconstructing the Montreal years. My French translators were Colleen Wilson, Anna Vance, and Christina Gutierrez.

I am also grateful to Cardinal Timothy Manning for the foreword to this work. Archbishop Robert Sanchez provided his loyal support and the introduction. Daniel Donohue of the Dan Murphy Foundation gave me several hours of his time and evaluated the material on Los Angeles. Brother Camillus Harbinson, B.G.S., Brother General, was supportive throughout the entire project and made possible my access to the order's archives. Brother Pierluigi Marchesi, Prior General of the Hospitaller Order of St. John of God in Rome, was most gracious and helpful to me. Brother Hugo Stippler, O.H., Provincial of Los Angeles, gave me tremendous encouragement and made the arrangements for my Los Angeles trip. Brother Anthony Jedziniak, B.G.S., was the quiet man-behind-the-scenes for two years, supplying me with copies of articles, photographs, and endless cups of coffee. Brother Jerome McCarthy, B.G.S., provided me with transportation and photocopying of documents. Brother Kevin Carr, B.G.S., shared his ninety-four years of wisdom with me during one memorable interview in June, 1984. Brother Laurier Ouellette, O.H., of Montreal, sent me a book and a tape of his recollections. Brother Thomas Byrne, B.G.S., sent me tapes of his conversations with Brother Mathias, Christmas cards, and raffle tickets for Waterford crystal, which, by the way, I never won.

Brother Benignus Callan, O.H., and Brother Finbarr Murphy, O.H., read the St. John of God sections of the manuscript. Demetria Martínez and Robert Bradley read the entire final draft. George Bello, principal of Albuquerque High School, Opal Stafford of the Business Department, and Marge Hicks of the English Department supported me in the mechanics of preparing the manuscript and buoyed me up with humor and encouragement.

To the many other people who assisted me in putting this book together, I am deeply grateful. I hope that in this remarkable story they will find part of themselves. It is a story that needs to be told, but without the help of those who participated with me in its creation, it would never have been written. God bless you.

— C.N.L.

Foreword

IT IS FITTING, SURELY, THAT SOME MEMOIR OF BROTHER MATHIAS Barrett should be placed on record. He walked out from the pages of the Gospel and lived its reality among us. The beatitudes were a backdrop for his personhood, his faith, and his dedication to the poor. He has in his heart that love that exceeds the eloquence of men and angels, that excels the gifts of prophecy and tongues, without which philanthropy — and even martyrdom — would be empty gestures.

From the moment of his arrival in Los Angeles, I was a witness of his single-minded dedication to the poor. In his simplicity he vaulted the barriers of officialdom. In a city where stardom is measured by glamour, affluence, and public relations, he entered by a lowly door and began the foundations of the work that has consumed him since.

This biography does not beatify Brother Mathias, nor should it do so. Let the evening of his life be serene, and when the curtain falls, may he shine from everlasting to everlasting.

Timothy Cardinal Manning
FORMER ARCHBISHOP OF LOS ANGELES

Introduction

A PERSON IS CALLED FAVORED IF DURING HIS LIFETIME HE HAS A SPE-
cial blessing in terms of meeting a person who is considered both a
saint of God and a legend in his own lifetime. To meet two such people
in one's life is considered to be a miracle, and I thank God for that
miracle in my life.

It has been my special pleasure and blessing to have met and
shared thoughts and feelings with two of the most outstanding people
that I have known in my lifetime: Mother Teresa of Calcutta and
Brother Mathias Barrett of Albuquerque, New Mexico. The former is
known throughout the world. The latter is known and beloved by
many in the United States, especially in New Mexico. It was my privilege to have met and talked with Mother Teresa on two separate occasions: once during the Eucharistic Congress in Philadelphia in 1976
and again at the International Synod of Bishops in Rome in 1980. Because of these two occasions Mother Teresa has become endeared to
my heart, and I pray for her daily.

Brother Mathias Barrett has been in my mind, my heart, and my
prayers for nearly thirty years. I first heard of Brother Mathias and
of his compassionate work for the poor and the needy when I was a
seminarian at the Immaculate Heart of Mary Seminary in Santa Fe
in 1953-54. However, it was not until my return from Rome in 1960 as a
newly ordained priest that I began to form a love, admiration, and
deep respect for this dedicated man of God. Since that time my admiration has continued to grow from year to year, watching and admir-
ing the wonderful works of God that he has continued to do for the
poor and the needy. In 1974, it was my privilege to assume the respon-
sibilities as the tenth archbishop of Santa Fe. This responsibility
brought me into a relationship with Brother Mathias in which I found
myself blessed to be able to work alongside him and to support his
magnificent vision of service to those in need. It soon became apparent to me that Brother Mathias was not only a humble and hard-
working servant of God, but more. He is a man blessed and possessed
with a very keen vision of bringing to reality those dreams that are
necessary to serve God's people at a particular time in life. He seems
to be a man beloved by all. His constant smile and wit charm the general public. His holiness and humility warm the hearts of those
closest to him, and his boundless energy at his age astounds us all.

This book about the life of Brother Mathias, dear reader, will fill your heart with a sense of goodness and peace. You will thank God that we live at a time when such outstanding men and women are still raised up to do the work of the Lord. You will smile with those who have smiled before you, and you will shed a tear in recognizing the goodness and simplicity of this man. I am grateful to Carol Lovato's sensitivity and love for Brother Mathias. These qualities have enabled her to compose a wonderful biography describing the life and work of Brother Mathias. How proud we are! The world will continue to admire and to love Mother Teresa of Calcutta, and we who are privileged to know and love Brother Mathias will continue to thank God for this privilege. God bless you, Brother Mathias, for what you have accomplished and God bless you continually for what you are and will do.

Most Reverend Robert F. Sanchez
ARCHBISHOP OF SANTA FE

Prologue

"ONCE UPON A TIME. . ." OLD TALES WOULD OFTEN BEGIN WITH these words, and the reader was thus prepared for a chronicle of fabulous and extraordinary events. In our time, skepticism has edged out the magical, and pessimism has eroded our ability to believe in the extraordinary. Yet, in the life of Brother Mathias Barrett, founder of the Little Brothers of the Good Shepherd, one finds all of these attributes.

A simple yet profound man, Brother Mathias has moved men in ways reminiscent of the "Great Age of Faith." Never doubting, never allowing obstacles to defeat him, or even to slow him down, he has forged an impressive organization of houses for the transient, the retarded, the elderly, and the derelict in seventeen American cities, as well as in Canada, England, and Ireland. Brother Mathias has raised poor men from the gutters, has cared for the rejected of society, the desperate, the unloved, the alcoholic, and has done so without passing judgment on anyone. He has been available at all hours of the day and night for seventy years of religious life. For this, he has been honored by many private organizations, governments, fraternal societies, and religious entities. He has been called the "Mother Teresa of America," a living saint. Yet, the man himself, eighty-six years old at this writing, is unaffected by the publicity. His clothes are simple, even threadbare; his face is worn, and he can hardly see. But he radiates a presence that observers find compelling.

Brother Mathias has said that he leaves the care of the soul to others and that all he has done in his years of service is provide food, clothing, and shelter. But it is a disclaimer that says more about his humility than it does about the actual facts. Hundreds of people have sought him out for advice. Perhaps thousands of men have felt the power of this remarkable, homely, nearsighted Irish Brother. Many have joined him and his community and have tried to live out the vision of life as he does: to view the poor as deserving of "Charity without Limit."

Brother Mathias currently lives at the motherhouse of his religious order in Albuquerque, New Mexico. The several buildings that comprise the motherhouse are of red brick construction, and they display the middle-class solidity popular during the first quarter of the century. There is a small garden in front, ringed with hedges. A sign announces that every blade of grass represents a benefactor. One climbs several steps to reach the front stone porch. There, a second sign proclaims that "Jesus is Master of this House," and a third, on the door itself, says, "Enter here to holiness and happiness." Everything has a slightly dilapidated look. A large plaster statue of the Good Shepherd stands in the front yard holding a light bulb, and a wooden cross looks down from the roof on visitors.

Inside, the chapel (a former dining room) has been fitted with long wooden pews and a small, wooden seat with a kneeler. This latter is Brother Mathias's accustomed spot and is placed between the radiator and the door. The altar, imposing for such a small room, is a made-over fireplace. On it are positioned six large candlesticks, like queens from some outsized chess set. Overhead, there is a gilded canopy, to which a wooden dove is attached, its claws gripping painted rays of the sun, its eyes fixed on a neon light that illuminates the altar below. A large wooden table is covered with a heavy green cloth on which are emblazoned the words "I am the Good Shepherd." Visible through the legs of the table is a reproduction of the Last Supper by da Vinci, which, on closer observation, turns out to be a jigsaw puzzle glued to a piece of cardboard. This was the project of a member of the second judicial district bench. A figure of the Virgin Mary, a bouquet of chrysanthemums clustered at her feet, holds out her hands as if to embrace visitors. Under the small table on which she stands, there lies a bowl of water, put there for neighborhood cats who arrive from time to time through the open window behind her.

In the interior of the house is the present dining room, with brick walls that look as if they were designed more for the outside than for the inside. Here, extra chairs are stored; and here, photographs, framed awards, laminated newspaper clippings, plaques, and letters are all arranged on the walls without any obvious order. The room has the air of a museum. Visitors sit here and are served breakfast, or coffee and cookies, or sandwiches, as the need requires.

Brother Mathias greets all guests with the same warmth. His hands grasp those of the person to whom he is speaking, and his gnomish countenance lights up, especially at the sound of children's voices. For them, there is often a statue of a saint, a holy card, or a picture of the Sacred Heart in a little plastic envelope. The heavy lenses of Brother Mathias's spectacles seem more a hindrance on his face than a help. His sparse hair has become quite white and wispy. He wears the white habit of the order, with the rosary at the waist and the cowl in back, which bobs up and down when he is in animated conversation.

One Sunday in September, 1984, I observed an incident that il-

15

lustrates the unique nature of Brother Mathias. Several visitors were talking in the hall between the chapel and the kitchen, beside a red-carpeted staircase that led to an upper level of the house. Three small children were milling around, one barely a year old. This child had been chortling and singing during the Mass, and now Brother Mathias was asking, "Where is the little one who was singing?" The child was held out by his mother and cries of delight followed from both Brother Mathias and the infant. Then, wriggling from his mother's arms, the baby worked his way to the floor and headed for the stairs. Up the faded carpet he went on all fours. To the amazement of the audience, Brother Mathias soon followed, going up the stairs on all fours and encouraging his little companion. The child had a head start and was swift and determined, but so was Brother Mathias. They reached the landing in a dead heat. Then, catching hold of the rope that rang a bell at the head of the stairs, Brother Mathias pulled it. The bell rang. The child — obviously startled — burst into tears. Brother Mathias put the rope into the child's hands and said, "You do it." But the infant continued to wail. Then, unaccountably, he stopped and reached for the old man's hand. The two came down the stairs together to the group of observers, some with mouths agape at what they had witnessed.

It was a pristine sight, but it was not out of the ordinary for this extraordinary man. He has a talent for making the remarkable happen daily, seemingly without effort. As seen through his eyes, life is simple and human needs are easily satisfied. If Brother Mathias has a secret, it may well be this childlike simplicity, but simplicity raised to the level of art and firmly embedded in faith. People hunger to believe that it is real. Thus, like St. Thomas before Jesus, they seek out the one who has lived it. People want to touch Mathias. If they cannot give of their time, they give of their money, sometimes openly, often anonymously. He has affected people from all walks of life: those in the professions and the trades; the unemployed; judges, lawyers, and mayors; doctors, bishops, and archbishops. Everyone wants it acknowledged that he or she has known Brother Mathias. Those who have never met him are reluctant to admit it, as if they had missed something essential to living.

Each year on March 17, hundreds of people flock to Albuquerque's annual St. Patrick's Day corned beef and cabbage dinner. It is the principal fund raiser for the Little Brothers of the Good Shepherd in Albuquerque. In 1986, almost six thousand people ate corned beef and cabbage and listened to homegrown Irish entertainment. Every year since 1952, Brother Mathias has been there, his green eyeshade and diminutive figure a familiar sight. Every year he sings the Irish classic "Danny Boy" with Joe, a resident of the motherhouse, who has only one eye. Their singing is not always in tune. Yet, somehow, all this is beautiful in the ears of their listeners. It is through their eyes, moreover, that Brother Mathias has taken on the attributes that are larger than life. It is in their eyes that he has become a "living saint." His care for others has made thousands of people love him.

— C.N.L.

1 .... Irish Childhood

BROTHER MATHIAS BARRETT WAS BORN IN IRELAND AND — LIKE
George Bernard Shaw — lived the first twenty years of his life in that
enigmatic country. Thus, it is appropriate that a chronicle of his life
should begin with a brief discussion of Irish history, for the turbulent
story of this land affected his life, character, and outlook. It created
the influences that molded the man. It shaped the kind of person he
would become, the thoughts he would think, and the schemes he
would pursue. To a large extent, his tenacity, his shrewd judgment of
men, his devout and humble Catholicism, his pursuit of opportunity,
his unfailing optimism, his stern role as a taskmaster, and his skill as
a teller of stories, can all be traced to his having been born Irish.

Ireland lies off the west coast of Europe and to the west of its
companion island, England. Situated at the edge of the Arctic Circle
and yet simultaneously warmed by the Gulf Stream, it has a climate
that alternates between bewitching sunshine and an all-pervasive,
gloomy dampness. In fact, its climate is one that can give "rheu-
matism to a duck."[1] Yet, there is a compelling enchantment there. In
the words of George Bernard Shaw, "Your wits can't thicken in that
soft moist air. You've no such colors in the sky; no such lure in the
distances, no such sadness in the evenings. Oh, the dreaming! the
dreaming! the torturing, heartscalding, never satisfying dreaming!"
Perhaps such memories of his native land inspired Shaw to write:
"Eternal is the fact that the human creature born in Ireland and
bought up in its air is Irish. . . . I have lived for twenty years in Ireland and for seventy-two in England, but the twenty came first and in
Britain I am still a foreigner and shall die one."[2]

Unlike England, Ireland was never invaded by the Romans. Irish
humor ascribes the Romans' reluctance to invade the Emerald Isle
both to the dampness and to the isolation of the island. This same
isolation also accounts for the fact that the English were never successful in assimilating the Irish, despite over seven hundred years of
determined effort.

The Irish are a people set apart from the traditions of Western
Europe, and yet, curiously enough, they have been at their center. It
was the Irish who sent the early evangelists of the seventh and eighth
centuries to Christianize Europe. St. Patrick was the great Irish saint
whose appointed day is now religiously — and irreligiously — ob-

served worldwide. Both the Irish proclivity for strong drink and for strong religion have entered into the common experience. So too has respect for the long and tragic history of the Irish race. The Irish will tell you, "We say that we have suffered more wrongs than any people in history, and the world, ignoring all reality, believes us, and weeps for us, and dyes its beer green on St. Patrick's Day and gives us money so that we can go and suffer more wrongs in the North of Ireland."[3]

The burden of Irish history is very real. Beginning in 1170, the English began their attempts to subjugate Ireland in whole or in part, attempts that reach into the present day. The names of Irish freedom fighters have also entered into the legend — Rory O'Connor, Hugh O'Neill, Red Hugh O'Donnell. All fought the Tudors, and all were defeated, their crusades ending in famine and despair.[4] Cromwell's infamous punitive expeditions in the seventeenth century further exacerbated what became known as the "Irish question." But it was the great Protestant hero William of Orange who, as William of England, enacted the infamous Irish penal laws in 1695.[5] These edicts banished the Catholic religious orders from Ireland, restricted resident priests to their parishes, and disarmed and excluded Catholics from both the legal profession and Parliament. Catholics could not establish schools or educate their children abroad. Perhaps the most devastating clause lay in the regulation that Catholics could not own property. The only recourse was to convert to the Protestant faith. Although the penal laws were relaxed gradually in the eighteenth century, and completely abolished in the nineteenth, their legacy remained to poison and embitter the Irish, turning some into patriots, others into opportunists, some into liars, and a few into madmen. Religion and patriotism became one and the same. Irish Catholics did not defend the one without including the other, and Irish children grew up with the knowledge that to argue with a cardinal, bishop, or even a priest, was to "cross swords with God himself."[6]

Surviving under siege, the Irish Church became inflexible on one hand but resilient on the other, conservative, and strong. The power of the Church was unsurpassed. It held more influence over the lives of the people than any other institution.[7] When Brother Mathias was born, public elementary education was controlled by the Catholic Church. The local priest hired the principal and approved the selection of teachers.[8] The Irish found most of their recreation in seasonal religious festivals, during which drunkenness and fighting were sometimes part of the social events.[9] The Irish poet Heany wrote that in the evening a visitor might arrive, "sometimes when the Rosary was dragging, mournfully on in the kitchen."[10] Even Irish suffering was Christian, as seen through the eyes of the rebel — and martyr —

of the Easter Rebellion, Patrick Pearse: "The people itself will perhaps be its own Messiah, the people laboring, scourged, crowned with thorns, agonizing, and dying, to rise again immortal and impassible."[11]

Together with the struggle to preserve its Catholicism, the country developed a perhaps lamentable provincialism. In one of Shaw's plays, the main character, Mrs. O'Flaherty, believed that "Shakespeare was born in Cork, that Venus arose out of the sea in Killiney Bay, and that Lazarus was buried in Glasnevin."[12] There was vigorous and lively belief in the efficacy of the saints, and one of a hundred or so would be "imagined as messengers constantly on the run between Irish Churches and the throne of God."[13]

Consistent with their role as victims in the British Empire, the Irish have also had to endure prejudice on a scale that has made them, in one historian's view, "the Blacks of British history."[14] Both Disraeli and Salisbury thought the Irish were savages, as incapable of self-government as the Hottentots.[15] Even advanced Liberals (such as Sir Charles Kikle) and Fabians (such as Sidney and Beatrice Webb) wrote, "We will tell you about Ireland when we come back. The people are charming but we detest them as we should the Hottentots for their very virtues. Home Rule is an absolute necessity in order to depopulate the country of this detestable race."[16] Opinion of the Irish in the United States at the time was hardly more inviting, as the following attests: "This would be a grand land if only every Irishman would kill a Negro and be hanged for it. I find this sentiment generally approved — sometimes with the qualification that they want Irish and Negroes for servants, not being able to get any other."[17]

During the American Revolution, Ireland improved its position, for the British were nervous about facing a revolution closer to home. Land leases were extended to nine hundred ninety-nine years, which for all practical purposes amounted to ownership.[18] Likewise, the French Revolution eased conditions in Ireland. Trade restrictions were relaxed and the iron hand of British mercantilist policy lifted. The Irish Parliament achieved concessions. Irish Catholics won the right to open schools, enter the field of law, vote, and bear arms.[19] The Act of Union followed in 1800, and by the following year, Irish members of Parliament sat in the British House of Commons and Irish peers in the House of Lords. Yet, the "Irish question" remained unresolved.

By the end of the nineteenth century, Gaelic organizations had proliferated in Ireland, giving vent to the demand for independence in culture, language, and national life. In 1884, the Gaelic Athletic Association was formed to promote, among other things, the game of hurling, an ancient field game mentioned in the sagas of Cuchulain, the Irish epic hero.[20] A middle-class movement, the Gaelic League was organized in 1893 and was dedicated to restoring Gaelic as the national language.[21] Waterford, the city of Brother Mathias's birth, was considered by the league to be a stronghold of "peasants uncorrupted by Anglo-Saxon culture."[22] In 1900, William Rooney and Arthur Griffith founded the *United Irishman*, a remarkable journal with artistic and scholarly contributions that made it one of the best periodicals of its time.[23] In December, 1905, Sinn Féin had its first meeting. The name means "Ourselves Alone" or "We Ourselves." The party was modeled on the example of the Hungarian People's Party and sought to follow its successful example in wresting concessions from the Austro-Hungarian Empire.[24]

These, then, were the forces coursing through Irish social and political life when Brother Mathias was born in Waterford on a fine spring day, March 15, 1900, and was christened Maurice Patrick Barrett. For convenience, and out of Irish patriotism, Brother Mathias has claimed March 17, St. Patrick's Day, as the day of his birth and it is this day that he celebrates.

Waterford, located on the southern coast of Ireland, is a proud city with an ancient heritage as a medieval free city, able to bestow privileges on its citizens and to procure their protection. It was also a hotbed of Gaelic sentiment and often led in the production of rebels for the various rebellions and uprisings that rocked Irish history. As a result of the disturbances of 1848, for example, martial law was declared in Waterford.[25] At the time of Maurice Barrett's birth, Waterford was known for its fine glass, leather, and sausages. Waterford beer took its reputation from the purity of the local water. Maurice's mother, Margaret Foley, was from Dunhill, Waterford, four miles from the ocean. His father, Tom Barrett, worked in the brewery, as did his maternal grandfather. There were three breweries in Waterford at the time, all owned by the English.[26]

The family lived on Yellow Road in a modest cottage.[27] A sister, Johanna, and a brother, also named Maurice, had both died before Maurice was born. But the second Maurice proved a healthy child. His parents had married while both were in their early twenties, with Margaret possessing the better education of the two. In recognition of this fact, Tom Barrett would often introduce himself as, "Maggie Foley's husband." This disparity may have been a source of pride, but it also produced some tension at home as Maurice was growing up.

Among his earliest memories were those of his father taking the family for walks in the country, during which they would often play the Gaelic game of hurling. Maurice, his sister Mary, and his older brother John were all very close. While they had arguments and did their share of fighting, it was never serious. As Brother Mathias later recalled, "Mary could give you a swipe in a hurry."[28] For his part, Maurice would tease her about her long plaits of hair, which he threatened to cut off with the scissors. "I'll settle you now," he would say. "You're a clown," she would retort. Maurice idolized his brother John, who grew up to become a schoolteacher in Dublin.

The central focus of life for the Barretts was the Catholic Church. All members of the family participated in its events. The personality and presence of the priests were of overriding importance in the Catholic child's life. For example, the De La Salle Brothers ran the local school and, as Brother Mathias recalls, "My Father thought they were Almighty God."[29] When the Brothers would take their annual vacation, they would give Tom Barrett their keys and he would take care of the school grounds. Arising at 6:00 A.M., he would brusquely call Maurice, who invariably went with him, to get out of bed. To have stayed in bed would have been disobedience to parental authority and, Brother Mathias remembers, "I got up immediately."

Maurice's early memories of the Dominican Fathers in the church where he went every evening are haunting and beautiful. The vision of the Fathers saying their prayers quietly during their choir rehearsals is a vivid memory. As Maurice recalls, the priests seemed almost ethereal, disembodied, free from earth. As a member of the boys' choir, Maurice would tiptoe past the praying figures on his way to the choir loft, where, by contrast, a less exalted scene awaited him. The choirmaster was a stern, unforgiving man. He once gave the boys a beating because they had come up the spiral staircase and made too much noise. Since this occurred at the same time that James Larken was organizing unions in the city, the boys came up with a plan. They determined they would go on strike by refusing to sing. After Mass, the superior held a meeting with the boys in the sacristy and solemnly informed Maurice, "I'll speak to your father. That will be enough."[30] The elder Barrett arrived home later, whistling under his breath, and said, "The priest told me to do it and I'm going to do it." With that, he gave his son several slaps on the face. The memory of this incident has always been a source of sadness to Brother Mathias, since his father never bothered to hear his side of the story.

The church carried on the custom of the "stations" in the community where Maurice grew up. This custom apparently dated from the days of the French Revolution when suspicion of Catholics as subversives led to the celebration of the Mass in private homes.[31] On Monday, Mass would be said in one house in the neighborhood, and the boy chosen to serve would ring the bell from the front steps of the house. The priest would be fed breakfast while the people would visit with one another. On Tuesday, the celebration would take place at someone else's house. Then yet another house would be chosen for Wednesday's Mass, and so on for the remainder of the week.

At the age of fourteen, children became confirmed. As the time drew near for Maurice, he began to worry. He was actually not quite fourteen, and might be asked a direct question on the subject that he could not evade. The clerk of the church was called "Johnny Amen" by the boys, due to his vigorous acclamations at Mass. It was his task to query the candidates for confirmation. When he reached Maurice, he said, "How old are you?" The answer came loud and clear, "I'll be fourteen!" Truth had not been sacrificed. The ruse had worked. Thus the thirteen-and-a-half-year-old aspirant passed his examinations, despite their difficulty. Brother Mathias recalls that "you had to be practically a theologian to pass them. You had to know the difference between 'contrition' and 'attrition,' and to be able to explicate the parable of the sower to the bishop's satisfaction."

The year 1913 saw the British Parliament considering the Home Rule bill, which had been introduced in 1912 by Asquith in the House of Commons.[32] Winston Churchill remarked, with pointed reference to the Ulster Protestant opposition, "Orange bitters and Irish Whiskey will not mix."[33] Further, 1913 proved to be a year of bitter labor struggles in Dublin, which culminated in charges of police brutality and paralyzed the city.[34] In Waterford, the fact that Maurice Barrett had passed his confirmation examination went quietly unnoticed.

School days for Maurice, at St. Stephen's School, run by the De La Salle Brothers, were a combination of work, drudgery, and discipline. There were, of course, rewarding days, and a few instances of spirited pranks pulled by overzealous pupils on unsuspecting instructors. Maurice was enrolled in St. Stephen's at the age of four years.[35] The Brothers ran a tight ship and permitted no infractions of the rules. There was a key that hung on a nail by the blackboard in each room, to be used for the bathroom. One did not even raise a hand to ask to be excused if the key was not there. Maurice thrived on the strictness and was especially fond of one Brother John, who found an apple for him from time to time, and urged him to say the Rosary on his way to school. So, rosary beads in hand, the child walked the brick streets. But he had to be careful not to become too absorbed in prayer while traversing the area they called "Ballybricken," a place where horses, cows, and pigs were regularly sold and where one had to watch one's step for obvious reasons.

In 1910, a revolt in Portugal was accompanied by persecution of

Catholics. As a consequence, the Dominican nuns fled Portugal. Since several of the nuns had ended up in Dublin, Ireland, young Maurice was assigned a composition on the subject.[36] In 1913, the Brothers built a hall across the street from the school for the training of teachers, in concert with the College of Waterford. Aspirants for teaching certificates would teach at the hall under the tutelage of the indefatigable Brother Thomas,[37] and they would use "volunteers" from St. Stephen's School as pupils. Rumor had it that the most successful strategy was to pick the "dumbest" pupils for the task. Sometimes, the students who helped those nervous, fledgling teachers pass their exams were rewarded. According to Brother Mathias, "The Franciscans and Dominicans were poor. You couldn't expect a penny from them." The lay teachers, however, were another matter. Some of them came from wealthy families and would pass out candy at the end of the two-week period.

During the tumultuous period in 1913, when James Larkin was organizing plasterers and carpenters in Waterford, Brother Hubert announced in class, "It's going to be a tough year." The class booed. Outraged, Brother Hubert picked a pupil at random and used his cane on him as an example to the others. The unfortunate pupil was Maurice. In the confusion that followed, Brother Hubert pushed him and then slipped and fell himself, claiming that Maurice had pushed him. The next morning, the class was paraded in the halls and Brother Gall caned every one of them.[38]

School was often demanding and frightful. In a later interview, Brother Mathias recalled his fear of failure as a schoolchild. "I didn't think myself too intelligent. I might be no good. I was always fearful of exposure in school. I knew my arithmetic, but I couldn't go up to the front of other pupils and demonstrate. I could go to the blackboard only because my back was turned."

Pupils at St. Stephen's School moved together through the grades, and Maurice moved from year to year in the company of Larry Schmidt and Jimmy Cooney. Once, a magician put on a show for the school and, as a result, Maurice arrived home later than usual. His irate mother raised her voice and said, "I don't send you to school for that! He might be the devil himself!" While the magician probably was not the devil, rumor had it that he may very well have been a German spy. Jimmy Cooney saw him later, with paper in hand, furtively checking out the understructure of the old and venerable Waterford Bridge.

Probably the most hair-raising escapade that the future founder of the Apostolate of Charity Unlimited did as a youth came with his "lark" to the town of Tramore, six miles from Waterford. The summer he was fifteen, he caught the train — which cost ten cents — to attend a party. One thing led to another, and everyone missed the last train home. Panic ensued. One of his friends conceived of the wild idea of giving champagne to the engineer, who agreed to take the group back to Waterford and then passed out. The students brought the train in and got the engineer to his house, whereupon his startled wife called both the doctor and the priest. When he asked his wife, "What happened?" she retorted, "You should know!"

Maurice's social conscience began to develop as early as age seven. He was exposed to the poor in many ways during his childhood. Several examples delineate his emerging social awareness. As part of Catholic observance, the Barretts regularly gave to charity. From time to time, they assisted the Little Sisters of the Poor in their work.[39] There was nothing extraordinary about this relationship. It was simply expected. One of Maurice's early experiences with poverty was seeing a crippled man working in the cobblestone quarry, cutting heavy stones while kneeling on some folded-up burlap sacks. Even in this posture, he was able to wield a hammer over his head. The man spent his free time catching birds by gluing food to a board. The birds would alight on the board and then stick to the glue. He kept them caged for a while to hear them sing, and then he freed them. This example of a man, crippled and unable to walk without pain, yet fascinated by the flight and song of birds, impressed itself on the young child's memory with vivid intensity.

Another early memory concerned the saga of the Hoolihan family, who had gone to America like so many other poverty-stricken Irish families to seek a better life. But the Hoolihans had returned to Waterford in dire straits. Maurice saw them as two old people, sitting on a bench with nowhere to go. Tom Barrett helped them find a place to live that, according to him, wasn't even on the map. The Hoolihans were not alone in having returned disillusioned from the promised land. Maurice often listened to the tales of Paddy O'Grady, whose father had been killed in the railroad excavations, and who knew all about New Orleans. The father had preceded the family to America and was supposed to meet them when they arrived. He never showed up. They never found a trace of him, although Paddy combed the Louisiana delta area from Mobile to New Orleans looking for him.[40]

A third erstwhile resident of the United States, Ned Scully, was then an inmate of a home for the aged run by the Little Sisters of the Poor. Ned had spent time in the States making moonshine in Buffalo, New York, and selling it to the lumberjacks who would come in from the woods in need of his wares. He made enough money to finance periodic return trips to Waterford. Maurice would often see him in his last years, riding the trolley cars and throwing sixpenny bits into the street, yelling, "Blow them up! Blow them up!"[41]

In addition to physical poverty, Maurice also noted a poverty of spirit among those with the means to afford an otherwise comfortable life. A family by the name of Whittles lived near the home of one of his aunts. They owned a bakery, a farm, and other income property. But the family had disintegrated to the point where its members were no longer on speaking terms. One of the sons, Willie, had become an alcoholic and was dying. The mother was old and feeble. Maurice would stop by from time to time, just in case he might be needed. His mother encouraged him in this early charitable endeavor by telling him, "Maurice, don't abandon them now."[42]

Beyond the experiences of Maurice Barrett in Waterford lay the general face of Irish poverty. Ground down for centuries by dispossession from the land and English mercantilist policies, Ireland had become a land of want. Most city people worked and lived in overcrowded tenements and were malnourished. Tuberculosis was a scourge, and infant mortality high, the results of chronic underemployment and low wages. Prostitution and alcoholism were the refuge of the desperate.[43]

The Countess of Fingall has left a vivid description of the Dublin poor:

> There was a crowd about the gates of the Castle. The Dublin poor always turned out to see any sight that there was. They shivered on the pavement in their thin ragged clothing, waiting for hours sometimes, so they might see the ladies in their silks and satins and furs step from their carriages into the warmth and light and gaiety that received them. The poor were incredibly patient. Even then I was dimly aware of that appalling contrast between their lives and ours, and wondered how long they would remain patient.[44]

In 1908, James Larkin, a Liverpool-born Irishman, organized the Irish Transport Workers Union, an organization with Syndicalist leanings. He signed up ten thousand men and won some concessions from Dublin employers. Then a combined consortium of employers mounted a massive resistance effort, and through the use of heavy-handed police action and lockouts, broke the union's strength.[45] One of Larkins's colleagues, James Connolly, organized a citizen army to fight back.[46]

All of this appeared in the newspapers and was read in Waterford. But the union was not discussed in the Barrett household. Tom Barrett had no use for unions. His contention was that the lot of the poor should be alleviated, but not through unions; it should be done by charity and good works. (Brother Adelbert, as we shall see later on in this chapter, also greatly influenced Maurice's thinking concerning the poor.)

At an early age, Maurice began to formulate a desire to enter religious life. Some of the Brothers of St. Stephen's School already sensed this desire. In a friendly way, they would tease him and demand to know which he would be when he grew up: a Brother or a priest? They would raise their caps to him in mocking good humor, which Maurice would doggedly ignore. Eventually, he kept his desire for religious life to himself, a trait that would serve him well later in life. He decided to wait until the time was ripe.

In 1914, the time was ripe. That June, the Austrian Archduke Francis Ferdinand had been gunned down at Sarajevo, and the crisis brought both Irish factions — Ulster and home rule — together. When John Redmond, the Irish leader, rose in the House of Commons to make a speech, it brought the delegates to their feet.[47] In Waterford, Maurice Barrett had just been confirmed. He returned home one fine day and announced to his mother that he was dropping out of school. Moreover, he intended to join a community of Brothers and enter the religious life. The exchange that followed made it clear that Margaret Foley would not acquiesce in this decision without a fight. Maurice enlisted the aid of one Father Ducey, who was told by his mother, "Father, you have enough to do taking care of your parish. I'm taking care of my home."[48] A Dominican priest by the name of Fahey, whom his mother regarded as a saint, made no more headway. But he did arrange a compromise. The Dominican told Margaret Foley, "Give him six months and if he still insists on going, you will have to let him go."[49]

In the interim, Maurice got a part-time job at a furniture factory that manufactured pews and kneelers for churches and religious houses. During this time, he also stayed in school, bowing to his mother's wishes. Because of his factory job, Maurice had access to the office and its telephone directories and newspapers. From them he gleaned the addresses of various religious houses. Secretly he wrote to several of them. He wrote first to the Holy Cross Brothers in Indiana but received no answer.[50] He sent the next letter to the Hospitaller Order of St. John of God, an address in England. He then haunted the mailman's route so as to intercept the reply before his mother saw it. Finally the answer arrived. The Brothers of St. John of God had a house in Dublin. That was close enough to be real. Maurice eagerly wrote to his older brother, John, who was by that time teaching in Dublin, and begged him to visit the house. John's report was classic. He wrote, "Good Lord, boy, it is a lunatic asylum they have there and everybody speaks French!"[51]

Shortly thereafter, there was an explosion at the furniture warehouse and Maurice was injured. At first he was afraid to seek medical help, but the burns on his face demanded aid. When he arrived home, bandaged across his face and jaw, his startled mother cried out, "Jesus, Mary, Joseph, what happened to you?" When his father came home, his mother said with some bitterness, "Well, you asked to get rid of him and he was nearly gone."[52]

On March 17, 1916, Maurice's father took him by train to Stillorgan, the house in Dublin operated by the St. John of God order. They were shown around the grounds and the hospital by a Brother who, when the tour had ended, paid his respects to Tom Barrett. Then he turned to Maurice. "You stay with us," was his invitation. So Tom Barrett did what he had not really intended to do — he went home without his son. Maurice took a deep breath. The new life was about to begin.

2 .... St. John of God

THE HOSPITALLER ORDER OF ST. JOHN OF GOD HAD A HUMBLE BE-
ginning in Spain in the person of its founder, a sixteenth-century Por-
tuguese-born soldier. Following his service in a number of wars, he
underwent a powerful religious conversion and turned to a life of poverty and hardship in order to help the poor. Overcome by his sins, or
what he perceived to be his sins, John wandered about the streets of
Granada doing public penance. He appeared to passersby to be mad
and soon ended up in a mental hospital where he was regularly
flogged, as this was the accepted treatment of the time for such
maladies.[1] But John turned the floggings into penance. This was a
unique turn of events, which eventually led to his release by the authorities, but only after Father John of Ávila intervened on his behalf.
While in the hospital, John had begun his habit of washing patients'
hands and faces and sweeping floors.[2] It is John of God who originated
the idea of the "knights of the road," his term for the transient, itin-
erant poor for whom he aspired to do deeds of chivalry in the name of
the Virgin Mary. According to Brother Norbert, historian of the order, "His fair lady was the Blessed Mother and he was on his way to
pay homage to her."[3]

John set up a night shelter with mattresses to accommodate poor,
homeless men. Often he brought them there on his own back.
"Certificates of character were not demanded," Brother Norbert
writes. "Poverty and need were the credentials for admission. . . .
Obviously he was often imposed upon, but that in no way discouraged
him."[4] John's sense of overriding Brotherhood drove him into the
streets to beg for the men he had taken in so that he might feed them.
His voice could be heard at the dinner hour, calling loudly, "Do good
to yourselves, Brothers. For the love of God, do good." Among the
apocryphal stories that abound is one that tells how he burst into a
rich man's home and took the pots and pans off the stove in order to
feed some hungry wanderers outside.[5]

One of the virtues of John's activity lay in his bridging the gap between the resources of the rich and the needs of the poverty-stricken.
Prior to the Reformation, this role had been filled with some success
by various religious houses. When these were closed in Protestant
areas, the conduits by which money had found its way into the hands
of the poor often dried up. But John of God had no such conscious in-

30

tent in mind. As his reputation grew, the demands for his help became overwhelming. He seldom slept and often ate meagerly. Unable to refuse anyone who came to him, he gave away to the needy on the streets the alms he had collected for his own poor group. Blessed with limitless energy, however, he soon began helping widows, the impoverished aged, and orphans.[6]

Saintly as these acts now appear, in his own lifetime John was frequently vilified. At his death in 1550, however, the city of Granada gave him a magnificent funeral, and "grandees of Spain vied with each other for the honor of bearing his coffin on their shoulders."[7] Following his death, the little band of followers he had gathered around him persevered. They built hospitals and served as nurses in the various Spanish armies. By 1585, they had opened seventeen hospitals in Spain and five in Italy.[8] They went to China, India, the Philippines, Africa, Australia, and South America. In due time, their medical training programs were among the finest in Europe. By 1800, the religious order had amassed an empire of 298 hospitals in Europe and South America, staffed by 2,731 Brothers.[9] The Brothers began their Irish venture in 1877 by founding a house at Stillorgan, near Dublin.

It is interesting to speculate on the connections between the charismatic founders of religious movements and the personalities of those who join those movements. Many of the character traits exhibited by John of God can be found among those who have chosen to follow in his footsteps. The resemblance, in the case of Brother Mathias Barrett, is uncanny. John of God never turned anyone away, regardless of the circumstances and bad character of the person involved. He would give up his own bed, if necessary, and sleep on the floor. His concern for his charges was deep and genuine. It lasted until he was physically broken and no longer able to care for them. He saw Jesus in the most wretched, loathsome, and rejected of men. Six letters written by the saint have survived. In one he wrote, "If you come, be prepared to sacrifice all for the sake of God. Be determined to do good works, if necessary at the cost of your skin. . . . You will have to work, for the hardest work is reserved for the favorite child. Have God continually before your eyes and never miss hearing Mass every day. . . . Love our Lord Jesus Christ above all things. The more you love Him the more He will love you."[10] Unwittingly, Maurice Barrett had entered an order whose founder's personality was remarkably like his own. Although he would not remain a Brother of St. John of God all of his life, Brother Mathias carried the spirit of this austere and selfless sixteenth-century soldier of God into his Little Brothers of the Good Shepherd.

The history of the Brothers of St. John of God in Ireland began in

1877 in Glen Poer, County Waterford.[11] Originally, the foundation at Stillorgan Castle was started as a convalescent home by French members of the order, but this was soon changed into a private psychiatric hospital. Due to the fact that the French government had expelled the Jesuits and other Catholic orders, additional French Brothers arrived in Ireland. Purchase of the castle was completed in 1882 for 4,000 pounds sterling plus an annual rental fee of 160 pounds.[12] Its location was superb, with magnificent views of Dublin Bay and the Dublin Mountains. By 1897, 24 Brothers and 10 paid staff members looked after nearly 100 patients.[13]

The order of existence was severe. The Brothers rose at 4:30 A.M. and worked until ten at night. The first two hours were spent in prayer and at Mass. There were prayers again before noon, at six, and at bedtime. Twelve hours were spent with patients. Thirty minutes were allowed by the superior for recreation. After 1901, sugar was permitted, and after 1908, an afternoon cup of tea. Politics was not to be discussed. No magazines were to be read, especially serialized novels.[14]

In 1908, a disastrous fire swept through the old sections of the building, including the chapel. As Mary Purcell has described it, "The Prior must have had mixed feelings when he sat down to write to the Provincial in Lyons. The latter would not be pleased to learn that Stillorgan had been insured for only 6,500 [pounds] while the fire damage was far in excess of that sum. On the other hand, the Provincial was responsible for thinking that a hand pump would suffice in case of fire."[15]

The Stillorgan records for the years 1908-1918 reveal only the day-to-day operation of the facility. The purchase of a new washing machine is noted, but the whole gives the impression of life "lived in a tiny enclave. . . . There is no hint of the tensions building up in Ireland at that time, of the labour unrest then coming to a head."[16] One searches in vain for mention of Unionists, home rule, Ulster Volunteers, or the Irish citizen army. As Mary Purcell writes, "Such matters might preoccupy patriots and politicians and the authorities, civil and military. They did not seemingly impinge on the lives of the Brothers or patients at Stillorgan."[17]

Even though it was only five miles from Dublin, Stillorgan remained remote from the great strike of 1913. The historian Seamus O'Brien, writing in *Dublin's Fighting Story*, describes the poor of that city as a "silent bitter mass," living in the "most abominable hovels of any European city."[18] Workers labored for a mere pittance and had no power to demand decent working conditions, wages, or "any protection from the harshest and most overbearing accumulation of masters ever gathered together."[19] The average weekly wage was sixteen shillings, or about four dollars, but many worked for far less. There were some women whose employers paid them anywhere from one to four shillings for sixty hours of work.[20] Driven to desperation, and under the inspired leadership of Larkin, the working poor of Dublin rose up in a general strike in 1913. Police attacked the lines, killing two men and injuring hundreds. "Most of these men had no strike funds to fall back on. They had wives and children depending on them. Quietly and grimly they took, through hunger, the path to the Heavenly City. . . ."[21]

Out of the trials of this time, an Irish saint for the working class arose in Dublin, a former drunk and day laborer named Matt Talbot. Considered a lunatic by some, Talbot was a part of these disordered times, spending all of his free time (including his lunch hours) praying or attending Mass. At the time of his death in 1925, it was discovered that he had taken chains and wrapped them around his body under his clothing so that some were actually imbedded in his flesh.[22] Such was the spirit of the times, and such the events in Dublin when young Maurice Barrett arrived at Stillorgan at the age of fifteen. The future Brother Mathias never met Matt Talbot. But in later years, he would name his new foundation in Ireland, a refuge for the poor and homeless, "The Matt Talbot House."

Life at Stillorgan made demands, but Maurice quickly fell into the daily routine. As he recalls, "I did not care if they were French, or Alsatians, or anything else. I was a postulant. I was part of it," referring to the Brotherhood. He rose at 5:30 A.M., a privilege, considering that the professed Brothers rose an hour earlier, at 4:30. He was placed in the kitchen washing dishes, and served in the dining hall under the tutelage of an elderly Brother named Adelbert, whom he grew to love and who developed a special love for and rapport with him. The house was run by a Frenchman who had the reputation of being hard but holy. There were many priests in the house, some of them quite elderly. Others had physical and mental problems. Maurice felt a certain awe in their presence.

His first misfortune was a swollen knee, which developed from too much kneeling on the hard floors. A certain Dr. O'Connell, a little man with a quick sense of humor, committed Maurice to the infirmary. It turned out that the doctor was a member of the Fenians (a secret society seeking Irish independence), and the night watchman played a trick on Maurice one night by telling him, "You're lost now. The doctor has gone off with the leprechauns!" Maurice fought back his tears, but some hot tea brought him out of it. Such incidents softened life in an otherwise difficult environment. But the knee did not improve, and Dr. O'Connell at length drained it with an ice pick. Afterward, Maurice was promoted to the linen room, but there he took his duties so seriously that he was soon back in the infirmary in acute pain. The little doctor put a rubber hose in his knee and said, "I'll have you here for a long time." Maurice was frantic. What about the laundry? Would he lose his new position? Would they send him home an invalid? He hobbled down, stiff-legged, to the kitchen and confided his worst fears to Brother Adelbert, who took one look at the bandaged knee and inquired, "Have you tried goose grease?" No, he hadn't, Maurice admitted, but he was willing to try anything. The goose grease cured the knee and Maurice kept his job.

Maurice also made a valiant effort to learn French, but he found the language difficult. At times people would have to stifle their laughter at his attempts to use the frustrating words and phrases, but he bore up under the strain. There was always the haven of the kitchen. In the practice of hospitality, Brother Adelbert was a formative influence on his young friend. When it was the feast of a particular Brother, Maurice would help him make a cake "on the quiet." Everyday, following the noon meal, the old cook would take the leftovers — usually potatoes, cabbage, meat, and rice pudding — and give them to the poor. This simple Brother, unfailing in his support, was a living example of what Maurice came to emulate.

As part of his duties in the linen room, Maurice would place a little package of clean laundry in every room. Once, when he came to the superior's room, he found a candle had been left burning. Fearing to put it out without permission, he left it burning. That evening he was reprimanded. Furthermore, it was discovered that he had spoken to an employee, an infraction of the rules of the house. That night he ate his dinner kneeling on the floor. Although officially he was to have no bread with the food, he recalls that the Brother superior "pitched me some bread."

The Brothers confessed in public, and the order of who went first was decided by a system of rotation. Minor infractions, such as being late, or eating between meals, all brought various punishments. One evening it was Maurice's turn to go first. Brother Adelbert helped him prepare for the ordeal. When it was over, the Brother superior observed that Maurice's room had been found in an untidy state: "The state of your room tells the state of your soul." Maurice was instructed to say the Rosary to atone for the sin of a messy room.

As he was the youngest postulant in the house, Maurice often found himself the butt of practical jokes. On one occasion, a French Brother, who was disliked by many of the residents, became ill and died. It was reported that his ghost had been seen hovering around the laundry room, and Maurice was petrified that he would run into the ghost there. He had no choice, however, but to continue to perform his laundry duties. Two employees decided to have some fun at his expense, waited upstairs in the linen room, attired themselves in bed sheets, and hid behind the door. When Maurice entered the room, they jumped out at him with a blood-curdling yell. Terrified, he threw the packages of laundry into the air and rushed headlong down the stairs, not stopping until he had slammed the kitchen door behind him.

The war dragged on and so did Maurice's duties at Stillorgan. Tom Barrett came to visit his son only once. It was during the feast of Corpus Christi in 1916, and Maurice was too busy to pay him the attention he expected. Brother Mathias recalls, "I put him with a priest from Waterford. Then it got to be 4:45 and I thought, 'My God, I forgot to get my father something to eat.' " The oversight was hastily remedied. Maurice asked if he could accompany his parent to the railroad station, but the superior said, "He knows the way well enough." With that, they parted and Tom Barrett went home to report in amazement, "What a reception. I wasn't even with him half an hour!"

The Easter Rebellion in 1916 was one of those chaotic events that only take shape and acquire meaning as the distance between them and the present lengthens. At the time, the population of Dublin was hardly affected by it, did not take part in it, and aside from cleaning up the debris after the rising ended, people carried on their lives with little interruption. But the legacy of the event quickly bloomed into a legend of sacrifice, honor, patriotism, and death.

The Home Rule bill had been presented to the House of Commons, but action was delayed due to the outbreak of World War I. The struggle between the two Irish factions — those in favor of home rule and those against it (the latter primarily in the North) — was further complicated by war-related issues. Of these, the most volatile was the question of Irish conscription.[23] Both in Ulster and in southern Ireland, private armies organized with impressive strength and resolve, bought arms and munitions in Germany, and smuggled them past British authorities.[24] The Easter Rebellion was in fact a complex event composed of strains of Irish nationalism, cultural nationalism, Catholic revivalism, rebellion against British imperialism, and the beginnings of urban radicalism.[25]

Roger Casement, a pensioned member of the Foreign Office staff, whose health had been damaged in the Congo, was in the United States recruiting for the Irish Volunteers when the Great War broke out. He went to Germany, where he maneuvered the Kaiser's government into supporting Irish freedom. He further raised an Irish brigade in Germany.[26] The British undersecretary, Sir Mathew Nathan, was inept. He did not censure the openly seditious *Irish Volunteer*, and his intelligence sources were poor.[27] By the end of 1915, the war outlook for Britain and its allies was bleak, and revolt was simmering in Ireland.

At twelve noon, Easter Monday, 1916, the Sinn Féin seized the General Post Office (GPO) in Dublin. A barrage of musket fire hit Dublin Castle, and the policeman at the main gate fell, shot through the heart.[28] On the night of that day, an observer wrote, "There was enough in the streets of Dublin that night of wild passion and fierce hope to convince the most careless of us that the country stood on the edge of an abyss."[29]

Trying days followed. Some people for the first time in their lives saw men killed. British defense was in disarray. Officials tried to use telephones, but when a telephone was found that worked, they were afraid to say anything for fear it was tapped by the rebels.[30] Nathan took refuge in the stables so that the castle could be occupied by the military. From there, he kept up a continuous flow of telegrams to London advising the Irish Office of the situation.[31] But there was no hope that the rising could succeed. By May 1, it was over.

All in all, only about a thousand people had taken part. Although there were isolated incidents elsewhere, the Easter Rebellion was mainly confined to Dublin. Success had been forfeited by indifference on the part of the population, discovery by the British of the German gunrunning operation, and confusion over whether the Volunteers should rise. The rebels in the GPO surrendered because they were surrounded and without food. Patrick Pearse wrote to his mother on May 1, "Our deeds of last week are the most splendid in Ireland's history. . . . You too will be blessed because you were my mother."[32] The rebels were executed. Their bodies, including that of Pearse, were buried in quicklime without coffins in the Arbour Hill Prison grounds.[33]

The house of St. John of God at Stillorgan, on the outskirts of Dublin, was hardly affected by the turmoil of the rising. The Brothers heard the noise of firing and watched the British army tramping through the village on the way into the city. They did without bread and there was a lot of confusion, but they stayed put. Butter became scarce, Brother Mathias recalls, and margarine replaced it, which he didn't like. He took over other jobs, scrubbing floors and washing more dishes than he had ever washed in his life. More soldiers landed and came up the coastline from Dun Laoghaire through Stillorgan. Irish rebels met them on the tops of houses and fired from the roofs. All the rebels were shot and killed. Not one survived.[34]

Out of the turmoil of the war years and the rising, the story that has impressed Brother Mathias the most was the saga of John Redmond. People loved the man and elected him member of Parliament for County Waterford. In 1913, he dedicated the new Waterford Bridge, and the most prominent men in the city vied with each other to pull his carriage by hand through the streets clogged with his supporters. Yet, by August of 1914, he received a different reception. Promising freedom for Ireland if he got fifty thousand Irish recruits for the British armies, he was met with rotten eggs and onions. The shock was too much for him, and he died shortly thereafter.[35] Of the rebellion itself, Brother Mathias has said, "They weren't at all well prepared. It was a tragedy. What use was it to take the barracks?"[36]

It was shortly thereafter, on July 16, 1916, that Maurice became a formal aspirant to the order. He received his habit and the name by which thousands of people have come to know him — Brother Mathias. Not long after that, he met a man who was to influence his life profoundly. The man, a doctor by training and early profession, was called Dr. Whitaker before becoming a member of the Hospitaller Order of St. John of God. Thereafter he was known by his professed name of Brother Francis de Sales. The two first met in the dining room at Stillorgan during the war. Brother Francis de Sales was moving the archives of the order from England to Ireland for safekeeping.

Although the novitiate of the order was located in Lyons, France, the prospect of going to France had never really dawned on Brother Mathias. Yet, in 1920, the order prepared to send two men to Lyons to the novitiate and he was one. The other was a thirty-two-year-old postulant from Waterford and the two stuck together. France was an unknown quantity, and it made sense to have a friend from home close at hand.

The assistant novice-master in Lyons in 1920 was none other than Brother Francis de Sales. Trained as a physician, successful in his practice, and with a bright future before him, Dr. Whitaker at age thirty-six had suddenly resolved to become a "humble postulant" in the Hospitaller Order of St. John of God.[37] No one seems to have known why. He was treated with a mixture of awe and suspicion by his superiors. They questioned his seriousness, and thought that his dalliance with the religious order would be short-lived. The doctor's avid attachment to sports, especially cricket and cycling, further deepened their suspicions. Most difficult to understand was his proud status as a founder of the Bohemian Football Club.[38] So it was not surprising that the prior dragged his feet on the subject of investing this unpredictable Brother with the religious habit, until, as the story goes, the two were sitting in the middle of a pond and Brother Francis threatened to submerge the boat unless he got his habit.[39]

Quickly rising to a position of responsibility because of his medical training, Brother Francis de Sales served as medical superintendent at the Hospital of St. John of God, Scorton, England, during the war. He also stepped in to act as administrator of the Scorton house because the British authorities were keeping German prisoners down the street, and they suspected the Alsatian Brothers of fraternization with the enemy.[40] In addition, he took over the practice of a country doctor who had left to be with the troops in France, and found the affections of his patients to be such that he barely extricated himself from them at the end of the war.[41]

Arriving at Lyons in 1920, Brother Francis became assistant novice-master for young men joining the order from England and Ireland. He became famous for his counseling of those who feared that their dedication to the work was wearing thin. For this purpose, he kept a tray of fruit, sweets, and a glass of wine to fortify flagging resolve. As a teacher, he had the facility of imparting knowledge to his students that "could not be surpassed."[42] This, then, was the man who, as counselor and teacher par excellence, would form the basis for Brother Mathias's experiences as a novice. He had, perhaps, the most profound influence upon Mathias.

Sent first to the clinic in Paris, Brother Mathias and his Waterford companion were met by the superior, who remarked, "I never saw two fellows like you in all my life. You don't even know the language!"[43] Not far from the clinic, which catered to an upper-class clientele, was a home for crippled children. Later, Brother Mathias would serve in both places, but at first he was sent south to the novitiate of the order in Lyons to prepare for his taking of temporary vows. After three years in temporary vows, the novice would proceed to final vows.

The hospital at Lyons was a large and imposing edifice. It was a "great hospital for poor infirm people, entertaining about 1500 souls with a school, granary, gardens and all conveniences, maintained at wonderful expense. . . ."[44] There were bars on all the windows and around the grounds because the "poor infirm people" were mental patients. Once they had arrived, Brother Mathias confided to his companion, "I think we will never get out of here."[45] It was a considerable relief to discover that the assistant novice-master was Brother Francis de Sales, to whom Brother Mathias had served meals in the dining hall at Stillorgan. In his other capacity as doctor, Brother Francis was also in charge of a ward of fifty-six epileptics.

Brother Mathias plunged into a schedule that would have daunted

38

a less committed and fervent soul. He tackled the French language with a vengeance and also took classes in anatomy and physiology. When the work seemed to be overwhelming, Brother Francis served as counselor and judge of human nature. On one occasion, Brother Mathias was on the receiving end of some severe language from his own ward supervisor, a hard man at best, but one who showed little compassion when under pressure himself. Brother Mathias barged into Brother Francis' office, boiling with anger and steaming with a sense of injustice. He was invited to sit down. After a short space, Brother Francis quietly informed the scowling novice that the superior in question had been up five times the previous night with the sick and dying. He went on to suggest that it might be useful for his religious development if Mathias would apologize. "If you want to be a good religious, tell him you're sorry." Sometimes Brother Mathias was able to comply with this advice, and sometimes his Irish temper got the better of him and he did not.

As an instructor of anatomy, Brother Francis had no peer. On one occasion, he strode into class, whose members had been idly talking together, and without introduction said, "Mathias, give a description of the liver." "Oh my God," thought Mathias, who was unprepared on the subject of the liver. He said nothing. "Well," said Brother Francis, visibly irritated, "you've had it with you all along. What is the problem?" With a flourish, he reversed the portable blackboard to reveal a full-color drawing of the liver and all its parts. The class swallowed audibly. Brother Mathias recalls, "He left us for fifteen minutes and we learned it."[46]

Then, on November 21, 1921, Brother Mathias Barrett, native of Waterford, Ireland, took his formal vows. The ceremony was solemn. It was an occasion for both joy and sadness. Not one member of his family could attend. As one of the professed Brothers, he was now sent to Paris, to the high-class clinic. He cared for about nine to ten patients, the normal load for a Brother at the facility. But Mathias was no ordinary Brother. He would keep a couple of big apples, bread, and some butter and cheese on the windowsill in case one of the patients had relatives who were hungry. Since there was no refrigeration, the windowsill served to keep the food cool, and he was able to pursue his desire to feed people in need.

He also served some months at the crippled children's hospital in Paris. Here, he was in his element. He found in himself a real delight in young people, coupled with a gift for gaining their trust and confidence. He would often take the children in their wheelchairs down into the tourist sections of Paris. There, they would find themselves a likely spot to beg, and settle down for the afternoon. The best places for begging were on the thoroughfares and by the Magdeline Church. The youngsters would sit, hour after hour, smiling, cheerful, and hopeful. He discovered that blind children could push the sighted children, because it was the sighted children who did the steering. This responsibility gave the blind children a feeling of usefulness that they might not otherwise have experienced. People would walk up and put money directly into their hands. It was an experience of direct charity, the kind that benefited both the giver and the receiver. It taught Brother Mathias that it was not difficult to ask for the needs of others.[47]

After six months at the children's hospital, he was abruptly sent back to Lyons. There had been some discussion among the Irish Brothers of getting away from the control of the French and establishing their own province. At one point, Brother Mathias had approached his superior and remarked, "Would you like me to cook in Ireland?" He had received the ambiguous reply, "The world is big and you'll be sent somewhere."[48] For the moment, however, that somewhere appeared to be Lyons. This time, he was assigned to the ward of St. Mark, under the supervision of Brother Laurent, a Canadian with a dour personality. It was not a pleasant assignment. There were ninety mental patients on the ward, and sometimes it was necessary to feed four or five simultaneously, with tubes down their noses. Brother Mathias dreaded the night watch most of all. One could become distracted by the needs of one patient and thus forget to turn the key which registered in the superior's office and which had to be turned hourly. It also seemed that there was more disorder at night and that more patients died. Brother Joseph Mary, an old ex-butcher, regularly picked the first night watch and would load coal in the furnace to the accompaniment of the gnashing of teeth.

Working with mental patients was a difficult and taxing job. Brother Mathias forced himself to make the best of the situation and attempt to communicate kindness to them. Once, he was put in charge of a young man who was a convicted murderer. The patient escaped, hid with his mother in Lyons, and killed a second time. He was apprehended and returned, only to develop typhoid fever and hover between life and death. Brother Mathias nursed him with a combination of hot water and cognac. He recalls, "I cared for him as if he were an angel. He really wasn't responsible." Then, on top of everything else, the murderer developed meningitis. But Brother Mathias refused to give up. Inexplicably, he was transferred back to Paris, and the desperately ill patient was left in the care of others. Years later, by chance, the two men met in the linen room at Lyons. The murderer had survived and was working there. He recognized Brother Mathias, now a middle-aged Brother, and said, "I remember you. You're the one who saved my life."

The Irish Brothers did get their separate province and were able to get out from under the French. Brother Francis de Sales reorganized the nursing school at Stillorgan. Irish Brothers serving in France were given the opportunity to return home if they wished. Some of the Frenchmen, who departed from Ireland for France at the same time, told their Irish brethren, "You will all be back in the French Province within three years because you Irish can never agree among yourselves."[49]

Again in Paris, Brother Mathias went to the provincial who told him, "You'd better get a couple of warm habits because you'll be going to a very cold country." The news got around. The rumor was that the "very cold country" was Canada, and that Mathias would be going with Brother Laurent, the Canadian under whom he had both suffered and served in Lyons. The Irish Brothers were upset and thought he should refuse to go, but Mathias knew he had to obey.[50] He was, however, anxious to see his parents before he made the trip. When he voiced this concern to the provincial, he got the reply, "When we get to that bridge, we'll cross it."

The day of departure was delayed. After weeks with no news, Brother Laurent suggested they write again to the provincial. Brother Mathias wrote that he had not yet had his annual retreat because when he was transferred from Lyons, the retreat had not yet occurred, and when he arrived in Paris, it had already taken place. The provincial wrote back saying, "You'll make a good retreat on the boat." Then more weeks passed. The delay was caused in fact by the negotiations with the archdiocese of Montreal. By the end of March, 1927, however, news arrived from Montreal that they had been accepted. The St. John of God order would cross the Atlantic in the persons of Brothers Laurent, Mathias, and Hilary. That night, the chaplain gave his usual grace at supper, but indicating Mathias, he added, "Ireland gave him, France is sending him and Canada is receiving him."[51] Not only was he bound for the New World, but the journey would open up a new world in the future for him, both as a Brother of St. John of God, and then, when that life reached its conclusion, as the founder of a new order of Brothers that would realize ambitions only dimly imagined in 1927. It was to be a journey that would change his life.

3 .... Montreal

BEFORE EMBARKING ON THE TREACHEROUS AND UNCERTAIN AT-
lantic voyage, Brother Mathias was granted a three-day leave to visit
his parents. He had not seen them for seven years. During the reun-
ion, Mathias hoped to convince his mother to have her picture taken,
something that she had adamantly refused to do. Since she would not
go to the photographer's studio, it seemed that her wishes in the matter would prevail. However, as Brother Mathias recalls, "We got it
settled. I brought a photographer to the house!"[1] This way, he got his
photograph to take with him to America, and to Montreal, the largest
city in the Canadian province of Quebec.

Brother Mathias remembers Montreal as a multicultural metrop-
olis that flourished on the maritime trade, exhibiting the charm,
character, and qualities of a large polyglot city with more than its
share of both social amenities and problems. There was a certain
mystique about Montreal that had always set it apart from other
North American cities. Travelers said that it was more open, more
willing to live its life in public view, to dress up its streets, and to celebrate lavishly. Its people, according to this mystique, were a happy
and vivacious lot, and as portrayed in the travel literature, always
hospitable to strangers. Other observers, however, saw beneath the
charm. The future World War I poet Rupert Brooke wrote, "There is
a Scottish spirit sensible in the whole place — in the rather narrow,
rather gloomy streets, the solid, square, gray, aggressively prosper-
ous buildings, the general grayness of the city. . . ."[2]

There was an underbelly of crime and misery beneath the glitter.
During the Prohibition Era in the U.S., Canada's trade grew by leaps
and bounds. Rum-running rivaled fishing on the Great Lakes. American "tourists" flocked across the border in Henry Ford's automobiles
with suspicious cargo in tow.[3] There was a drinking problem in Montreal, and there were "pockets of slums" where conditions became
increasingly poverty-stricken.[4] These pockets had all the depressing
characteristics by which sociologists were later to describe them.
"The air is heavily polluted, the side streets are littered and dirty, the
roads are crammed all day with cars and lumbering trucks, most
buildings, including churches and recreational facilities, are ugly or
depressing, and the majority of the houses have deteriorated or are
sub-standard."[5]

In 1915, a forty-eight-year-old electrician named Achille David had rented a loft in an old dilapidated building; managing to acquire ten broken-down bedsteads, he provided shelter for ten infirm and homeless men who had nowhere else to go.[6] It can be said of this enterprise that it was a spontaneous act of charity, and that the furniture and surroundings were no more dilapidated than the human beings who used them. Achille David begged for food to feed his charges and, when he was unable to pay the rent in one building, they would travel to another. The residents would carry their meager belongings through the streets. For ten years, living from hand to mouth in this fashion, David and a fellow electrician staggered under the load of charity they had shouldered. By that time, they had acquired twenty-five men who were housed in an old munitions factory. Then, abruptly, David, who was something of an eccentric, dumped the whole enterprise into the lap of a local journalist, Olivar Asselin, who happened to be a member of the St. Vincent de Paul Society.[7] When Asselin saw the refuge for the first time, he nearly fainted. "In a room that was obviously a dismantled factory with grimy floors and rough walls were scattered about 50 bedsteads. . . . On these beds were lying 50 pitiable specimens of human nature. Some were paralyzed, others crippled . . . all were old, dirty, decrepit, friendless and unwanted."[8]

Rather than bowing out of a task that he had not chosen, and which seemed overwhelming, Asselin and his wife took on the responsibility. They set up committees to raise funds, tried to clean the facility and its occupants, and began to collect old clothing and bedding. Prominent citizens were enlisted in the effort, and Asselin even obtained a small government grant. Continuous public exposure of the needs of the men elicited concern, and gradually more people stepped forward to help. One of these turned out to be Brother Laurent Cosgrove, a member of the Hospitaller Order of St. John of God, who met Asselin quite by accident in 1926 during a vacation to see his family in Montreal.

Apparently, the meeting between Brother Laurent and Asselin occurred after Laurent had gone to visit the Blessed Sacrament Fathers. One of them, a Father Carrier, said to him, "Let me show you this dump." Brother Laurent was deeply moved by the plight of the poor struggling inmates of this remarkable homemade refuge. He was equally impressed by the overextended resources of the *ad hoc* group that had been pressed into service to care for them. When he returned to France, he took up the question with the provincial of Lyons, and thus negotiations began with the archbishop of Montreal to bring the Brothers to Canada.[9] By his letter of September 20, 1926, to Arthur Gagnon, president of the Refuge of Notre Dame de la Merci, Brother Cortail promised that Brother Laurent with two companions would go to Canada to reestablish the Hospitaller Order of St. John of God there after an absence of over a century and a half.[10]

In a very real sense, the order was simply picking up where it had left off in Canada. The Brothers (who had been in Canada between 1716 and 1758 at Louisbourg) had been forced out when the English Army took the city in 1758.[11] Even so, it was a momentous undertaking. The three Brothers who would make the trek were Laurent, Hilary, and Mathias. They embarked at Cherbourg on a vessel, the *Valendance*, after a hair-raising train ride during which Brother Laurent nearly got stranded. It appears he had gotten off the train with all their papers and passports. He had not returned when the train began to pull out of the station. Both Brother Mathias and Brother Hilary were leaning out the window when they caught a glimpse of Brother Laurent running alongside the train. He managed to climb into the baggage car, and from there he made his way up to the passenger section. Once on the ship, Brother Laurent became quite seasick and continued indisposed for the duration of the voyage.[12]

The vessel arrived in Halifax, Nova Scotia, at 11:00 P.M., on April 14, 1927. Brother Laurent had brought with him a large assortment of luggage, including a six-foot statue of the Little Flower and several chandeliers. He whispered to Brother Mathias not to reveal the contents of the baggage to the inspectors. "Don't tell them or it will be expensive," he said. Fortunately, the inspector spoke only English, and the Brothers pretended to know only French. Thus, babbling something about the lateness of the hour, they escaped inspection.

Their troubles, however, were not over. There was no one to meet them in Halifax. Consequently, they spent the night stretched out on the hard wooden benches in the terminal building. In the morning, they boarded a train to Montreal. Brother Mathias purchased a couple of mildewed pies at a place called Fox River, but threw them out the window after a few bites. Luckily, a kindly conductor took pity on them and supplied them with bread and chocolate. It was fifty hours by train from Halifax to Montreal, and when they arrived at 2:00 A.M., they lay down on a bench in the depot and slept for three uneasy hours. It was Holy Saturday, April 16, 1927.[13]

At five o'clock, Brother Laurent roused his companions. "Let's go," he told them. "Where?" asked Brother Mathias. "I don't know," was the answer. "That's a fine how-do-do!" retorted the irate Mathias. Nonetheless, they had to do something, so they caught a taxicab and reached the residence of an old priest on Dempster Street, just as the priest was hurrying out. "I have no time for you," he called cheerfully as he disappeared into the distance. Brother Laurent sat down and said, "We'll go back." Brother Mathias also sat down and said, "I won't go back over that ocean for anything." The dispirited trio located the nearest church, Our Lady of Bon Succors, prayed, bought some coffee, and felt their spirits revive. At that point, the administrative committee for the refuge, headed by Olivar Asselin, discovered the Brothers, whom they had been seeking at the train station. They made profuse apologies, and then took the Brothers on a tour of the institution they had come across the Atlantic Ocean to operate. The refuge was located in an old brewery on Rue Saint-Paul. The visit was a sobering experience.

Later, the Brothers took a walk down the street, rosary beads in hand, praying absently together, and asking themselves in which corner of that hovel they were to sleep. They could not stay at the old Notre Dame Hospital, since it had temporarily been turned into a hospital for typhoid cases.[14] Brother Mathias insisted on bedding down right next to the men on old sacks. All kinds of discussions ensued. Since there was no room in the refuge itself, the committee rented an "uninhabitable" building next door as their residence. It was hardly more cheerful than the refuge. But the Brothers set to work. "They believed in soap and water as the best antiseptic and they got down on their hands and knees and scrubbed those old floors until they were as white as the deck of a man-o-war."[15] They did all the scrubbing, cooking, and nursing for forty old, decrepit men and, in addition to this herculean task, they repaired the houses.[16] Soon a chapel was added, the house next door was rebuilt (which was accomplished by burning the midnight oil after regular hours), and benefactors of the poor in Montreal began to sit up and take notice. It even became fashionable to visit the refuge, to watch the Brothers at their labors, and to contribute money to the cause.

The Brothers met formally with the administrative committee of the refuge on April 24 and determined the relationship that would exist between them. By the terms of the understanding, the Brothers would have charge of all internal affairs of the refuge, including administrative and financial decisions, in return for which services the Brothers would receive room and board from the committee.[17] The parties also agreed that if a difference of opinion came up, the settlement of the differences would be made by the diocesan bishop of Montreal.

Olivar Asselin, so long the rock on which the refuge had rested, was overjoyed at having the Brothers take over the practical matters of feeding and nursing the old men. He was ebullient in his praise of their efforts. He compared Brother Laurent to Alexander the Great and Napoleon, and praised his abilities as "architect, engineer, electrician, pharmacist, cabinet maker, nurse, artist, and spiritual director."[18] A ladies' auxiliary committee helped by declaring war on the vermin in the refuge. In addition, they organized visits to the facility which left visitors in a state of awe, and from which they emerged "enflamed with zeal."[19] The public gave generously of furniture, clothing, bedding, and construction materials, and local working-class men donated their time and skills.

The inaugural for the two facilities — both the refuge and residence — took place on June 3, 1927, and the formal ceremony marking the reestablishment of the order on Canadian soil occurred two days later. The refuge was blessed for the first time. "Everything smelled sweet, from the parlor to the chapel to the loft to the sacristy, which was situated under a staircase."[20] Checks piled up on the platters and in the boxes provided for charitable donations. It was truly a memorable occasion, and a tribute to the individuals who had made it a reality. There were only a few sour notes. Although the advertising of the ladies' auxiliary committee and the administrative committee resulted in the collection of $3,700, several prominent Montreal citizens had failed to attend. The committee ran an open letter in the local papers following the event in which it was noted that "an additional $10,000 will be coming from rich people who didn't show up."[21] Listed among the absent dignitaries were the mayor, all the aldermen of the city, various city officials, and legislators. Only one judge escaped Asselin's ire, due to the fact that he attended, and "one parish priest who has made admirable sermons on charity donated $100."[22]

Brother Mathias served as the cook of the establishment and was in charge of begging for food as well as preparing meals for the indigent residents. Miraculously, he appeared three times a day with appetizing meals, "the fruit of begging in the early morning markets and long hours in the kitchen."[23] In this regard, Brother Laurent proved to be a stern taskmaster; and, under his relentless eye, Brother Mathias became especially adept at begging. Once, Mathias went through the telephone book and picked out the names of several prominent attorneys. Then he paid a visit to one of them, a Mr. Hackett. Hackett, quite naturally, expected a client and asked, "How may I help you?" Brother Mathias said, "I'm begging." For a moment, the attorney stared at him. Then he realized who his visitor was and gave generously. He even provided Mathias with a list of his colleagues to call on.[24]

On another occasion, Brother Mathias went to visit a wealthy lady who, according to rumor, had been good to the Jesuits. When he had previously telephoned her home, she had hung up on him. Then he presented himself at her door, and when she opened it, put his hand in the opening. Angrily she said, through the crack in the door, "I told you I'd see nobody." "Well," said Brother Mathias, "I'm nobody." The door opened and, after being served refreshments, he told her about the men in the refuge having to sleep on newspapers. He left her home with a generous order for sheets and blankets.[25]

Brother Mathias plunged into the work at hand with a will. His first love was the down-and-out poor man. In the words of one slum dweller, "Down here, there's a sort of truth and basic reality. . . . There's no use putting on the old BS down here because if you haven't got it, you ain't got it and that's all there is to it."[26] Because he was not the principal in charge, Brother Mathias was subject to the demands, and caprices, of his superior, Brother Laurent. At times he feared that his health would break down under the strain, but it didn't. Every morning, Brother Laurent expected him to go out and beg. Once, he struck it rich early in the day in the business section of downtown — a man gave him $100 in bills. Considering his options, he thought, "I'll divide it into two parts." He gave $50 of the money to Brother Laurent, and then spent several hours in the cool of a church praying. When a suitable amount of time had elapsed, he came back to the refuge and gave him the other $50.[27]

> I always had a custom of putting things aside. I got a load of buns once that were a bit hard but not moldy. I dumped them all into a big box. The men were supposed to go to the bakery in the morning for day-old bread at 7 A.M. The man in the refuge who could drive went, and I was afraid this particular morning that he wouldn't get any bread. So I put these buns in a deep pan, sprinkled water on them and put them in the oven. I didn't say a word to anyone. He came back. "The bakery's not open. Why didn't you think of that yesterday?" Then I pulled out the buns. "Oh, look at this," I said![28]

The city of Montreal ran a municipal refuge with six hundred beds for night stays only. Men would be lined up in the winter for hours, beginning sometimes as early as 3:00 P.M., in order to get a bed for the night.[29] One evening, Brother Mathias decided to join the line. Standing in the snow with a hole in the bottom of his shoe was no joke, but he was consumed with curiosity to see how the men in the line were treated. Once inside, he relinquished his clothes and received a handful of soap. The beds were double-deckers covered with canvas. There were no mattresses. The night's sleep was fitful enough, but the events of the following morning came as a shock. The men were hustled awake and told to dress. Then they were sent out into the cold without a thing to eat or even a cup of coffee to warm them. Brother Mathias went to the directors of the shelter and pointed out the inhumanity of this approach. They became angry and said, "Aren't you in this business too? Are you trying to raise problems?" Brother Mathias shrugged his shoulders and said, "I only know I was there last night and the least you could do in the morning at 6 o'clock would be to give the men a cup of coffee and a piece of bread."[30]

In 1930, Montreal set up a day shelter for men, located at 514 Notre Dame Street, and named Ignace Bourget Shelter. It could accommodate two hundred men during daylight hours and supply them with sandwiches. In 1935, the shelter was taken over and administered by the Brothers of St. John of God.[31] Thus did Brother Mathias achieve his goal of a place for a man to get a "cup of coffee and a piece of bread."

Having been relieved of the day-to-day care of the patients, the committee that administered the refuge was now able to turn its attention to the erection of a hospital for the indigent and chronically ill. In this regard, November 27, 1927, was a festive day. The Honorable Athanase David, secretary of the province of Quebec, visited the refuge, and over one hundred people attended the ceremonies. A brass band in the street provided musical diversion, and the president of the committee, Arthur Gagnon, praised the secretary and his cousin Achille David, who had been the originator of the refuge twelve years previously. Pledges were given for $5,000 in government subsidies, and an additional $5,000 in discretionary funds. Over and above this, the provincial secretary gave another $5,000 to the committee.[32] The drive to raise funds for the hospital was moving into high gear. In March, 1928, $1,486 was raised at an evening of charity, and $5,745 was raised by collection during the day of forget-me-nots. This so-called "tag day" was organized by the Baroness d'Halweyn and was intended to raise funds by "tagging someone for a good cause."[33] The hospital of La Merci, projected at a cost of $800,000, would contain four hundred forty-two beds, be located on the Prairie River on donated land, and be financed by loans and public charity.[34]

By 1929, between two hundred and three hundred men were being housed in the old brewery. During the Christmas and New Year's holidays, Brother Mathias reasoned that a bottle of beer wouldn't do the residents of the refuge any harm, since "those poor old fellows were used to it anyway." Brother Mathias recalls, "I used to go to the brewery and get several cases of beer. They always wanted the bottles back. They were worth more than the beer."[35] The refuge had a top floor that required a ladder in order to be reached. Brother Mathias had his bed up there, along with some bunk beds for the overflow downstairs. One night, a man died in one of the bunks. Next to him was a drunk, who appeared dead too. The Brothers called the morgue, and when they arrived they took the wrong man. The drunk later woke up in the cooling room at the funeral parlor, scared out of his wits. When he got back to the refuge, he begged Brother Mathias on his knees, "Don't ever do that again!"

The threat of fire in the old building was ever-present, so arrangements were made with a Mr. Limburger, who owned the factory next door, that in case of an emergency the beds from the refuge would be transferred to his factory. Before it was necessary to accept this generous offer, one resident put his pipe in his pocket, went to bed, and set his pants on fire. Brother Mathias threw him out into the snow in his underwear.[36] In 1931, serious damage was done to the refuge by a fire that destroyed an adjacent commercial building. The flames were extinguished only by flooding the quays. The old people were transferred, some to hospitals, and some to the factory owned by Limburger. The public responded generously to the appeal for funds to rebuild the refuge with fire-resistant materials. As a result, the facility was also enlarged and improved. Thus, a near disaster was turned to good use.[37]

Brother Mathias lost part of his right index finger while he was in Montreal. One day, while operating an electric meat grinder, someone came up to engage him in conversation and he was momentarily distracted. That was time enough for the blade to slice through his finger. He ran to a doctor, had stitches put in, and then returned to finish serving breakfast. The stitches began to open up and he soaked his hand in bread and water. This turned out to be a mistake. Soon, the first joint was threatened by infection. Luckily, a young doctor who happened into the refuge took stock of the situation. As a result, Brother Mathias had to go several times a day to the local hospital for therapy, but the finger was saved. Later, in partial payment "for services rendered," he assisted the doctor with a difficult patient.

> He had to do some surgery on a patient who was very belligerent and lived in a poor section of Montreal. He called me and said, "Brother, can you help me?" The man had left the hospital without permission and had gone home to Corsair Street, a very miserable street. So I went down there and he was screaming and everything else, so I told him in French, "I'm taking you to my place and if you scream like this, you go right through the window." He went with me. We got two sheets and made a kind of emergency operating room. After the operation, I kept him with me.[38]

The Brothers could not have had a more able administrator than Olivar Asselin. Not only was he a skilled executive, but as secretary of the committee he took on the responsibility of speaking out on behalf of the fund-raising efforts. Money had to be raised, not only to cover the current costs of operation, but to finance the construction of the Hospital de la Merci. The committee envisioned raising $25,000 by the end of 1929, thus proving itself to be fatally optimistic. In one of his printed appeals for funds, Asselin displayed his oratorical gifts:

> The most difficult piece of furniture to place is an old, sick, indigent man. No one knows how long he will need to stay. He doesn't pass through the institution quickly to be on his way somewhere else. Poor, old people who stand at the door with a few dollars in their hands have been abandoned by their relatives. La Merci is forced to turn away several every day. We need another house for the Brothers. In such a difficult religious task, it is almost impossible to keep novices if they don't have a little garden to take some air in. Postulants who have the enthusiasm of youth can stand it for a few months but beyond that time span, it is well beyond human tolerance.[39]

When a man came to the door of the refuge seeking assistance, he might say, "I'm a cook." In that case, Brother Mathias would welcome him with, "Just the man I want! There's a man here who hasn't eaten for three days!" The newcomer would then enter, a little mystified, to be hustled in the direction of the kitchen. Apparently "three days" was the standard time to be down and out. "It was a custom that they had to say, 'I haven't eaten for three days.' It wasn't four and it wasn't two." Or, perhaps the poor derelict at the door would say, "I'm a carpenter." Then Brother Mathias would say, "Just the man I want! There is something wrong with this door jamb." The men at the door were thus made to feel like they had something worthwhile to give. Rather than being received reluctantly, they were being welcomed.[40]

Somehow, there were always musicians in the line. Where they came from, nobody knew. Once, a concert pianist showed up in need of a meal and a night's lodging. Brother Mathias organized a choir and engineered a "little procession" from the church of Our Lady of Bon Succors one Sunday after Mass. The company proceeded down the street to the refuge singing lustily and smiling at the passersby. This was another example of one of Brother Mathias's axioms — "All these things are very simple when you look at them properly. But you can complicate them and then you are wasting your time."

In October, 1932, late in the evening, Mathias got a telephone call from the police about a man who "shouldn't be here." The man in question turned out to be a priest from the United States, from Ogdenburg, Vermont, which was very close to the Canadian border. Brother Mathias went down to the police station, and on the way a remarkable thought occurred to him. He not only felt the presence of his mother, he had a vision that she had died and was somewhere in heaven conversing with the mother of this priest from Vermont. The essence of this extraordinary conversation was, "My son will not let your son stay in jail all night." When he had collected his man — who was quite drunk, had scratches on his face, and was unable to stand — Brother Mathias brought him home to the refuge and put him to bed. Then he quietly took out the priest's rosary beads and replaced them with his own. The next morning, he bought the man a ticket and put him on the train back to Vermont. Later, he heard that the priest had returned to his parish and was considered a fine, upstanding servant of God. The priest must have wondered, when he used his rosary beads, what had become of the ones he had taken to Canada.

Moreover, it turned out that Margaret Foley had, in fact, died. A letter arrived soon thereafter from the nuns in Waterford with the news. They told Brother Mathias that they had asked his mother if she wanted them to try to bring him back before she died. She had said, "No, he is where God wants him to be."[41]

The new hospital was to be built as a joint effort of municipal, provincial, and private contributions. It became the all-consuming passion of Olivar Asselin, whose tireless efforts in its behalf bore fruit. Meanwhile, operating funds for the refuge had to be raised. Benefit concerts were held, and auctions of artwork took place. Donations could be as practical as one-half the coal needed for one year, or as luxurious as a radio and record player. The committee enthusiastically accepted soap, woolen bedspreads, and light bulbs.[42] For the hospital itself, one appeal followed another. A total of $800,000 had to be raised. During 1929, $90,000 of this was obtained, due to heroic efforts by the Brothers and the generosity of the public. Three fourths of the amount could be secured by borrowing against the forthcoming government subsidies. Above that, the committee sold $150,000 in life annuities.[43] Olivar Asselin was quoted in the press as having said, "Contrary to rumor, we did not get a golden slipper from a fairy."[44] On another occasion, he upbraided a critic who had questioned the cost of the facility — presumably with the complaint in mind that such funds would be wasted on the poor — and retorted, "This won't be a tennis court."[45]

On June 8, 1931, the construction site was blessed. Slightly over a year later, on September 25, 1932, the hospital was completed. Un-

51

employed men terraced the grounds and planted trees "in exchange for supper." The facility was gaily decorated — as if for a parade — with garlands, flags, and banners of the French kings. "When the breeze made all its colors vibrate, one could have thought it was a huge dragonfly of beige brick. . . ."[46] The opening of La Merci was a stupendous event. The Brothers welcomed their new quarters, and the patients who were transferred into the sparkling surroundings were literally speechless. There was a chapel located in the center of the hospital complex, as if it were the heart. The building itself was 350 feet long, 40 feet wide, and had 316 beds as well as several elevators and offices; it also boasted 134 feet of river frontage and had 3 floors with a novitiate, infirmary, heating system, and laundry facilities.

What could the poor expect if they were lucky enough to become patients in La Merci?

> You will see in the hallway the silhouette of the small brother dressed in the white shirt of a nurse. He will bend over you as you are lying in bed just as your mother did when you were a child, during nights of fever and nightmares. He will encourage you with a smile and comfort you with a friendly word. He will care for your body with untiring dedication. He will also help your soul because he knows from long experience with human misery that as Thomas has said, man has a desire for a minimum of well being in order to be virtuous.[47]

If this sounds a little saccharine to the modern ear, it did not strike the public of Montreal as such during the years of the Great Depression. Certainly, the amount of private funds that poured into the coffers of the hospital was indicative of a nerve touched by the example of the Brothers. The need was real, and daily became more obvious. Citizens who were secure and provided for on a Monday, might suddenly find themselves out of work and with vastly altered circumstances by Friday. The biblical injunction "There but for the grace of God go I" was relived hourly in the consciences of people from all walks of life as the bread and soup lines lengthened and as the notices of unfortunates having frozen to death the previous night became more numerous in the papers.

> It is a moving spectacle to see this human mass of disheartened people tossed around between the Muerling refuge which houses them during the night, and the Ignace Bourget house which gives them shelter and nourishment during the day. If it is nice starting in May, the Square is filled with these summer guests in rags.

52

Once the cold has started, these miserable people cannot long remain outside. They come to smoke their pipes and cigars on the benches of the refuge where the smoke enshrouds the whole room in a bluish fog.[48]

In 1934, Brother Laurent was recalled to France, and Brother Mathias took his place, having been appointed by the superior general of the order, Reverend Brother Ephrem Blandeau. He was the former provincial of France, with whom Brother Mathias had established a good working relationship. It was due to the rapport between the two men, plus the obvious growth and vigor of the establishments in Canada, that led to the division of the French province. In 1939, an independent Canadian province was established. Thus, Brother Mathias became provincial of the new Canadian province. The promotion, however, did not change him. He continued to work at the refuge even though he was now administrator of the hospital and titular head of all the Brothers in Canada.

He soon turned his energies to the development of a "juniors program" for young men in their teens. The juniors program had evolved out of the need for caretakers for the chronically ill patients who were appearing with more and more regularity at the refuge. After the construction of La Merci, Brother Mathias acquired a home for the chronically ill by fortuitously purchasing a downtown building owned by Bell Telephone. The project was financed by a grant from the Canadian government. In addition, the government began paying thirty cents per day for indigents who were hospitalized in the big facility on the Prairie River. With some negotiation, those payments were transferred to the new convalescent facility. In January, 1934, as Brother Mathias recalls, "I had to fight the government to do it" (that is, to transfer the payments). Even with this assistance, the Brothers were $98,000 in debt.[49] But with the city of Montreal paying a dollar a day for each patient, the total cost was distributed.

The juniors program was a true inspiration. Brother Mathias had picked up the idea from the Good Shepherd Sisters, who took in orphan boys, aged fourteen or fifteen years. He saw the value of giving these boys an education, board, and room, in return for their services in feeding the chronically ill old men. Each boy had a patient assigned to him whom he fed three times a day. Concerning the boys, Brother Mathias tells us: "The first year I had about twenty. I was afraid to send them on vacation. They might not come back! But that year they all came back. And I got twenty more. So I established a scholarship. I went to banks and the St. John Baptist Society. I got $500 in scholarships. Between novices, postulants and juniors, I had over 90."[50]

Father Trudeau arrived at the convalescent hospital after the vicar general had made inquiries on his behalf. He was badly crippled from rheumatoid arthritis, which he had contracted after his ordination, and which a number of trips to prominent medical institutions, including the Mayo Clinic, had been unable to cure. Brother Mathias showed him a little room in the St. George corridor, outside of which hung a painting of the saint combating a fierce dragon with its head on Russia and its tail on England. Then he showed the priest a little oratory across the hall. They went downstairs and Father Trudeau asked, "Where's my room?" Brother Mathias looked surprised and answered, "I just showed it to you." "But," said Father Trudeau, "I only have $30 a month." Brother Mathias retorted, "Who's talking about money! I'm not talking about money." So Father Trudeau returned to his room. Later, he came downstairs to dinner looking wan and out of sorts. When asked how he was feeling, he responded, "Terrible." Upon further questioning, Brother Mathias discovered that his new resident had had a visitor, a Jesuit priest by the name of Brunette. This stern, intimidating individual had knocked on Father Trudeau's door and abruptly announced, "I am Father Brunette, spiritual director for the novices. I make no visits and I want no visits!" "Imagine that," said Brother Mathias.[51]

Later, when he needed a professor for his juniors program, Brother Mathias asked Father Trudeau to serve in that capacity. Father Trudeau responded with, "Look at my hands." Both men looked down at hands crippled by arthritis. Brother Mathias said, "It isn't your hands I need." When the new professor was introduced to the approximately sixty juniors whom he would instruct, he announced to them, "I have no hands and no legs, but I have a will and I have a voice." They loved him.[52]

A lay teacher had been originally hired for the juniors. He was very hard. The juniors had to wash cups and saucers, and now and then they would break one of them. The pieces went into a shoebox with the "guilty" boy's name on the outside. The ones who broke nothing would get a prize at the end of the month: a pen or a notebook. Soon, no one was breaking anything. The boys were expected to adhere to strict rules of conduct. Failure to do so would result in dismissal. Brother Mathias discovered that the lay teacher was judging certain boys with undue harshness. One day he picked up a report card on a boy named Paddy O'Brien that listed scores of 80% in math but only 20% in conduct. He changed the mark for conduct by making the 2 into an 8. Inwardly he said to himself, "Next time it will be 80%. I'm not sending him away!" This kind of trust won over some of the boys so completely that they became postulants in the order later on.

Not long after this incident, the lay teacher was dismissed and Father Trudeau took his place.[53]

In 1935, Brother Mathias gave an address to the ninth annual assembly of the refuge and hospital committees, and their supporters. Among his remarks were the following:

> It is a sweet and gentle task for me to come and thank you sincerely for all that you have done for us and our work. . . . The cooperation that exists between the Committee and us deserves mention, for it is through this cooperation that we shall be able to continue to do good; it is this spirit that we must keep and as long as the general interest is our ideal, and not our personal interest, we shall have success. . . . Our hospital was organized during the year in a better way and thanks to the precious assistance of all of my brothers — for there is a Brother in charge of each department, such as procurement, operating room, kitchen, laundry room, etc. — and this is why, Ladies and Gentlemen, you should attribute nothing to Brother Mathias for the success, but rather to the entire community. You know that union makes strength.[54]

Brother Mathias was directly involved in the construction of five institutions during the years 1927-1941. The Jesuit Father Brunette — referred to earlier in connection with his treatment of the mild-mannered Father Trudeau — often took Brother Mathias to task on this question. He would say, "Brother Mathias is making acts of construction when he should be making acts of contrition!" Others also lost patience from time to time. There seemed to be no end to Brother Mathias's ambitions to expand the order. In August, 1936, Brother Mathias decided he wanted to build two more wings on the hospital, one for novices and one for the professed Brothers. He brought up the idea to the board of directors, embroidering his ideas so that the board was told the structure would "look like an airplane." They were not impressed, and the meeting was adjourned. Going home on the bus, Brother Mathias told anyone who would listen to him, "Look what they've done to me!"

Two weeks later, the board met again, but Brother Mathias absented himself. He stayed in the chapel on his knees and refused to come out. Various delegations were sent, but he refused to budge. It got to be seven o'clock, then eight, then nine, and finally ten. The board then drafted a letter to Archbishop Gautier and invited him to the next meeting. This offered a marvelous opportunity, and Brother Mathias rose to the occasion. Preparing a big poster that said, "Arrived in Montreal on the road without a place to lay our head," he tacked it up in full view of where the archbishop would be seated.

Then he prepared a list of all that had been accomplished over the years, placing a copy on every plate.

The archbishop duly arrived and took his seat next to Brother Mathias, inquiring of his host, "I wonder why I am here tonight." He then turned to several members of the board of directors and asked, "What does Brother Mathias want to build and why don't you build it?" Protests followed from several members. One pointed out that construction on the university had been suspended because of the depression. Another countered, "We're not building a university, a hotel, a theatre, we're building a hospital and the needs are there. I think it's an insult to the archbishop to bring up the university!" Finally, one member proposed that the addition be built. The motion passed. On the way out, the archbishop remarked to Brother Mathias, "There is still too much Irish in you."[55]

On the ground floor of the hospital there was a room where the board of directors regularly met. On one occasion, a Brother remarked to Mathias, "It's a shame this room is only used once a month. We could put the tables double-decker in the corner and use it." Brother Mathias exclaimed, "You'll get me burned at the stake." But, fired by the idea, they went ahead anyway and moved the tables out of the way to make room for extra beds. In due course, the board members arrived for a meeting, and Brother Mathias had to convince them that they were not being thrown out of their jobs.

Construction on the new hospital wings broke down when the contractor struck quicksand and presented a bill of $10,000 in additional costs to put steel casings down to bedrock. The board refused to go along with the increase. One doctor declared angrily, "We knew that would be the case." The architect retorted, "Doctor, my case is not like yours. When your cases are not successful, they go six feet down." The architect then informed the builder that it was a "no go situation" with the board, and the builder announced he was going to go to court. Brother Mathias followed him out of the room and told him, "Give me the telephone. You know very well you are going to be paid. You should be ashamed of yourself! All those poor men waiting for work!" The builder asked for the foreman to be put on the line. He ordered the lights turned back on and they continued to build, twenty-four hours a day, until the job was finished.[56]

What these charming anecdotes illustrate is that Brother Mathias had a great will and persistence to get things done. They also illustrate the fact that his personality could occasionally alienate people who were willing to assist him and the Brothers in furthering their work. While no one person could claim sole responsibility for these achievements, his continual pushing and shoving may very well have been the catalyst for action. On March 10, 1939, Brother Mathias wrote a letter to the Fathers and Brothers of the Canadian province announcing the formation of the Canadian general delegation. He said:

The Father General wrote us: You are a General Delegate, your powers are those of a provincial, your obligations are equally those of the provincial. . . . I count on each of you as always but if possible more today because greater are our obligations, more important has become the need for help. It is only by your prayers that we will be able to attain the goal we have set. I ask you to have a special intention for me, for if you want me to be able to do some good, it is absolutely necessary that you pray a lot for me.[57]

As one of Brother Mathias's last projects in Canada, he conceived of a rather wild scheme to combine treatment facilities for tuberculosis patients with seminary training for priests. The location would be in the mountains outside Montreal. In addition, the mountain place would serve as a vacation site for the young juniors. For this purpose, Brother Mathias scrupulously saved any extra money he could salvage from the operation of the hospital, and eventually had a tidy sum, which he "watched like a hawk." It amounted to several thousand dollars. The property he wanted was owned by a priest who informed him that he would be in town on a certain day. He also told Brother Mathias that he "had better make up his mind because I'm selling." So they settled for $1,200 at $100 a year for twelve years. The property had a little shack on it, but the land was where its value lay — one hundred twenty acres with eight hundred feet of beach on the lakeside. The board of directors asked him, "Are you going to tell us what you've done?" Brother Mathias answered, "I've done it anyhow!"[58]

In the fourteen years that the Brothers of St. John of God had been in Montreal, they had built five institutions: a refuge serving 200 men and staffed by 4 Brothers; a hospital with 500 beds staffed by 70 novices, postulants, and Brothers; a soup kitchen staffed by 2 Brothers; a home for epileptics called St. Rose of County La Valle; and a convalescent home for 75 residents staffed by 3 or 4 Brothers. But change was in the air. Brother Mathias was tired. He toyed with the idea of returning to Ireland to join the other Irish Brothers in their new province. His father, a widower, was aging and ill. The achievements had been impressive, but the difficulties seemed overwhelming at times.

He wrote to his cousin John Barrett, in Los Angeles, informing him of his intentions, and John wrote back, "I never knew you were such a coward. Why don't you come to Los Angeles?"[59] Thus was the process set in motion that would bring Brother Mathias to the United States. We will look briefly at the details surrounding the transfer to Los Angeles in the next chapter. It was clear that the change would not be easy, but that it was, in all probability, necessary.

The Brothers in Montreal joined with the members of the administrative committee, the board of directors for the hospital, and many members of the community in bidding Mathias farewell. During the ceremony, a number of speeches were made in his honor. He was praised for his "enthusiasm and moderation, wisdom and prudence, finesse and vision." He was credited with taking over the administration of the hospital and offering that "sense of authority and spirit of discipline that the Order had bred in him." The question was rhetorically asked by one speaker, "From where does this vibration of his personality derive, and the charm of his bearing and the valor of his friendship?" Other speakers recalled events of the past fourteen years, and the result was described by one awed observer as comparable to "the stained-glass window in the monastic chapel." Brother Mathias was visibly moved. He stood up and enumerated all the efforts of each person that had resulted in the common success of the works of mercy. Then he gave a short speech himself. The thought that had been the inspiration of his life, he told the assemblage, was that "there is no love without devotion, and no devotion without love." He had loved all the jobs, the modest ones and the big ones. He had loved all the religious, those from France and those from Canada. Above all, he had loved all the poor that he had comforted.[60]

The day ended with a mixture of nostalgia and grief. Yet, it was not without those emotions that fire men to go on with tasks that they know will be difficult, based on the comradeship that those struggles have won for them in the past.

Brother Mathias left alone for the American West Coast in March, 1941. In October, when two other Brothers left Canada to join him, the emotional leave-taking was repeated. The seeds they would plant would bear fruit in the United States. Brother Mathias would return to Canada, but it would not be as a member of the Hospitaller Order of St. John of God. Thus, the good-byes said on that March day were final.

4 .... Los Angeles

THE OUTBREAK OF WORLD WAR II HAD A MAJOR IMPACT ON THE life of Brother Mathias. He was recalled to Ireland in 1941, but the war made travel impossible. As has been discussed in Chapter 2, rather than returning to Ireland when the new Irish province had been formed, Brother Mathias had remained in France, and had later gone to Montreal. Now circumstances combined to transfer his field of action to the United States. By 1941, he had become embroiled in conflict with other members of his order regarding priorities and goals. According to the "Draft History of the American Province," prepared by the St. John of God order in Los Angeles, "There was criticism and dissension concerning hospital administration and practice of religious life in Montreal, and in 1941, Brother Mathias was ordered back to Ireland. War restrictions made it impossible for him to travel so he obtained permission to go to Los Angeles where he knew that the Father General Ephrem Blandeau was interested in establishing the Order."[1]

Brother Andrew Aucoin, who was in Canada at the time, has written that the report submitted by one Jesuit Father Bourque to the superior general of the order in the latter part of 1940 became a crucial element in the decision to ease Brother Mathias out of Canada. The report dealt with certain difficulties, among which was the novice-master's insistence upon "living the religious life almost to the letter of the law."[2] Father Bourque interviewed a number of the Brothers, and apparently his recommendations (in conjunction with other information from the French province) brought about the Father General's decision of March, 1941. The decision stipulated that Brother Mathias be removed from his office as superior, and that Brother William be named in his stead.[3]

Another perspective on the Montreal difficulties has been offered by Brother Hugo Stippler. He has noted that the province was under a visitation at the time, that Brother Mathias was not "tuned in to education" and did not want the Brothers trained because he felt that "if they were trained, they would leave."[4] Moreover, Brother Mathias was "moving more to the poor than he was to the institutional type of facility."[5] Of course this was the model set by John of God in his time. Nevertheless, the Brothers in Canada were going to ask that Brother Mathias be transferred. "They all loved him but they just couldn't stand this movement that was taking place within him."[6]

Finally, there appears to have been a real struggle between the Irish and French-Canadian contingents of the religious order. This proved a source of abrasiveness that continued even after the order became established in the United States.[7] Brother Andrew explained, "At the same time, the [Father] General realized that by sending Brother Mathias to America he was eliminating the trouble in Canada and establishing a new foundation, so killing two birds with one stone."[8] But the transfer was wrenching. Brother Andrew described its effect upon him at the time as comparable to his later reaction to the death of President John F. Kennedy.

Knowing that change was in the air, Brother Mathias had written to his cousin in Los Angeles in December of 1940. He asked him to sound out the ecclesiastical authorities there on the possibility of bringing the Hospitaller Order of St. John of God to the United States. Brother Mathias had always hoped to come to the States, and now seemed a golden opportunity. In addition, he was not pleased with the prospect of returning to Ireland. The letter he wrote to Archbishop John Cantwell of Los Angeles on the matter made both sentiments clear. As a result of his request, the cousin, John Barrett, made some direct inquiries on his behalf. On December 27, he sent a telegram to Brother Mathias in Montreal. It said that he had had a productive interview with Archbishop Cantwell and that the latter was very interested in the subject of "starting a mental institution, not for lunacy, but mental ailments, and that he considers your order the finest."[9] Brother Mathias was instructed to write immediately to the archbishop.

Brother Mathias was not the first Brother of St. John of God to correspond with Archbishop Cantwell. The archbishop had grown up in Tipperary, Ireland, close to County Waterford, and had known about the Hospitaller Order from childhood.[10] Regarding the subject of bringing the Brothers to Los Angeles, he had written his first letter in 1930 to the provincial in Puebla, Mexico, when the provincial was bishop of Los Angeles and San Diego.[11] An exchange of letters had followed in which the Mexican provincial, Diego Palacios, had advised Cantwell that passports could not be obtained for the Mexican Brothers unless a letter from the sponsoring diocese could certify that an institution was already functioning where they could exercise their vocation. Due to the fact that such an institution was not in existence at the time, the bishop's secretary replied, "If it were necessary to make such a statement, the Right Reverend Bishop would prefer to abandon the project of an institution for the Order of St. John of God in this diocese."[12]

There, matters had remained until Brother Mathias's four-page handwritten letter arrived in December, 1940. It contained a painfully direct message: "Excellency, you can understand that a young Irish (Waterford) lad could not continue to be over a group of French Canadians."[13] He alluded to his having been recalled to Ireland and added that he greatly desired to see Archbishop Cantwell before complying. "I am sure that your Excellency would not like me to risk the crossing over to Ireland at the present time . . . if it was at all possible to make a stay in California. . ." he wrote.[14] The letter had the desired effect. On January 4, 1941, the director of Catholic Charities, Thomas J. O'Dwyer, sent a telegram in reply: "His Excellency extends cordial invitation to come to Los Angeles as soon as possible. He will discuss in detail your plans for foundation here."[15] This was followed two weeks later by a letter of welcome from the archbishop himself.[16] Brother Mathias prepared for the trip by train to the United States, with the permission of the Father General in Rome, and bearing the title of general delegate, which would empower him to establish new houses of the order when he arrived.

However, the American authorities at the United States border proved obdurate. Despite residence in Canada for fourteen years, Brother Mathias was not a citizen of that country. In fact, he had no identification that the border officials would accept. He solved the problem in typical fashion, deciding that if he "wrote to Ireland, it would take months and then, they would probably write back and ask for $5 costs. So, I wrote out a Baptismal Certificate and said on it, 'exact copy as found in the Archives, Waterford, Ireland.' They accepted that with no further questions."[17]

On March 25, 1941, Brother Mathias arrived in Los Angeles, carrying a cardboard suitcase and wearing old black shoes, one of which had a loose sole that flapped.[18] His first task was to pay his respects to Archbishop Cantwell, who proceeded to lay out an ambitious program. "We'd like to have a home for men on the road," he announced, "one for the chronically ill, and one for the mentally ill."[19] Cardinal Timothy Manning — who as Father Manning was serving as the archbishop's secretary at the time — recalls that Brother Mathias appeared "totally French, his accent was French, his outlook was French." But there must have been enough of the Irish to show through, because the archbishop, born in Ireland himself, formed a personal affection for him and recognized the "need that he would fulfill in Los Angeles."[20] After having listened to the dreams of his new and distinguished mentor, Brother Mathias swallowed his misgivings and took a tour of the city's facilities for the indigent. He was accompanied by the president of the St. Vincent de Paul Society, Wiseman MacDonald. MacDonald also took him to the top of a huge building and showed him the city, a sight that, according to Brother Mathias, "was like a bucket of water on me and didn't make any impression at all."[21] Then, armed with $10 from MacDonald and the $10 he had brought with him, Brother Mathias sought out the nearest Western Union office. He sent a telegram to the Father General in Rome that read, "Foundation established. Send Brothers." It was a vast overstatement. Moreover, the telegram cost him $5.65.[22]

His first act, after having sent this extravagant message, was to ask the people running the St. Vincent de Paul Society salvage store for some furniture. They said they first needed to see the house where the furniture would go. Brother Mathias told them they couldn't see the house because there wasn't any house. Undaunted, he then visited, by foot, the office of Catholic Charities where some kind soul directed him to a certain zealous Franciscan in Watts. The Franciscan, a Father Arthur, helped him find a house. The first floor was available for $35 per month, and with the help of the good Father, Brother Mathias paid the rent. He then took his receipt back to Archbishop Cantwell, and was reimbursed. Soon, he was again in the business of feeding people, and back on the streets begging in order to do it. In short, he was in his element.

Not long after, two more Brothers, Leonard Mondat and John Dubuc, arrived from Canada. They, however, were not impressed with the prospects that greeted them at the "new foundation." Brother Mathias even took them around the block several times before finally pointing out the house where they would be living. Upon seeing it, they groaned and said, "We knew that's what you would do."[23] Soon, things took a turn for the worse. One Saturday night, the upstairs residents carried on until the wee hours of the morning. Then the icebox broke, and water overflowed into the refuge below. As if this were not enough, the following Sunday, when the Brothers were at Mass, the refuge was burglarized. Everything was taken, including the sheets off the bed. Brother Leonard even lost his electric razor. In dismay, the Brothers borrowed a pickup truck and moved their operation to a safer location, on Twenty-second Street near Broad Street in the parish of St. Vincent's Church. Being forced to relocate in St. Vincent's parish turned out to be propitious for the Brothers' future.

After settling into the new place, Brothers Mathias, Leonard, and John went to pay their respects to Father Ward, the parish priest, who sized up their situation and seated them in the first pew on the right, next to a wealthy benefactress named Countess Doheny. As Brother Mathias soon learned, the Countess supplied flowers twice a week for use at St. Vincent's. He decided to inform her that he and the Brothers were planning to open a chapel in December and that "it would be nice if we could have some flowers too."[24] She responded by sending flowers twice a week to the new chapel, which she soon visited. Brother Mathias took that occasion to suggest that it might be even nicer if the price of the flowers could be divided into two portions, "one for bread and one for flowers." Soon he was receiving a check for $100 a month in the mail.[25]

Two more Brothers arrived from Canada in October, Brothers Andrew Aucoin and Vincent de Paul Rapin. It was time to establish a novitiate, a prospect Brother Andrew welcomed at the time because "fortunately, I did not cook."[26] The search for a location for this grandiose establishment soon took on elements of the comic. Brother Mathias had seen an advertisement for a nursing home in San Fernando Valley for seven hundred dollars per month, with five acres and an orange grove. Not wanting it known that he represented a religious community, he took along his cousin John Barrett to make inquiries about placing his wife. According to Brother Mathias, "He told the lady who ran the place that his wife had had a nervous breakdown. She said, 'We don't take people like that.' So he said, 'Well, I need a rest after taking care of her.' So she showed him the rooms."[27]

Meanwhile, Brother Mathias sat outside in the car, contemplating the orange grove. John soon emerged, grinning from ear to ear, and said that it was exactly what Brother Mathias wanted. Negotiations followed, and the Brothers were able to lease the facility for $400 a month. The archdiocese forwarded a check to cover two months' rent. Brother Mathias then sent three Brothers out to handle the new facility, while he himself remained at the downtown refuge with Brother Vincent de Paul. It was now November, 1941. The following month, the United States went to war with Japan and Germany.

Commuting to San Fernando Valley soon became a burden. The war was on, and increased workloads, shortages, gas rationing, and fears of invasion dictated the move to a place closer to the downtown refuge. Despite its allure, the orange grove had to be given up. Thus began the long and drawn-out process of acquiring the property on South Western Avenue. The house in question, originally built by the "cement king," was owned by the Bayly family. It was a stately white mansion set above street level in an upper-class residential district of the city and was being operated as a home for convalescents. Again, John Barrett went in as the front man to make discreet inquiries, but this time Brother Mathias tagged along. Again, John's enthusiasm carried him away, and he suddenly burst out with, "Wouldn't this make a lovely chapel, Brother Mathias?" The lady conducting the tour turned her eyes directly on Brother Mathias, who retreated further into his habit. The cat was out of the bag, but in the end it did not matter.

The initial attempts to raise money to buy the place bordered on farce. Mathias and another Brother went down to a bank and sat in a plush office with a loan officer. The officer asked the Brothers, "How do you live?" The other Brother said, "Public charity," whereupon the loan officer cleared his throat, got up, and excused himself. As it turned out, a certain Mr. Martin, vice-president of the Bank of America, was willing to extend the money, provided he could also have the signature of the archbishop on the note. On May 29, 1943, Brother Mathias was authorized to buy the Glen Brae Sanitarium at 2445 South Western Avenue, with the archbishop purchasing the property but deeding it to the Brothers. The understanding was that they would pay it off within ten years.[28] The nursing facility at San Fernando Valley was now closed, and the Brothers and the patients moved to Los Angeles.

The combined hospital and novitiate facility on South Western Avenue was blessed by Archbishop Cantwell on Sunday, July 10, 1943. There was an open house throughout the day hosted by the Women's League of St. John of God, led by Mrs. Klinkhammer, Countess Doheny, and Miss Nellie Cantwell.[29] The women's league had been formed the previous year in August, with one Mrs. Pollock as its first president, and had set $1,000 as the first year's fund-raising goal. The amount had already been exceeded.[30] According to the *Tidings*, the archdiocesan newspaper, the need for the facility had been obvious. "On many an occasion, [the Brothers'] spirits were very low; but their Provincial, Very Reverend Brother Mathias, would not hear of failure. When turned down time and time again in the acquisition of a property, his battle cry was, 'Let's try again! Pray harder!' His indomitable Irish spirit and his trust in God overcame all opposition."[31]

The 1943 annual report of the religious order noted that at the San Fernando convalescent home, the Brothers had been caring for twelve patients. However, they had had to turn away about four hundred others, of whom seventy-five percent were mental cases.[32] One of these, who was accepted by the Brothers with a stipend of $10,000 to cover his lifetime care, was a young man who "believed in Santa Claus with the faith and excitement of a little child, and the light in his eyes and the air of expectancy about him as he would be put to bed on Christmas Eve were a delight to behold."[33] Another patient was a former San Francisco hotel owner named Shanley, who had moved into a Chinese neighborhood, opened a laundry he called "Shan-Lee Laundry," and had been picketed by the Chinese, who put him out of business.[34]

The early years on South Western Avenue were not easy. Brother Kevin Donohue, the first American Brother to join the order, recalls that the dedication of the older Brothers was remarkable and a source of inspiration for him. "Brother Leonard did laundry all day in the basement, carrying wet damp linen up the steps to hang out." When it came to making beds, no one could outdo Brother Vincent de Paul.[35] Moreover, the religious communities of women "could not have been better than they were to the Brothers." The Daughters of Charity sent hospital beds that were no longer in use. The Sisters at Queen of Angels Hospital provided hospital experience for the Brothers, and the Immaculate Heart Sisters took the Brothers into their college and "never sent any form of a bill."[36] Finally, the Brothers had a firm friend and benefactress in Miss Bernadine Murphy, who lived across the street from the home and who showed great concern for the patients. "On feast days and holidays, she always came over ahead of time in the morning with little favors to go on the patients' trays — thoughtful things like that, which in many places people don't even think about."[37]

Archbishop Cantwell had a "great admiration and respect" for Brother Mathias. But his support of Brother Mathias and his projects sometimes had a plaintive ring to it. The refuge continued to operate under the original arrangement, which stipulated that the Catholic Welfare Bureau would pay the monthly rent of $50, and then be reimbursed from archdiocesan funds. But the course of this relationship did not run smoothly. On one occasion, the auxiliary bishop wrote to Raymond O'Flaherty of the Catholic Welfare Bureau with the following observation: "His Excellency, the Most Reverend Archbishop, does not wish to place any definite term on the length of time for which he will continue to pay rent for Brother Mathias, but he hopes that the Brothers will soon establish themselves on a self-supporting basis."[38]

Then, within one week in 1943, the archbishop signed a thirty-thousand-dollar check so the Brothers could purchase the house next door to their sanitarium, and sent a letter that demanded payment for a $3.27 radiogram which Brother Mathias had sent to the apostolic delegate in Rome.[39] Archbishop Cantwell had been suitably impressed with the director of Catholic Charities' arguments in support of the purchase of the addition to the sanitarium: "The buildings are in splendid condition. They will accommodate about 35 patients . . . at an average income of $85-$90 per month."[40] In fact, according to Cardinal Manning, such support of a religious order had not been previously done in the archdiocese.[41] However, it appears that even in small matters, financial accounting was equally precise.

In late 1943, the Brothers acquired Rancho San Antonio, a home for delinquent boys in Chatsworth, California. Brother Kevin Donohue was sent as administrator. The Brothers working at the home received a salary of $75 per month from the administrators of the facility. But the work was difficult and, for most of the Brothers, unfamiliar. Moreover, there was a railroad track that ran right through the property, a fact that made it convenient for the errant boys to hop a freight train and escape. Brother Kevin recalls some of the difficulties that the Brothers experienced:

> We had to start from scratch. There was nothing. The boys in the recreation room — so called — were sitting on orange crates. They would break up furniture for want of a program of something to do, and throw things in the fireplace. I was astounded at the pittance the institution received [from Catholic Welfare]. We had to go and ask their permission and then it was "try and convince them" if you could. The layman who was in charge there had to think about his salary and what the community chest was going to say and all that sort of nonsense. When I realized the bills we had even for food, I called my father one night collect and he sent me $10,000. That paid the bills. . . . I hated keys. When I first went there, keys were for everything, even to put on the lights. I told the boys that the keys were not important to me and I was going to do away with them and that "they don't mean a thing to you because you know how to break in if you want to."[42]

Brother Mathias tried to alleviate the stress involved by organizing an orchestra for the boys and establishing a printshop for a school paper. In addition, the Brothers applied a "coat or two of paint" on all the outside walls of the buildings.[43] But Rancho San Antonio continued to be a bone of contention for other reasons. There were severe conflicts with the lay board that administered the facility, the Knights of Columbus who funded it, and the contact people at the Catholic Welfare Bureau who laid down regulations that were arbitrary, even damaging.

The problems of obtaining sufficient Brothers to staff the facilities and to care for the growing number of patients was a continual struggle. Brother Mathias made repeated efforts to get Brothers from Ireland and Canada. On August 10, 1943, he complained to Archbishop Cantwell that the Irish province "doesn't seem to pay any attention to my continual requests either by cable or letter."[44] Already one American, Brother Kevin Donohue, had joined the order. His arrival had been most auspicious for the Brothers, as he had brought with him a five-hundred-dollar check from his father in New Jersey to pay for the return trip, if needed. The Brothers used that money to eat. Archbishop Cantwell wrote Brother Mathias a letter of congratulations that said, "Bravo! I am glad to hear that your first novice will be inaugurated into the Society of the Brothers of St. John of God. The beginnings are always hard."[45]

In March, Brother Mathias got a letter from the Irish minister to the United States, to whom he had written about bringing Brothers over from Ireland. Due to the war, getting transportation was nearly impossible. The minister, Robert Brennan, had written back that he had suggested the idea of having priests come over in empty U.S. transports but that "nothing came of it." Perhaps, he suggested, British passenger boats could be used, since Irish boats were against the board of trade regulations.[46] As it turned out, no Irish Brothers were able to make the trip until the war was over. In 1946, however, two of the order's most stalwart members arrived.

In addition, there was the delicate question of getting military deferments for the American Brothers who were joining the order. In November, 1941, Auxiliary Bishop Joseph McGucken advised Brother Mathias that he would have difficulty getting Brothers deferred when they gave their occupation as cooks or gardeners. "They should say they are Ministers of Religion. If they do this, no difficulty will arise out of the failure of certain officials to comprehend how cooks, janitors, etc., can be Ministers."[47]

Meanwhile, Brother Mathias had not let grass grow under his feet with regard to community support, particularly fund raising by the newly formed Women's League of St. John of God. This group held luncheons, teas, and various other worthwhile functions to raise money for the Brothers. The efforts of these dedicated women, many of them wealthy and with notable social connections, aided the Brothers greatly. They made it possible for many projects that would otherwise have never been realized.[48]

In January, 1944, an article on Brother Mathias appeared in *St. Anthony's Messenger* with this description of the tireless Irishman:

As soon as lively little Brother Mathias, provincial and delegate-general, who has already established a night shelter, a hospital, a social center for soldiers and sailors and a novitiate for American vocations, had finished pouring tea at the night shelter, refusing a cup himself, I asked him about this matter of hospitality and if this "guest business" wasn't laying it on a bit thick. "Not a bit," he reassured me, repressing his broad Irish smile. "Our vow of hospitality commands us to see in the poor, the sick, the homeless and the needy, the suffering Christ. . . ." Unfolding his arms beneath the wide scapular of his black habit, Brother Mathias tilted back in the chair, his woolen cowl brushing against the wall. . . . "How do you manage to keep out the professional bums?" I asked, looking at this big-hearted Irishman, who would give his habit away if it wasn't forbidden by canon law. "We don't. If they come — and they do — they are received like the rest."[49]

The author of this article was later taken on a tour of the convalescent home and witnessed, in the course of the visit, a hunchbacked youngster curled up in a wheelchair, several loathsome cancer cases, and an old man who splattered his orange juice all over Brother Mathias. The reporter was told, "It's the difficult and repugnant ones that our vow of hospitality commands us to cherish and accept with open arms."[50] The reporter returned to his office, obviously impressed. Brother Mathias probably went to the kitchen and washed the orange juice out of his habit.

The Los Angeles years contained many stories of the individuals who came and went at the shelter and the various other facilities run by the Brothers. One man showed up who volunteered to wash dishes. Only later did he let on that he really was a priest. Brother Mathias told him to keep quiet about it.[51] Another "guest" arrived from somewhere back East on a Saturday afternoon and tried to get into the cathedral rectory. Brother Mathias recalls that "getting into the rectory there is like trying to get into heaven because there's a wrought iron gate." He was told to go to Catholic Charities, which was also closed. He ended up at a flophouse with a twenty-five-cent jug of wine. When Brother Mathias got hold of him, he upbraided him. "You're a mess," he scolded. "I'm even wasting my time." The man stepped out into the street and was hit by a car. People pulled him to safety and as he looked up at Brother Mathias, who was bending over him, he moaned, "If you had taken me in, this wouldn't have happened." It turned out that the man stayed for five years with the Brothers, during the course of which he stopped drinking.[52]

In April, 1944, Brother Mathias wrote to Bishop McGucken with respect to the availability of the MacDonald property adjacent to the sanitarium. He had discovered that it could be acquired for $17,500. In his letter to the bishop, Brother Mathias said:

It is possible that someone might acquire it for an apartment house and it would not at all do to have the novices so close to all this. . . . I would be glad if your letter would not seem to be an answer to mine, but coming directly from you. You can understand how they feel at Brother Mathias doing so much and of course there always creeps in a little jealousy but all will work out well please God. The others may change one day but Brother Mathias will be always on the spot so I am taking every precaution for the American province and I think that I have every right to do all I can for our American boys.[53]

This letter is an interesting hodgepodge of business and philosophy that reveals some of the pressures in Brother Mathias's life. By May, he was deeply involved in negotiations for the MacDonald house, pointing out to anyone who would listen what fine living quarters it would contain, that it had a larger chapel than the one the Brothers currently had; moreover, it had conference rooms and the possibility for one-third more income. He asked Bishop McGucken, "Will it be possible to borrow 10 or 12 thousand dollars?"[54] The archdiocese saw the wisdom of the purchase, and in July the deal was consummated. By August, Brother Mathias was jubilantly reporting, "We have already opened the driveway between the MacDonald property and ours — broke the wall and leveled the ground, took away the old shrubbery and indeed it looks very clean. . . ."[55]

Some problems remained to plague the order with regard to the training of the Brothers, and the regimen under which they lived. Some critics felt that the novices were not getting a solid enough foundation before being asked to man the barricades at one or another of the facilities. As Bishop McGucken wrote to Brother Mathias in March, 1945, "It is quite necessary that the young Brothers have a solid foundation in their religion and I am wondering whether or not it might be well to ask your Chaplain Father Schulte to give them a regular course in Christian doctrine."[56] Furthermore, the prior general in Rome was not pleased with certain changes that Brother Mathias had instituted on account of the pressures of the work — principally the shifting of meditation from the morning to the evening hours. The prior general was "greatly grieved at this change" and instructed Brother Mathias to go back to the usual practice of getting up at 5:00 A.M. and holding meditation in the morning. The latter complied "in filial obedience."[57] But it was not easy to maintain European standards of religious life in the American setting. James Barrett (another of Mathias's cousins, now deceased) recalled that as a young man he would visit the sanitarium and see the novices wearing T-shirts with their cigarettes rolled up in the sleeves. "That was unheard of. The rules of the Order did not allow it."[58]

After Brother Mathias transferred his efforts to Boston (a subject which will be detailed in the following chapter), Brother Patrick Corr became novice-master in charge of training the aspirants for membership. He recalls that Brother Mathias sent him young men from Boston, but that most of them did not stay. "They would knock on the door in the morning and say, 'Brother Patrick, we're leaving.' It was disheartening. Most of them were nice but sometimes you would get a not so nice one come and look over the place and say, 'Is that all you have?' Then I would say, let us look at it from the point of Almighty God. You've been asked to come forward and build up a tremendous Order from nothing in this great land."[59]

On July 10, 1944, the Women's League of St. John of God held its first annual garden party on the grounds of the hospital. It was a gala affair, which was accompanied by an impressive printed program containing articles about the Brothers all over the world. The advance billing for the event noted that "favorite film stars will attend."[60] The Brothers also began publishing a newsletter called "The Flame of Charity." It contained poems, news of hospitals in foreign countries, articles on how to nurture vocations, testimonials of gratitude from patients and their families, and ads from friends and sponsors. The September, 1944, issue noted that in the order's facility in Rome, "the Brother Dentist does extractions free." It also quoted Voltaire to the effect that "religious are people who live together without knowing each other, or without having any affection for each other." The paper commented that Voltaire was wrong, pointing out that "religious must love all fellow beings."[61]

Soon, however, life would change for all the Brothers in Los Angeles. In April of 1944, Brother Mathias had received a fateful letter. It came from Edward Sweeny, Jr., in Boston, asking if the Brothers could take over a hospitality house in that city. Other letters followed. Sweeny offered to ask diocesan authorities for permission. It appeared — a point which did not fail to appeal to Brother Mathias — that there were no Catholic-operated refuges in Boston. Initially, however, nothing came of the request due to the illness, and then death, of Cardinal William O'Connell, archbishop of Boston. No new archbishop was named until October 13, 1944, when Richard Cushing became Boston's new prelate. Brother Mathias sent a congratulatory letter. On January 25, 1945, Edward Sweeny wrote again: "There are two very good reasons why you should try and locate in Boston, the first is that Boston is one of the fertile fields in this country for vocations. . . ."[62] He did not need to give a second reason. With his ardent desire to obtain Brothers for Los Angeles, Brother Mathias seized the opportunity and, on March 3, 1945, he wrote to Archbishop Cushing. Thus began the sequence of events that was to take him away from Los Angeles and ultimately to return him to Ireland.

Shortly thereafter, Brother Mathias received an early morning telephone call from the gravelly voiced archbishop of Boston. The gist of the conversation was Cushing's invitation to the Brothers to take over the operation of Hammond Hall and make it a home for aged and infirm priests. Brother Mathias's reply at that early hour was, "Your Excellency, we'll go."[63] He hung up the phone and went directly to the chapel. What had he promised to do? Suddenly it seemed rather overwhelming. For one thing, who was he to consult? The war was on, and communication with his superiors in Rome was difficult. The next best course of action was to meet with Archbishop Cantwell. He called Father (future Cardinal) Manning, the archbishop's secretary, to arrange an appointment. Father Manning said that he would take up the subject at lunch with the archbishop. When he called the next day to check on developments, Brother Mathias was told that the archbishop was furious. According to Brother Mathias, Father Manning told him, "He is wild. Come down and see him yourself."[64] Full of foreboding, Brother Mathias went to see the irate Cantwell, who banged a few doors and yelled at him. "Nothing but pride and ambition!" he roared. Brother Mathias tried to counter with an explanation. "You want me to do this and do that," he said, "and I don't have the men." He was told to shut up. He rose, kissed the archbishop's ring, and left the room.

He then wrote a letter to Cantwell, apologizing for having put him into this situation, and saying that the matter had not been adequately explained. For his part, Archbishop Cantwell wrote to Dublin to the order in Ireland on behalf of the Brothers and to Archbishop Cushing in Boston. Then he sent a conciliatory reply to Brother Mathias, saying, "My dear Brother Mathias, I am in greatest sympathy with you, and am anxious that things should be carried out as you wish."[65] As one historian of the order has commented, "Archbishop Cantwell was understandably displeased when told that the dynamic if pint-sized Irishman was leaving the West for the East coast. Their parting was rather cool."[66] Cardinal Manning, however, recalls that "the Archbishop would have these outbursts of displeasure which did not at all reveal his normal state of mind. There was no radical displeasure with Brother Mathias to my recollection."[67]

In May, the council of Brothers decided that operation of Rancho San Antonio was not in accord with the work for which the St. John of God order has been founded. Auxiliary Bishop McGucken wrote a rather frigid letter to Brother Mathias noting that the Brothers were obliged to stay until suitable replacement could be found: "In the meantime, you have a very definite moral obligation to continue in the work that has been undertaken until you can be relieved of it without doing harm to God's work in the Archdiocese of Los Angeles."[68]

Ultimately, the Brothers relinquished the operation at Rancho San Antonio to others. Then, in June, the hostel building was sold, and, unable to find a new place to relocate, the Brothers stored the furniture in the St. Vincent de Paul warehouse and closed the facility.[69]

By September, 1945, Brother Mathias was beginning the struggle to open up a foundation in Boston while simultaneously handling the everyday problems in Los Angeles. He wrote to Archbishop Cantwell with elation in October that new applications were coming in and that he had great hopes for more. He promised that "the houses in Los Angeles will be fully staffed," and assured his prelate that he would be back in Los Angeles "very shortly."[70] He also sent photos of Hammond Hall to now-Monsignor Manning, who tactfully noted that "the Retreat House looked very much like your own novitiate here."[71] He continued to try to get Brothers from Ireland and France. Now that the war had ended, the prospects seemed much brighter. Archbishop Cantwell wrote to Brother Patrick Murphy in Paris at Brother Mathias's request and offered to pay his expenses to Los Angeles.[72] Brother Mathias wrote the Los Angeles prelate in January, 1946, and called him "the Father of St. John of God in America." This letter was filled with optimistic news of the Canadian and Irish postulants. "It should be a great consolation for your Excellency to know that the Province of Our Order [Our Lady Queen of Angels] with its center in Los Angeles is called to be one of the finest in the Order, and extending from the Pacific to the Atlantic."[73]

In January, 1945, he was back in Los Angeles. On the nineteenth, Archbishop Cantwell visited the patients in the Mount St. John of God Sanitarium and presented the Brothers with vestments that he had procured for them from Canada. Further extending himself on their behalf, the archbishop signed affidavits of support for two Irish Brothers and thus made possible the journey to America of Brothers Patrick Corr and Enda Farrell, two men who would later make their mark in the New World. Brother Patrick would become an indefatigable worker and a first-rate fund raiser for the hospitals built by the order in California. Brother Enda put in many long, productive years with the various Los Angeles institutions. Then, in October, the archbishop signed affidavits for two more Irish Brothers, Kieran O'Reilly and Oliver McGivern. To add to the headaches suffered by Brother Mathias during this period, letters arrived from Gloucester, Massachusetts, with news of troubles back in Boston. Once, they were even sent by special delivery.[74]

In a very real sense, the move to Boston caused irreparable strain on the operations in Los Angeles. It created what amounted to a "family rift" among the Brothers that reached even into Brother

Mathias's own family. Some Brothers supported the Boston effort, while others felt that the strain upon the overtaxed American province was more than could or should be borne. The Brothers who were left behind were thrown back on their own resources, where indeed they had been placed by Brother Mathias anyway. But now they did not have the benefit of his unique and driving personality to turn to. Gradually they learned to operate without him.

The Brothers of St. John of God have mixed memories of Brother Mathias's years in Los Angeles. On the one hand, there was open admiration for the man of vision who came alone from Montreal and succeeded in founding an impressive hospital and associated institutions in a relatively brief span of time. Brother Hugo recalls that Mathias was "young, strong and vigorous and didn't want the structure to hinder him."[75] Brother Andrew remembers that "if everyone had the same zeal, you could do wonders."[76] Brother Oliver praises him for being "willing to do anything, and for having the gift of drawing people to himself."[77] On the other hand, there are criticisms of his administrative practices. The whole picture was undoubtedly influenced by the conditions of chronic overwork faced by most of the Brothers most of the time. For example, Brother Oliver was put in the difficult position of working with too many people in Rancho San Antonio. "They put in a social worker who was liaison and we were pushed to one side. I went to [various] courts to interview boys and learned to deal with probation officers, etc. I took care of the cooks, and with the spiritual needs of the boys. . . . I've shut out a great deal of this." Clearly, Brother Mathias was not responsible for much of the confusion that resulted from administering Rancho San Antonio, but he did not always deal effectively with the complaints that were brought to him. As a superior, he often felt it was enough to say, "Leave it to God."[78] The difficulties were also structural. Brother Hugo notes that "he was opening too many houses and did not have Brothers prepared to run them."[79]

Cardinal Manning has reflected on his long association with Brother Mathias in these words: "He has an extraordinary humility and perseverance. Nothing could suppress the man. He is so utterly transparent. People are won to him. He belongs to a texture of people who have that same simplicity."[80]

According to Brother Kevin Donohue, who later left the order but remained one of Brother Mathias's friends and benefactors:

He has the theory that you are dedicated to what you are doing. It may be a source of trying you out and also a way of studying just what kind of material you are made of for the future. . . . Brother

73

Mathias is a very unique person and also a man who is difficult for the average person who is very methodical and lacks a certain sense of humor, to understand. Yet as driving a force as he is, he is most forgiving and a very loving man. . . . When I was young in the community, there wasn't anybody who was kinder or more understanding of me than he was.[81]

Donohue's assessment has endured. Many today would recognize it as the essence of Brother Mathias. Today, Los Angeles boasts a thriving province of the Hospitaller Order of St. John of God. The strength and vitality of its institutions stand as a tribute to the Brothers who have built them. Not the least among them was Brother Mathias, who arrived in 1941 on the train from Montreal with an old pair of black shoes, one of which had a sole that flapped when he walked.

5 .... Boston

BOSTON, THE CRADLE OF THE AMERICAN REVOLUTION, HAS THE third largest Catholic population in the United States, after Los Angeles and Chicago. According to a study done by the staff of the South End House in 1898, the city was also the home of the poor. Why Boston — with its illustrious history, its stunning location, and its charming architecture — became, like other American cities, the victim of blight, should not have been a surprise. The inner city had been decaying for a half-century, beginning with the first wave of out-migrants to the areas in the Back Bay and Beacon Hill. Thus it was that the South End became synonymous with poverty.

Within an area of roughly one-half square mile, according to the 1898 study, there were three Roman Catholic churches (German, French, and the Cathedral), seventeen Protestant churches, and two Jewish synagogues.[1] Four of these institutions operated rescue missions. In addition, two corps of the Salvation Army worked to alleviate the misery of transients, mostly unemployed dock workers.[2] St. Stephen's Rescue Mission, run by members of the local Episcopal church, hired men to do seasonal labor in their wood and coal yards, while the Berkeley Temple, the largest and most widely known "social gospel" institution, managed a diversity of operations: recreation room, lunch counter, kindergarten, stamp savings bank, lectures, pool table, and the free services of a lawyer.[3] For shelter there was the Workingman's Hotel run by the Salvation Army, which offered the homeless, working or not, a place away from the cold.[4] Little mention was made of Catholic action in the settlement study, but one can assume that the usual individual charity was dispensed without an organized front to advertise its existence.

By 1908, the Catholic community in Boston had acquired its own newspaper, the *Pilot*, which published news of a local and regional nature of interest to Catholics. The "ghetto mentality" of the Church at this time was still a powerful presence, although in Boston the preponderance of Catholics made its effects of minimal importance. In fact, there were so many Irish Catholics that the obituary sections of the local newspapers were called the "Irish funnies."[5] It was a time in the city's history when politicians were made on the strength of the ethnic vote. The comment "Arrived on the boat Monday, voting by Tuesday" was frequently heard by those who preached the dangers of the immigrant tide and its potential for overturning American values. It was a long time since the punishment for drunkenness had been the whipping post, or the sewing of a *D* to the offender's clothing, and individuals were no longer publicly whipped for "lying, swearing, perjury, drunkenness, selling rum to the Indians, sleeping in church and for slander."[6] But by the early twentieth century, social problems were increasing in severity and reaching the point where both the government and the Catholic Church would be forced to respond.

According to George Weston in *Boston Ways*, "Many of the little hidden courtyards of the South End are used as outdoor drinking places and are all paved with 'empties,' mostly wine bottles."[7] There was even a species of "cat" said to inhabit the South End, distinct in manner and breeding, or lack thereof, from any other feline in the city. ". . . The nearest thing to a wild animal to be found in the city, the Skid Row cat may be seen only at dusk or in the very early morning — a shadow among shadows, a derelict among derelicts. He slinks furtively along, close to the sides of buildings, never in the open. His life is precarious and he dies a sudden and mysterious death. One never sees an old cat on Skid Row."[8]

During World War II, the Boston Navy Yard brought thousands of sailors to the city on their way to the war or back from it. Every public facility was strained to the utmost by this transient, patriotic, but unsettling throng of eager, often rowdy, and undisciplined young men. Every Sunday morning the populace would breathe a sigh of relief and then brace itself for the following Saturday night. Lunchrooms, dance halls, tattoo parlors, burlesque theaters, penny arcades, and all the other trappings of a staging area at the fringes of war became fixtures of the area adjacent to the Boston Navy Yard. Particularly affected was the old historic Scollay Square, dubbed by one Boston judge the "Crossroads of Hell."[9]

Boston's Catholic hierarchy was one of the most conservative in the nation, especially under Boston's archbishop at the time, Cardinal William O'Connell, who died in 1944 and was succeeded by Richard J. Cushing, destined to become "one of the nation's most prominent ecclesiastical figures during the middle third of the 20th Century."[10] The new archbishop swept into the bishop's residence and immediately his energy was felt. Dispensing with the bevy of intermediate personnel, he was apt to pick up the telephone himself and roar into it, "This is the archbishop!"[11] He inaugurated the first radio program in which an archbishop addressed the faithful, and his gravelly voice could be heard three times daily saying the Rosary.[12] He put in an eighteen-hour day not only doing the administrative and spiritual work that his office required but also in dashing here and there in order to appear at various functions, such as officiating at a groundbreaking ceremony, speaking at a graduation, or appearing at a celebrity funeral.

> The river of psychic energy was swelling within the Archbishop at its broadest crest during the late forties and all of the fifties. How else explain the multiplicity and diversity of his formal and informal acts of charity, many of them the subject of his intense personal ministrations; the daily radio broadcasts of the Rosary and later, TV masses for shut-ins, the incessant jolly visits to his cherished hospitalized groups: the ailing old, the afflicted young.[13]

As a fund raiser he was legendary. There were emotional appeals to the faithful in the pew that reached over three hundred parishes. There were coin containers on bar counters and used license-plate collections. But the most famous were the archdiocesan waste-paper drives.[14] Parishioners were exhorted to save up their old newspapers for months, bale them, and deposit them on the sidewalks. Volunteers would drive up and down streets all over the city collecting the bales. Then these would be "roared at full throttle down to the freight yards — by-passing the junk yards and on to the paper mills." The unsightly mass of papers piled in small mountains on residential streets, and the reckless manner in which some drivers went about collecting the offerings, earned Cushing the unofficial title of "archdiocesan ragman."[15] For major fund raisers, the archbishop brought in name figures in movies and entertainment, including such luminaries as Dennis Day, Bob Hope, Jimmy Durante, Fred Waring, and Perry Como.[16]

Most remarkable about the new archbishop, however, was his devotion to bringing in new religious orders to Boston. "Archbishop Cushing lowered the O'Connell curtain, threw open the door, and steadily invited units of almost all the orders of the Catholic Church into the Archdiocese. As fast as he could buy, build, rent or lease institutional and residential accommodations for them, Archbishop Cushing kept the religious orders coming."[17] Between 1945 and 1950, twenty-eight new orders arrived; between 1951 and 1962, thirty more entered the archdiocese.[18] It was a bewildering array of habits, cowls, vestments, and caps — Dominicans in white cowls, Capuchins in sandals, Benedictines in black-hooded habits, and Sisters of Charity with white hats that looked like they would take off and sail into a high wind. It was, of course, this man who brought the Brothers of St. John of God to Boston in the fall of 1945, after a series of fortuitous events, the first of which was initiated by Brother Mathias himself.

Brother Mathias had written to the new Boston prelate to congratulate him on his ordination and to feel out the possibilities for opening a foundation in his archdiocese. After giving Cushing the usual information about the purpose and extent of his religious order, Brother Mathias made a reference to Montreal, Canada, "where I happened to be the co-founder of the first house in that country" (that is, since the order was forced out by the British in 1758), and then went on to extol the blessings showered upon the American province by Our Lady Queen of Angels. He then proceeded to the point:

> The most of our Vocations come from the East, and that is why I am hoping that one day we will see a House in your Archdiocese, Excellency. Now His Excellency Archbishop Cantwell who has done so much for us is anxious to have us establish a Mental Hospital and other institutions which are in great need out here, but I recall His Eminence Cardinal Villenueve's remark when he wanted the Brothers to go to Quebec and take over an Institution for Epileptics, "do not keep all your eggs in the same basket, Brother Mathias."[19]

The original letter now resides in the archives of the archdiocese of Boston. One can read, in a clear hand across the top, the note that Archbishop Cushing appended to it: "Have him call. We need this outfit."[20] The matter seems to have rested here for the time being. In July, Brother Mathias tried again to interest the Boston hierarchy in supporting a move by the Brothers. This time he wrote to Cushing's secretary, Monsignor John J. Wright, concerning "a shelter, or Hostel, or Refuge for the poor homeless men."[21] (Wright was created a cardinal in 1969 and eventually named prefect, Congregation for the Clergy, at the Vatican.)

This time, the reaction was immediate. The letters almost crossed in the mails, so prompt was the reply from Boston. Monsignor Wright wrote that Brother Mathias's letter had seemed to him — and to the archbishop — "like the answer to prayer,"[22] adding, "I am sending this reply by air mail and even before seeing Brother Leonard because His Excellency is extremely anxious to offer you a temporary foundation here in Boston which would give you an opportunity to get established, to make friends, to acquire vocations, and to look about for such a place as you might prefer."[23] The Brothers were invited to take over the care of elderly, sick, and infirm priests at a "large mansion on the North Shore." Written across the top of the copy of this letter is Cushing's script with the words "Hammond Hall."[24]

Brother Mathias answered that he had instructed Brother Leonard to go and take a look at the place outlined by Wright in his letter, "if there is no objection." He thanked the archbishop for his "delicate attention toward our Order and we promise to be always loyal to all."[25] He stopped short, however, of making a definite commitment to go to Boston. Then Archbishop Cushing made his early morning telephone call to Brother Mathias and extracted the promise that indeed the Brothers would come to his archdiocese. Brother Mathias's next communication by letter referred in rather mild language to the confrontation with Archbishop Cantwell. "I did inform His Excellency Most Reverend Archbishop Cantwell of this foundation, and of course he was afraid of losing me, and he expressed his opinion, that he would be very happy to hear from Most Reverend Archbishop Cushing concerning this foundation in Boston."[26]

On September 8, 1945, Brother Mathias again wrote to Monsignor Wright to announce when the Brothers would arrive, reassuring the secretary that there were at least four or five young postulants "already lined up" to swell the ranks. The letter said:

> To tell you the truth I am anxious to get this foundation going and I am sure that it will be the last Diocese that I will go into. You know that I am now nearly 20 years making foundations and as you fully understand, it is a very strenuous job — no wonder my hair is as white as snow at only 45, while my companion who is Brother Camillus Monaghan from the middle west, a fine nurse, a veteran of this terrible war, and he has not a grey hair on his head at 44. . . . I don't want to give any direction, but I think that we should not give any news of our arrival until we are actually there and the work going. I might be an organizer, but I am not too much of an exhibiter.[27]

The move to Boston was probably a mistake. Certainly the circumstances under which Brother Mathias left Los Angeles were not auspicious. Even though he did return to visit the institutions in that city, to all intents and purposes his energies were now being expended on the East Coast. Secondly, the Brothers were spread very thin as it was, and although it is true that additional vocations were gained from moving into Boston, additional demands were also made on their manpower. Brother Mathias himself, practically single-handedly, kept the Rollins Street refuge going, feeding eight hundred men a day on donated food.[28] It turned out to be an exhausting period in his life, and although he called on all his reserves of talent, energy, and ability to move men and institutions, he discovered that even these splendid qualities had their limits. The Boston years did not produce the fruits that had at first appeared so dazzlingly within reach. The more difficult things became, the more he tried to create temporary

79

solutions, and the more the traditional structure of the Brothers — with its community life, ordered existence, and group commitments — was altered.

Brother Norbert McMahon, who played a crucial role in the recall of Brother Mathias to Ireland in 1949, has this to say about the move from Los Angeles to Boston: "Once the Brothers had taken firm root in California they were able to give a wider scope to their charitable ambitions. They cast their glance over to the Eastern border of the United States. The opportunity came when his Eminence Cardinal Cushing invited them to open a house in the Archdiocese of Boston."[29] It is debatable how accurate the assertion is that "the Brothers had taken firm root in California." Brother Vincent in his unpublished "History of St. John of God" says simply that Monsignor Wright and Bishop Cushing of Boston "invited the Brothers to take over a soup kitchen on Rollins Street."[30] Brother Mathias was motivated principally in terms of the vocations he believed could be obtained in the East more readily than in the West. It is true that membership in the order did fluctuate from 1941 through 1949, but the American houses came to be more dependent on Brothers sent from Canada and from Ireland than they were on Brothers recruited in Boston.[31]

On September 19, 1945, seventeen days after World War II ended in the Pacific, Brothers Mathias and Camillus Monaghan arrived in Boston.[32] There, on the steps outside his office, Archbishop Cushing said to Brother Mathias, "You have all of New England to recruit in." Then he put his hand into his sleeve and withdrew $500 and the keys to Hammond Hall.[33] It was a heady welcome for a man who had always operated on a shoestring and who had arrived only four years earlier in Los Angeles with little more than $10 in his pocket. Moreover, Hammond Hall proved to be an estate whose beauty and size were awesome. The mansion was the former home of Jack Hammond, famous for the organ that bears his name. Brother Mathias described his first impressions of Hammond Hall as follows: "Everything was there. There was a gorgeous chapel. There was a Martha Washington room and a George Washington room and an Oriental room. There were beautiful paintings hanging on the walls. I thought, 'This must be a joke. They're making a movie and I'm going to get caught.' "[34] It was the latter suspicion that led Brother Mathias to spend the night in the bathroom where he thought he would not be discovered. Obviously, the Brothers were impressed.

Aside from the gorgeous surroundings, there were the immediate problems of how to meet the utility bills and to pay for some of the needs not covered by the archdiocesan support fund. The first task was to find a parish in Gloucester, where Hammond Hall was located, that would be sympathetic to the Brothers and their aims. "I got a newspaper and saw only Portuguese and Italian names. It seemed that we were going to go hungry here!" he later asserted.[35] On a Saturday, he went down to St. Ann's Parish and introduced himself to Fathers Costello and Sullivan. It turned out to be a fortuitous visit.

As fate would have it, the pastor of St. Ann's Parish was Father Ready, an aged, infirm, and senile priest. Brother Mathias was ushered into a rear room in the rectory to meet this invalid, who was seated in an old upholstered chair, had long fingernails, and needed a shave. True to form, the Irish Brother responded to the situation with honest outrage. He turned to Father Costello and announced, "I'll have you arrested for neglect, and I'll be the first to testify!" The two priests made profuse apologies, uncertain how to react to this unexpected assault. Then, several days later, Monsignor Minnear showed up at Hammond Hall and asked Brother Mathias to take over the care of Father Ready himself. He rose to the occasion. As he put it:

> I cut his hair. I cut his nails. I washed him. He was mad, of course. I got him a better chair. Then I asked the cook for two boiled eggs and some toast. I sat in front of him with a spoon and said, "You know that Cadillac you've got in the garage? It's getting rusty. I could use it to drive down from Hammond Hall." When he opened his mouth to say, "Ay!" I got in the eggs. Then I said, "You know that yacht you've got out in the ocean?" Another scream. Another spoonful of egg and a piece of toast went down. And so on.[36]

Upon hearing the saga of Father Ready, Archbishop Cushing exclaimed with enthusiasm, "Those are the men I want in my diocese!"[37]

More and more priests were arriving at Hammond Hall. Soon there were twelve in residence. Brother Mathias recalls one with special affection: "I'll never forget this one man, a lovely man from New Jersey, with snow-white hair. He was standing at the entrance early one morning, crying like a child. He said to me, 'If only I had my dogs with me.' So I replied, 'Go and get them.' 'Do you mean that?' 'I certainly do,' I assured him. 'There are two kennels down by the ocean and we'll put them there.' "[38]

Under the circumstances, it wasn't long before Brother Mathias cast around for a suitable dwelling in which to establish a novitiate. He had his eye on a vacant house next to Hammond Hall that he believed could serve the purpose. Within a few months, the financial arrangements were completed with a bank in Gloucester and, on August

25, 1946, the novitiate was formally opened. The Boston *Pilot* carried the announcement under the headline "First Novices to Be Invested at Gloucester," noting that "the special works of charity undertaken by the Hospitaller Order have attracted a large number of interested candidates, many of whom have applied to the Gloucester foundation for admission. The formal opening of the Novitiate will now make it possible to receive a number of these men."[39] Among the eleven postulants was one Benedict Doucet, who would later become prior at Hammond Hall.[40]

The Christmas season brought to Boston, for those who could afford tickets, the famous Trapp Family singers in a "gay Christmas concert." Those who were more politically inclined could attend former communist Louis Budenz's "Crusade Against Communism," and moviegoers flocked to see Louis Calhern in "The Magnificent Yankee." Three days after Christmas, 1946, the Brothers of St. John of God opened the South End refuge.

The order had been in Boston for a little over a year when the Brothers were asked to take formal responsibility for the soup kitchen on Rollins Street. The enterprise, according to Brother Vincent's "History," was being run "in a tenement house in very poor condition and was administered as a work of true Christian charity."[41] In this case, "true Christian charity" meant that no one else wanted to take on the responsibility. According to the Boston *Pilot*, in its article headed "Hospitallers of St. John of God Open House in South End," the services rendered at the refuge were necessarily limited, but that the Brothers hoped to be able to offer shelter for the night in the near future. The article added, "In the humble dwelling, Brother Vincent de Paul and Brother Raphael daily dispense food and clothing to more than 150 needy men irrespective of race, color, or creed."[42]

Brother Mathias began making connections with local food outlets and suppliers to donate unsalable and surplus food to the refuge. Day-old bread was procured in this fashion, and a local butcher donated bones for soup. War surplus was moved from pickup points to the downtown facility. In this regard, Brother Mathias got wind of the plan by the U.S. Navy to dump several carloads of dehydrated carrots into the ocean. Borrowing a truck, he presented himself at the loading dock and announced to the startled workers, "You'll go straight to Hell if you dump that food!"[43] The carrots were quickly consigned to his custody and from there they found their way into the refuge soup.

The line of hungry men increased daily. Soon, the Brothers were feeding eight hundred a day. In December, 1946, the prior general of the order, Ephrem Blandeau, arrived from Rome on a tour of the order's New World foundations and visited both Boston and Los Angeles. He announced a five-year program of expansion to include hospitals for the mentally ill, centers for those suffering from epilepsy, shelters for homeless men, homes for delinquent boys, and facilities for the care of the mentally retarded. Further, he appointed Brother Mathias prior of Hammond Hall and vicar provincial of the order in the United States.[44] Later, when there arose the nagging question of "expansion," and how much of it had been feasible or necessary, this visit remained as evidence that Brother Mathias's view of the future of the order was certainly no more grandiose than that held by the authorities of his order, and that he was no more or no less visionary than they.

Boston held some unforgettable experiences for Brother Mathias, who never seemed to tire or to lose his zest for the work. In fact, these qualities seemed to gain in intensity with the passage of time. Shortly before St. Patrick's Day, 1947, the doorbell rang at the refuge in the early evening. When Brother Mathias went to the door, he was greeted by a well-dressed man holding a letter of introduction from a local parish church. Brother Mathias recalls:

> I asked him to come in and I went down to the basement to get him something to eat. Upstairs we had a fireplace with a mantel and on that mantel was a statue of Jesus with a glass bank which held several nickels and dimes. I brought up the tray of food and saw his eyes on that glass bank. He said, "I don't want the food." Then he said, "I just got out of Sing Sing." I thought, "Oh my God, I'm finished," and held on to my knees. "Gee, that's too bad," I said. "Won't you take the cup of coffee?" He replied, "I don't want your coffee." Then he said, "Over there in that thing there might be a couple of dollars. I was down at the race track and I used to make a couple of thousand." I thought, "He's going to hit me over the head now and take that couple of dollars." I couldn't offer him a cigarette because I don't smoke. I couldn't say a "Hail Mary," and if I moved he might think I was going to the phone. Just then the doorbell rang. I got up quickly, gave him a couple of dollars out of my pocket and said, "You can get a room for the night with this."[45]

The ex-convict took the money and left. Brother Mathias breathed a sigh of genuine relief, and shut the door behind him. The man spent the night in a rooming house down the street but returned the next day to thank Brother Mathias for his kindness. He had, of course, meant no harm.

On another occasion, Brother Mathias was finishing up the food line for the night when he noticed a well-dressed man on the other side of the street. The man finally crossed the street and announced simply, "I'm hungry." Mathias engaged him in conversation and ended up telling him about his own life in Ireland and France, partly to fill the silence while the man ate, and partly to cheer him up. The man finished his meal without acknowledgment, and then said, "You didn't ask me any questions." Brother Mathias countered, "What questions did you want me to ask? You told me you were hungry, so I made scrambled eggs and toast." At this, the stranger reached into his pocket and pulled out his card. It identified him as a doctor and gave an address in the state of Massachusetts. He had been taking care of a patient who had died, and unable to cope with losing the patient, he had gone on a drunk. Several months later, around Christmas, Brother Mathias received an envelope from Worcester, Massachusetts. Inside was a one-hundred-dollar bill folded carefully in a blank sheet of paper.[46]

Not only did Brother Mathias make himself available, he made arrangements to ensure that Boston's wealthy Catholic ladies' society became involved in the order's work. The Ladies' Guild of St. John of God was organized to support the Brothers with fund raising and publicity. On November 23, 1946, the guild assisted in the celebration of Brother Mathias's observance of thirty years in religious life. The Boston *Pilot* carried the announcement and noted, "His career in the community has been closely associated with Our Lady's feasts. He became an American citizen on the Feast of Our Lady Help of Christians."[47] The ladies' guild held bridge and whist parties from time to time and arranged for at least one major concert or lawn party per year. The guild was an invaluable addition to the efforts of the order, not only providing funds for necessary projects, but serving as a liaison between the busy, overworked Brothers and the outside world.

But it was not only the ladies of Catholic society that were pulled into service by Brother Mathias when the need presented itself. The U.S. Navy also got commandeered to assist the Brothers. Having ended the Second World War with mountains of war surplus — chairs, tables, desks, pickup trucks, and the like — the navy was often at pains to find enough space to store the overflow, but that did not mean that it was any more amenable to parting with specific items. Brother Mathias wanted one of the navy's surplus trucks. Unable to get anywhere with the local commander, he went to see John McCormick, who had an office in the Federal Building and was speaker of the U.S. House of Representatives. He was also, incidentally, Irish. Brother Mathias told him that the navy wasn't giving him a fair shake. McCormick picked up the telephone and said to unknown parties on the other end, "I have Brother Mathias here and you should be able to take care of him." After hanging up, he advised Brother Mathias, "You go down there and don't come back here anymore." Returning to the Boston Navy Yard, Mathias was accosted by several irate naval employees who made it clear that "we didn't need John McCormick to call." In any event, Brother Mathias left with what he had wanted: the pickup truck and an extra set of tires.[48]

In January, 1947, the *Pilot* announced that a new downtown center for Catholic social action would be opened to include offices of the Holy Name Society and that "his Excellency likewise plans in the immediate future the opening within the limits of St. James Parish of a hostel for needy men. This refuge will be conducted by the Brothers of St. John of God and will be known as 'The House of St. John of God.' "[49] Coincident with the establishment of this center, and the increased interest that Archbishop Cushing was generating in the South End, the *Pilot* carried an article detailing the history of the famous old church where the center would be housed, St. James, and also discoursing on its dedication (which was held on July 25, 1875) and on its architecture — an "outstanding example of classic ecclesiastical architecture."[50]

Wherever Cushing went, news reporters followed to snap pictures of the prelate at his duties and to interview local participants. Thus it was that the *Pilot* ran a major full-page article on the Brothers of St. John of God in March, 1947. Headlined "Brothers of St. John of God Conduct South End Soup Kitchen," the article described the facility as follows: "Just a few blocks from Dover Street, in a somewhat 'down at the heels' neighborhood, two religious . . . figuratively work their fingers to the bone to accomplish an almost insurmountable task. At 4 P.M. the line begins to form. Hot soup and bread are served. . . . The glorious welcome held out to our returning heroes in most cases did not materialize and there were those who could not take the shock."[51] Brother Vincent informed readers of the paper, "It takes a long time to train our men. For nearly three years the boys are of no practical use to us."[52] He made a plea for more vocations and expressed the hope that Boston would bring in the recruits the order so earnestly sought.

Meanwhile, the nation was gradually reverting to peacetime pursuits. The war veterans' columns disappeared from the pages of the newspapers and were replaced by news of communist maltreatment of Catholics in Eastern Europe and the Far East. Columns on communism began to appear on editorial pages. In the *Pilot*, the column "Sidelights on Communism" became "The Communist Conspiracy."[53] These concerns, however, did not filter down to the level of feeding and clothing men in the South End of Boston. The Brothers

85

had never considered the social causes of economic inequities which may have caused the plight of the men they served. Simply to provide for their basic needs was enough.

Beginning in July and running through August 8, 1947, Brother Mathias placed ads for vocations in the classified section of the Boston *Pilot*. It is interesting to note that this was the only time in the four years that he headed the order in Boston that these ads appeared, and they ran only one month. The ads that appeared included the information that the order was seeking young men no older than thirty-five, who were "desirous of consecrating" themselves "to Almighty God and suffering humanity, an opportunity to be of very valuable service to the Church and Society because this Religious Order embraces every form of Catholic Action."[54]

In September of 1947, the Ladies' Guild of St. John of God held a lawn party at Hammond Hall to benefit the work of the Brothers. It was advertised as an occasion to give everyone "the opportunity to meet the Brothers in this Order and enjoy the beautiful grounds surrounding the hall." Chartered buses would run from Boston up to Gloucester, and it was announced that Bishop (future Cardinal) John J. Wright would address the group and conduct the Benediction of the Blessed Sacrament. The ladies' guild added, optimistically, "A large attendance is expected."[55] The occasion also marked the second anniversary of the arrival by the Brothers in Boston. At the outdoor extravaganza, the Reverend Stephen DeMoura, representing Archbishop Cushing, "praised the work of the Brothers in caring for the aged, retired and invalid priests and in teaching Sunday School at his parish Church." A choir composed of the Brothers who were musically inclined entertained the visitors, and refreshments were generously dispensed by the ladies' guild.[56]

By the end of 1947, the Brothers of St. John of God could truly thank the people of Boston for their encouragement and support. They did so by placing a notice in the *Pilot* extending to all "a very joyful Christmas and a Happy New Year."[57]

But already there was dissension. It had begun with the arrival of the two Brothers from Ireland. They were not happy with the conditions at the refuge on Rollins Street where they had been assigned. According to Brother Mathias, "They wanted to install showers and everything else in a hurry and that's not done like that. Feed the men first."[58] In addition, the refuge was considered an eyesore by those in the surrounding areas and, located as it was near the cathedral, it became an embarrassment to one Father Gallagher, the cathedral's pastor. Father Gallagher was continually demanding that they find what he euphemistically termed "a more suitable location." Archbishop Cushing even entered the fray and reportedly told Father Gallagher not to worry until the men were actually sitting on his doorstep.[59] The problem turned out to have an ingenious solution. Brother Mathias had noticed that there were a large number of old, oak pews in the basement of the cathedral and learned that the pastor intended to cart them away to the dump. Brother Mathias seized upon this opportunity and suggested that the men from the shelter could refinish the pews if given the materials to do so. Having received permission to try, Brother Mathias outfitted his crew of workers with gloves and the men sanded and painted. Almost miraculously, the old grimy pews emerged as sturdy — even beautiful — pieces of furniture with their new coats of varnish. Father Gallagher was "converted," both to the need for the refuge and to the suitability of its location.[60]

Father Gallagher and his congregation were not the only opponents of the Rollins Street refuge. Brother Mathias wrote to Archbishop Cushing with some solutions to the dilemma on February 7, 1948. The letter is worth quoting in part as it gives insight into the difficulties that were proving so burdensome.

> Excellency, much money has been devoted to this work, and you have generously contributed towards the upkeep of the poor men to now leave it fall through. Even if we did find a place we should get it into order and it would take funds for that too. To build at the present day is completely out of the question, but there is nothing to prevent us from making the work a success even in that very place, 25 Rollins Street. I am sure that when we get the members of St. Vincent de Paul really interested in the work we shall make greater headway.[61]

In July, Brother Mathias wrote Cushing on a related subject, one which has echoes of Montreal and Los Angeles contained within it, and that was his desire to establish a hospital for the chronically ill.[62] Also included in this long letter was the information that there were sufficient vocations to the Brotherhood, not only to staff the order's facilities at the time and the projected facility mentioned above, but also to send Brothers to Los Angeles. The letter ended on the hopeful note that "nothing prevents us from looking around for a . . . place which could be made suitable for a little Hospital for Chronics or invalids, not too far distant from Boston."[63] The assertion that there were enough Brothers not only to staff current operations, but to justify contemplating new ventures, may have been overstated. Certainly we know that one of the major difficulties that Brother Mathias faced was in staffing the institutions that had already been established. But he resolutely refused to admit either stalemate or defeat.

In 1948, the refuge was moved to another part of the city. In this connection, Brother Norbert McMahon commented that "one of the advantages of the change-over was the opportunity given to the Brothers of leading their community life and practicing in full the spiritual exercises that are an essential part of the religious life." This was followed by the observation that "this has had a stabilizing effect upon the work."[64] Reading between the lines, one can sense that the superiors in the Hospitaller Order of St. John of God were also concerned about conditions in the refuge, but for different reasons than those of the neighborhood or the Boston hierarchy. Apparently, the "stabilizing effect" noted by Brother Norbert was the end result of a struggle over whether the Brothers in the refuge were indeed living a religious life, or whether they were serving simply as dispensers of food and clothing to derelicts. The latter, however laudatory in practice it might be, was not sufficient to meet the standards of the order's hierarchy.

By 1948, according to Mary Purcell, "Reports that Brother Mathias Barrett was making decisions that should be made only by the heads of the Order began to cross the Atlantic."[65] In May of 1948, Brother Norbert arrived from Ireland on a visit, in part to investigate those reports. Brother Mathias recalls one of the "decisions" under investigation. The community of Welfare Island in Boston had petitioned the Brothers to open a refuge there and he had agreed. The superiors in Rome overruled the idea, but Brother Mathias had gone ahead and promised the community that they would get their refuge anyway.[66] It was following this incident that Brother Norbert was sent. Upon arriving, Brother Norbert appointed Brother Enda Farrell — one of the two Irish Brothers who had arrived in 1945 — as prior at Hammond Hall. He also appointed a delegate provincial for the West and one for the East, each to have his own council. In June, Brothers Norbert and Mathias visited Los Angeles together.[67]

By November, there were difficulties with still another project that the Brothers had undertaken at Downingtown, Pennsylvania, to work with mentally ill priests. Brother Andrew Aucoin returned to Boston and Brother Benedict Doucet took his place at that facility. Brother Norbert then left the United States, only to return in January, 1949. At this point, he took charge of the novitiate at Gloucester personally. He transferred two Brothers to Canada, and changed Hammond Hall from a facility for priests into a nursing home for long-term patients.[68]

These changes left Brother Mathias in charge of the refuge, and little else. Brother Mathias was convinced that Brother Norbert was "working to get me out of Boston completely."[69] What had earlier been cordiality between the two men rapidly evaporated and was replaced by hostility. Brother Mathias was told that he was "killing himself" with work and needed a rest. There were acrimonious discussions about his being bound by the vow of obedience to the superiors and the order. The overworked Brother Mathias unburdened himself of two convictions. One was his compelling desire to finish the work in America as he saw fit. A second was to be able to make decisions regarding the needs of the people he served, as he, not as Brother Norbert, saw fit to make them. Harsh words passed between the two men. As Mary Purcell has tactfully described it, "It was one of those misunderstandings between those who follow Christ, misunderstandings which God permits for his own good reasons."[70] Having come from a European tradition, Brother Norbert took a dim view of the publicity that Brother Mathias had found to be a welcome part of his work among the American people. When a local newspaper ran an article on the refuge calling Brother Mathias the "Angel of Mercy of the South End," Brother Norbert acidly inquired if he also intended to become mayor of Boston.[71]

The public, of course, saw nothing of this internal struggle. For all apparent purposes, the Brothers of St. John of God were achieving enviable progress in 1949. The Ladies' Guild of St. John of God followed up its successful Christmas sale and bazaar with a bridge and whist party at the Hotel Lennox in March.[72] Then, on March 25, the new hostel for the needy at 8 Fayette Street was blessed by Archbishop Cushing.[73] The building had been purchased for the Brothers by the archbishop, and the *Pilot* noted with approval that "the interior has been completely renovated, a chapel installed and every convenience provided for the benefit of the residents."[74]

It is not easy to arrive at an explanation for Brother Norbert's conduct. His history of the Hospitaller Order of St. John of God makes no mention of his own role in extricating Brother Mathias from Boston. It is difficult to be certain as to the sequence in which events occurred, yet the picture that emerges is quite clear. Things came to a head in July of 1949. Brother Mathias was planning to hold his annual fund-raising organ concert at Hammond Hall. On July 2, the *Pilot* ran a notice that the Ladies' Guild of St. John of God would sponsor a musicale on July 31 at the Hammond Museum. One week later, it was announced that William Daly, organist at Holy Cross Cathedral, would play on the "worldwide famous Hammond organ, assisted by other well-known artists."[75] Then, on July 16, the paper printed a photograph of six members of the ladies' guild with Brother Mathias planning the gala event.[76] Brother Norbert was nowhere in evidence. He allowed the concert to take place. Then, as he and Brother Mathias were returning to Hammond Hall that evening, he dropped the return-to-Ireland order in his lap. It was short and to the point: "You are obliged to proceed without delay to the house in Ireland."[77] It was signed by Ephrem Blandeau, prior general of the order.

In the weeks that followed, Brother Mathias sought solace from Archbishop Cushing. Their correspondence is revealing. Here was a man who was prelate of one of the largest and most prestigious dioceses in the United States; yet, Brother Mathias had put an apron around his waist and stationed him in the serving line at the refuge to hand out turkey on Thanksgiving Day. The relationship between the two men had grown to be one of mutual trust. Brother Mathias received the following note from the archbishop: "I thought you should have a copy of the letter I sent to Brother Norbert. It is enclosed."[78] On September 2, 1949, The archbishop wrote again: "I will confer with you on the way to Ireland. The Lord is good. He will show us the way to save the work. I will do everything I can in God's good time. . . . I will see you on the *Brittanic*."[79]

The reference to "see you on the *Brittanic*" held more than passing interest for Brother Mathias. The pilgrimage to Ireland, billed as "Back to Eire," had been in the planning stages for almost a year. Archbishop Cushing was to be the leader of a large group of Boston pilgrims scheduled to sail on the Cunard liner from Boston on September 9. It was a major event for the city. On Saturday, September 3, the *Pilot* noted in an article headlined "Local Pilgrims Complete Plans for Ireland Tour" that five hundred twenty-five tourists would sail with the archbishop and his auxiliary bishop, John J. Wright. "The ship is making her first post-war call at the port of Boston, and is the largest motor ship in trans-Atlantic service," the paper informed its readers.[80] It was a magnificent show. The group left as scheduled and sailed for the Emerald Isle to meet with the archbishop of Dublin, the president of Ireland, Sean O'Kelly, and Premier John Costello. Also meeting them would be the legendary Irish patriot Eamon de Valera. The list of pilgrims filled three columns in the paper. Brother Mathias would also sail with the pilgrims, but his name was not among them.[81]

There was a certain irony in a situation that made Brother Mathias, a son of Ireland, part of this experience. Rather than a pilgrimage of joy, this tour became an occasion for private grief. The time of trials had begun in what would be the most difficult part of his life. Certainly without any knowledge of the meaning it might have had, the *Pilot* ran a poem entitled "On the Wreck of the St. John." It read in part, "From sinless fathoms peer you for a tryst, / and there, there, there, the Paraclete that came / as a Dove, a Thunder, or

Tongues of Flame / over the Gray glass graves, moves as a mist."[82] The poem appeared the day after the *Brittanic* sailed.

The crossing was marked by a week of storms alternating with "calm, shimmering seas."[83] The ship narrowly avoided the tail end of two hurricanes and was caught in their choppy backwash. At one point, the passengers were confined below decks, and the crew strung ropes in the corridors to assist the less sure of foot from taking a painful fall as the big ship rolled. The evening hours were enlivened by popular lectures on the saints, scholars, and history of Ireland. But it was Cushing's sermon as the vessel approached his native land that burned itself into the memory of the Irish Brother who was going home: "We are approaching a Holy Land, our Holy Land, and we must enter it in the spirit of true pilgrims, humbly, gratefully, reverently, and always mindful of our own dear departed loved ones who once upon a time called it home. Their spirits will be marching with us as we go from shrine to shrine and gaze upon hallowed spots they loved so well."[84]

On September 16, the *Brittanic* docked at Cobh Harbor, Ireland, and amid fanfare and celebration the American visitors were welcomed to the island that many called their second, spiritual, home. There was hardly a dry eye on deck as the passengers cheered and waved. The dignitaries who met the vessel even rode out in small craft to escort it the final distance to shore. The travelers disembarked with their baggage, ready for the trip to Dublin and the "many formal receptions planned in their honor."[85] But Brother Mathias did not go with them. He took the train for Dublin, and Stillorgan, alone. The images of the ship's crossing faded from his mind and another host of memories crowded around him as he stared out the window. One thing was painfully clear: Ireland was no longer home.

As will be related in the following chapter, Brother Mathias did not stay in Ireland. He returned to the United States the following year, having broken with the Brothers of St. John of God. He would shortly thereafter begin a new group of Brothers in Albuquerque, New Mexico. But his relationship with Archbishop Cushing would continue strong. On February 12, 1951, scarcely a month after the Little Brothers of the Good Shepherd came into being, Archbishop Cushing wrote to Brother Mathias, "Wishing success in new project." He had been among the first to be told. The letter, however, also added, "I never see or hear from the Brothers of St. John of God [anymore]. I did much for them because of you, but it seems that all is forgotten."[86] The note of sadness is sounded again in a letter from Cushing that arrived in August of that year: "I miss you very much. We could have accomplished a great deal but the Lord wanted you elsewhere, that is why He gave you such a heavy cross during the last days you spent in Boston. You carried it well."[87]

In the years that followed, the archbishop of Boston and the founder of the Little Brothers continued to correspond. It was clear that a bond had been forged in Boston that would last a lifetime. In 1952, during his second year in Albuquerque, Brother Mathias received a letter from His Eminence pointing out that the archbishop had seen a picture of him in a T-shirt. "I wish more of the workers in the vineyard would be photographed in that attire."[88] Then in 1967, Brother Mathias wrote Cushing that he wanted to believe that the news concerning the closing of St. Francis Refuge was false. He stressed the fact that during the two years he was at the refuge he fed some eight hundred men daily. He went on to say that he realized "there were many opposed to this work which, as well you know, is Christ's work, helping the poor needy and unwanted. . . . I do recall on one occasion your Sermon at Holy Mass there when you exclaimed: 'If Christ came on earth, where would we find Him? Right here on Rollins Street.' "[89] This letter closed with a plea to the archbishop to write and assure him that the refuge was still in operation. Shortly thereafter, Brother Mathias received a reply from a Monsignor O'Brien that the refuge had been closed for two years.[90] The writer reminisced, "When I think back and remember how proud you were when you got that plot of land from the City for $1.00. . . ."[91]

What thoughts were his as he stood on the deck of the *Brittanic* in September, 1949, and watched the shoreline of the New World fade from view, we can only surmise. In obedience to the call of his superior, Brother Mathias had given up both the honors and the drudgery of his work on behalf of the poor of Boston. It is not clear which he would miss more. The man had reached mid-life with a passion for action, a unique ability to galvanize the high authorities of Church and State, and a compelling devotion to the outcasts of society. Certainly his superiors could have seen that to recall him to a life of quiet obedience, perhaps even of boredom, in the same house where he had begun his religious life over thirty years earlier, would not succeed. It remained for them, and for him, to discover just how strong his attachment to his work had become and just how much he would suffer before being allowed to return to it.

6 .... Back in Ireland

ST. JOHN OF GOD HAD ONCE ADVISED AN ASPIRANT TO RELIGIOUS life, "If you come, be prepared to sacrifice all for the sake of God. . . . You will have to work, for the hardest work is reserved for the favorite child. Have God continually before your eyes and never miss hearing Mass every day. Love Our Lord Jesus Christ above all things. The more you love Him the more He will love you."[1]

Brother Mathias had entered the Hospitaller Order of St. John of God accepting this discipline, and the entire rule of the Brotherhood itself with its rigor, sacrifice, and difficulty. But all of it had seemed easy. Caring for the sick, the poor, the rejected, the unloved, had been liberating. Working at what he loved had tired other men but not him. Now, the "hardest work" awaited him. He was being asked to give up all that he had done, everything that had been accomplished in the United States. He was being asked to start over, humbly, trusting in the wisdom and accepting the power of the superiors over his life. Perhaps he was that "favorite child," but even that was small consolation.

Bitter days lay ahead: days of recrimination, self-doubt, and even shame. It was to be an inner struggle asked of a man who had hitherto met only with success in outer struggles. To say that he was unprepared for this retreat from the world would be an understatement. Had the sacrifice been asked in anticipation that he would willingly respond, perhaps the result would have been different. But the sacrifice was demanded. It was imposed with a finality that, in the end, savored of injustice. No matter how fair and kind his superiors were in their attempts to understand this famous and impetuous member of their order, they had failed to assuage that sense of wrong that he carried in his memory. Thus, in the absence of perfect justice, there was also the absence of perfect obedience.

The historian of the Brothers in Ireland has this to say about Brother Mathias's return to Stillorgan and his attempts to adjust to its routines: "He obeyed, but the hospital at Stillorgan was for paying patients and the man dedicated to helping underdogs became unhappy there. His years of working for and among the poor had changed his concept of his vocation."[2]

His superiors had told Mathias, "You killed yourself. You're too generous with your life." But he felt this was untrue. Faced with the

93

daily fact that his former life had evaporated before his eyes, he felt desolate. "I felt that I would die of a broken heart," he confessed.[3] The fact that he had become an American citizen was apparently his secret. As far as he could tell, no one knew, not even his family. "Sometimes I would get a box of chocolates or coffee in the mail. People had sympathy. They saw that I was an exile. I would put the coffee on the kitchen table and the chocolates in the recreation room. Then I got notice that I was to cut off all communication with America completely."[4]

He went over and over the last year in Boston and tried to see where he had erred in judgment. He asked himself where he had done something wrong, or been out of line. Perhaps, he reasoned, it was because "I seemed not to be able to refuse anything that was offered us." Or, again, perhaps it was because "I became too popular and must have made some people unhappy."[5] At times, it seemed that Brother Norbert had been the villain: "In 1948, he wanted to close the house in Boston, only I objected. As you understand, to close a house of the poor is not Brother Mathias."[6] The Brothers in Ireland, most of them younger men who had not known him personally, were not especially friendly. Brother Mathias recalls, "All day I heard from everyone, 'My poor Brother, look how they treat you after so many foundations you have made.' " But he heard a touch of malice in their concern. He told himself, "Do I have to endure all this for many years? I have seen that sympathy like this is worse than all the rest."[7]

Archbishop Cushing had not only given him the money for the trip back to Ireland, he had also given him money for the return voyage to Boston, once things could be arranged. Now the prior of Stillorgan was requiring that he surrender all of his money to the order. He was frantic. He begged the prior general to send him back to America in any capacity. He begged him not to leave him in Ireland folding linen in the laundry room where he had served as a boy of fifteen.

The prior general, Ephrem Blandeau, responded, "I have received your last four letters. Be calm . . . you must wait for the moment wished by God in order to accomplish His Holy Will."[8] Then, in a rather curious reference, he brought up the subject of Boston: "I know what Monsignor Archbishop of Boston wishes . . . among his counsels is one which is: that you have need of rest, that it is necessary that certain affairs calm themselves in Boston."[9] The letter closed with the paternal admonition to be strong, and the assurance that he would not be forgotten. But not only was there scant sustenance here, there was the intimation that somehow Archbishop Cushing had been a party to the recall. That was difficult for Mathias to bear.

Brother Mathias increased his petitions for redress and his pleas that he be allowed to return to the United States. In November, Ephrem Blandeau suggested that he could go to another of the order's houses in Ireland or Paris, or, if Mathias wished, he could accompany Blandeau on one of his trips of inspection. The superior wrote, "I received your last two letters. You cannot return to the U.S. for the moment and your pleas to go to the Franciscans in New York will not be approved by anyone." He offered this comfort, "The tests pass, the merits live."[10] But if he could not return to America, to the Franciscans in New York, or in any capacity, Brother Mathias declared that he would go nowhere. "I preferred to reside at Stillorgan and carried on just like a little novice, following all the practices, both religious and otherwise, so much so that they wondered why I should go."[11] In the meantime, he continued to write to Rome, trying by persistence alone to make his superior, Ephrem Blandeau, bend.

Blandeau responded again in January, 1950. "I have received your letters of December 18th and January 12, but I have been sick for three weeks." He again offered an assignment at any of the houses in Paris, and added Marseilles to the list of possibilities. He urged Brother Mathias to be resigned until "the moment chosen by Him." In the meantime, "the tribulations pass, to suffer passes, to have suffered and offer this suffering to God endures."[12] But Brother Mathias, stranded in Ireland in the dead of winter and folding laundry, could not follow this advice. After having spent his life alleviating the suffering of others, how could he quietly acquiesce in his own? The superior general, as far as Mathias was concerned, was asking the impossible. He fired off another letter to Rome.

In February, Ephrem Blandeau took action. Brother Mathias was ordered to return to France. He was to report to the provincial in Marseilles. There, the two would meet.[13] Eagerly, Brother Mathias packed his little bag and obtained his tickets. Thus began a saga that was both heroic and pathetic. The pilgrim was confident that a face-to-face interview with his superior would finally bring about his most ardent desire. Blandeau agreed to the meeting only because letters had been unable to communicate the force of his decisions. It would be a fateful encounter.

Brother Mathias arrived in Marseilles at midnight. It was cold and dismal. The last bus had departed, or so he thought, but he managed to catch it after inquiring of a taxicab driver whether he could take him to St. Bartholomew's House. The cabby had looked at the diminutive figure in black and informed him that the distance was too far for a taxi. But he showed him where to find the bus. On boarding the bus, Mathias recalls, "The driver asked me, 'American? Ever been in Boston?' I said, 'Sure,' and he said he had been in Bedford, Massachusetts during the war in the merchant marine. When we arrived at St. Bartholomew's, he said, 'I shouldn't let you down but I will.' ''[14] Brother Mathias watched the bus retreating in the distance. Then he tried the big iron gates at the house and found them to be closed and locked. He sat down. It was cold and it was more than an hour after midnight. He found himself reflecting on his past and present fate: "Here I am. I had beds in Los Angeles and beds in Montreal. It could've been worse. It could be pouring rain and it's not. There could be dogs barking around me and they're not. But it's bad enough. . . . The door opened at 6 A.M. and the Superior came out. 'Oh, Mathias! Traveling all night?' 'Yes,' I said, 'and dead tired.' ''[15]

There was a letter waiting for him from Archbishop Cushing that said, among other things, that they had not heard a thing from Jack Hammond since he, Brother Mathias, had left Boston. He almost resented the letter being there at all. It was only a painful reminder of that other universe which he must now look at from the outside. He thought, "Why can't they leave me alone?"[16] But there was another blow to come. The superior of the house told him, after breakfast, that Blandeau would not be coming back to Marseilles after all. Instead, he would be going right from Paris to Rome. It was unbelievable! Looking down at the cup of coffee in front of him, Brother Mathias fought his emotions. Then, after a short rest, and a trip to visit the shrine of Notre Dame de la Garde in Marseilles, he set out for Paris by train to confront the prior general before the latter returned to Rome.

In Paris, he was pulled aside by Brother Vincent de Paul, with whom he had worked in America, who counseled him to be calm. Brother Vincent also informed him — reluctantly — of the prior general's schedule and when he would arrive at the Paris house. Mathias and Blandeau met, by accident as it turned out, at the Brothers' residence at the Paris clinic. Brother Mathias was coming down the stairs, and suddenly there he was. But Ephrem Blandeau was not alone. As fate would have it, Brother Norbert McMahon was standing there in the hall with him. Recalling the scene as being not unlike the appearance of Jesus before Pontius Pilate and Caiaphas, Brother Mathias describes what took place: "The Father General said, 'Oh, Mathias, I thought you would stay in Marseilles.' I replied, 'I don't think that was fair. I worked there years ago and I've done my share here in France.' He said, 'Why don't you stay here?' I answered with, 'I'd rather go back to Ireland if that's where you want me.' I came down the rest of the stairs where I met the Provincial from Ireland and I told him.''[17]

Back in the linen room at Stillorgan, Brother Mathias prayed that somehow his situation would ease. He entertained the wild thought of going to Haiti, or even to Martinique. At least he knew the language there. But then he might get malaria and be in worse difficulty. Then he thought he would enter the priesthood and, armed with this new idea, wrote two more urgent letters to Ephrem Blandeau, who by this time had returned to the order's headquarters on Tiber Island in Rome. On June 24, 1950, the superior general gave his opinion of Mathias's latest plan. "I can assure you," he flatly stated, "that God is not calling you to the priesthood. Be patient. I am not forgetting you, the moment has not yet come. . . ."[18] Brother Mathias was exhorted to offer his sufferings to God and to pray for works behind the Iron Curtain.

Mathias's one solace was visiting with his sister's children. There were now six of them and they were bright, lively, and genuinely fond of their "American" Uncle Mathias. In their presence, it was possible to forget the weighty matters that otherwise concerned him. On one occasion, they invented a game named "Operation," where one child played the role of the doctor, another that of the anesthesiologist, and one took the patient's blood pressure. Uncle Mathias played the part of the poor patient. He happily lay down on the table and let them put a sheet over him. His sister Mary arrived in the doorway during this activity and, taking one look at the busy group, remarked, "I don't know which of you is the crackedest!" On other occasions, he would regale the family with Boston jokes and anecdotes. He told the story about the man whose wife had put a violin on top of his coffin. A visitor at the wake inquired why the violin was on the coffin; he was told that the deceased had played it. His comment was, "It's a good thing he wasn't a piano player."[19]

By August, Ephrem Blandeau's patience was clearly wearing thin. It had been a year, and the errant Brother from Boston had not yet accepted his lot, nor had he been seen settled in some Irish or French house. Brother Mathias was now questioning his vocation, even thinking of breaking with the order itself. The superior general launched an impassioned plea for forbearance. After making reference to an unnamed number of letters that had awaited him upon his return from Germany and Austria, Blandeau said, "Do not for long work for the appreciation of men. And if in the past our intentions have not been supernatural enough, God permits that we do penance in this life." There followed the dire example of a Brother who had insisted on becoming a priest, had gotten his dispensation in January to leave the order, fallen ill in April, and died in August. "In spite of my counsels," Blandeau stressed, "he wanted to follow his ideas." Responding to Brother Mathias's various schemes to return to America, he said, "I fear you will be the victim of your illusions." As if this were not sufficient, the letter carried a sober postscript: "Brother Arbogaste has just returned to his vocation. Another one who did not want to listen."[20]

On August 27, 1950, Ephrem Blandeau wrote his longest and most impassioned letter to Brother Mathias, in an attempt to forestall what he had most dreaded.

> I received your letters of August 13 and August 24. If people respect you, it is because you are a Brother of St. John of God. I beg you once again not to go to your whims. Be faithful. Do our religious who are suffering in jails or concentration camps ask to be unfaithful or to suffer less? . . . I fear that in spite of my warnings you will leave and at the end of your life when you appear before God, you will be neither Brother of St. John of God, nor priest, nor anything other than a poor man who has ruined his life.[21]

It would be the last letter he would write as the superior of the stubborn Irish Brother who had so tested him. On September 6, 1950, Ephrem Blandeau forwarded a dispensation to the provincial in Ireland, thus ending the ties that bound Mathias to the Hospitaller Order of St. John of God. In the letter that he sent to Brother Mathias informing him of his action, Blandeau expressed his great sadness: "If you ever decide to return, I will do everything possible to help you."[22]

It is now necessary to relate a parallel series of events that involve the career of Father Gerald Fitzgerald, founder of the Servants of the Paraclete in Jemez Springs, New Mexico. The lives of Father Gerald (as he was known) and Brother Mathias had only incidentally crossed in the past, like proverbial ships in the night. Fate would now bring them together in altered circumstances.

Father Gerald had served as a chaplain in the armed forces during World War II and, upon his release at the end of the war, had approached Boston's Archbishop Cushing with a proposal to set up a facility for aged, infirm, and mentally troubled priests. For various reasons, the proposal did not materialize in Boston and he went to Cardinal Spellman in New York, who gave him some seed money to go wherever he wished to establish the enterprise. The search took him through many locations, until he finally found himself in the archdiocese of Sante Fe, New Mexico, where Archbishop Edwin Byrne offered to obtain a site in Jemez Springs for the facility.[23] Meanwhile, Brother Mathias had arrived in Boston and taken on Hammond Hall, a similar enterprise. From time to time, he would receive mail addressed to a Reverend Father Page. Somewhat mystified as to the identity of this shadowy "Reverend Page," he returned the letters unclaimed to the chancellory office. Then one day he learned that Reverend Father Page was in actuality Father Gerald Fitzgerald, who had adopted this pen name in order to avoid the displeasure of a certain former prelate of Boston, who had not approved of his priests writing for the press.[24] Becoming interested in this individual, Brother Mathias had jotted down the Jemez Springs, New Mexico, address in his little black book in case it might be needed for future reference.

Once back in Ireland, one of a host of worries that Brother Mathias had to face was the fact that his passport was rapidly expiring. Somehow he had to arrange a way to visit the American Embassy in Dublin in order to renew his passport without arousing suspicions. It so happened that a certain Brother from Stillorgan became ill and was admitted to a Dublin hospital, and when another Brother wanted to go to see him, Brother Mathias attached himself to this expedition. As part of the outing, he paid a visit to the American Embassy. He was asked, "Why do you need a passport? You're not traveling." He retorted, "Mind your own business."[25] The passport was extended without further ado.

Also, some weeks before, Brother Mathias had opened his little black book and come across Father Gerald's name and the address in New Mexico where he operated a facility for priests. Convinced that here was a man who would understand him, Brother Mathias had written to New Mexico to make inquiry. The reply came quickly. This was in June, 1950. There had as yet been no break in the wall that faced him with respect to his own religious order. The stalemate continued into the fall, and when, on September 6, the dispensation was mailed, Father Gerald also put a ticket in the mail for Brother Mathias to fly to the United States. The dispensation and the ticket arrived on the same day.

Within forty-eight hours, Brother Mathias found himself in New Mexico. It was the end of an extraordinary series of events. Trans-World Airlines had called him in Stillorgan to advise him about the ticket. There was no one to take him to the airport, and he had to take a bus. Before leaving, he arranged for the doctor of the house to supply him with a certificate of good health in case he needed it. Then he went from Stillorgan into Dublin by himself. It was pouring rain. He took the train from Dublin to Shannon Airport, and his brother — John the schoolteacher — came to the station from his home in Marlborough to say good-bye. Tears were streaming down his face. Brother Mathias recalls, "He was afraid I would become a rebel and join Billy Graham! He wept like a child. I told him, 'We'll never meet again. It's finished, John. No one will ever again know where I am.' "[26]

As the train lumbered on through the rain toward the airport, Brother Mathias sat up and stared into the distance. He felt almost like a political rebel fleeing some unknown danger. But nothing out of the ordinary occurred and he boarded the aircraft for the long flight to New York. He had told his brother as he gripped him in that last embrace at the train station that it was his intention never to be seen or heard from again. He would disappear in New Mexico. He had said it also to himself, "Never again will anybody know where I am, never! I'll be up in those mountains taking care of those priests and I want nothing more to do with anybody."[27]

As matters turned out, of course, that did not happen. Within months, Brother Mathias was back in the public eye. He moved cautiously at first, but nonetheless he was determined to continue the work that had so absorbed him in Boston and that had been so unexpectedly interrupted. This time, the foundation that he would establish would be his alone. It would be one that no one could ever again take away from him.

7 .... The Good Shepherd

THE FLIGHT TO ALBUQUERQUE WAS UNEVENTFUL. AFTER LEAVING the crowded East Coast and the congested Midwest, the plains of the Southwest opened out beneath the wings of the aircraft. It seemed as if there was no further sign of human habitation below. Brother Mathias was on his way to a place about which he knew very little indeed.

New Mexico had been the prehistoric home of the Mogollon and Anasazi Indians. It was in New Mexico that the Spanish established some of the earliest settlements in what later would become part of the continental United States. The landscape was bleak but stunning, open, and largely uninhabited. Its wild beauty had entranced the native peoples for centuries and had given them cause to worship the Great Spirit in their own unique and powerful way. Their confrontation with Coronado's soldiers, Oñate's settlers, and the Franciscan friars who brought Catholicism to New Mexico was painful. After colonization had taken hold, the Indians came to a reluctant accommodation between their own traditions and the demands of the white man's religion. Catholic historian John Tracy Ellis points out, however, that "the Spanish had more compassion for the red man as a child of God" than did the English.[1] He views the influence of the *leyenda negra*, or "black legend," as having been bequeathed by the English, thereby transmitting to the new American nation an anti-Catholic bias that was also virulently anti-Spanish.

For example, Herbert Eugene Bolton, one of the most eminent historians of the American West, held some startling opinions on the nature of Catholicism, betraying a bias that undercut his otherwise superb history of the former Spanish colonies: "No band of conspirators was ever more closely welded together. The one will of the Pope rules the creed, the politics, the conduct of all. The selfsame malign influence is at work in Spain, in France, . . . and in the United States."[2]

Another American historian, Arthur Schlesinger, Sr., who died in 1965, once remarked to a prominent member of the American Catholic hierarchy, "I regard the prejudice against your church as the deepest bias in the history of the American people."[3] Ellis observes in this regard that "Catholic-baiting is the anti-Semitism of the liberals."[4] It is interesting that long after Catholics and Protestants had come to an acceptance of each other in the Eastern part of the country, there remained a separation and a mutual hostility between the two camps in the West.

Until the American conquest in 1846, only the Roman Catholic Church had built churches and financed friars, and subsequently secular priests, to minister to the people of the region. After that year, however, increasing numbers of Protestants filtered into the new territory, convinced that it represented a frontier for conversion of a misguided, heathen, "priest-ridden" people. Even the new American hierarchy of the Church — in the persons of Archbishop Jean Baptiste Lamy and his friend and close associate Vicar-General Joseph Machebeuf — viewed the people of New Mexico with a jaundiced eye. Both were judgmental toward the heritage, the standards of cleanliness, the food, and even the art of the Southwest. Willa Cather, in her famous novel *Death Comes for the Archbishop* (1927), introduced millions of Americans east of the Mississippi to the people and customs of New Mexico. Unhappily, her judgment of these subjects was often less than favorable. During an imaginary conversation held in Rome in the early 1850s, Cather has several high-ranking prelates in the Church discussing New Mexico. One of them comments: "This country was evangelized in 1500 by the Franciscan Fathers. It has been allowed to drift for nearly 300 years and is not yet dead. It still pitifully calls itself a Catholic country and tries to keep the forms of religion without instruction. . . . The few priests are without guidance or discipline. They are lax in religious observance and some of them live in open concubinage."[5]

Recently, two Hispanic historians have written about the situation in New Mexico during the Lamy years, in part to rehabilitate the reputation of the most famous of the native priests, Father José Antonio Martínez of Taos. One of the historians, Ray John de Aragón, has reversed the Cather model and given Lamy a black eye — in many places — simply by quoting him directly: Lamy suspended native priests, threatened those parishioners who did not pay the tithe with being considered "outside the fold," ordered *santos* (that is, statues of saints) removed from churches and burned, and demanded the destruction of the forty costumes woven for La Conquistadora, Our Lady of Victory.[6] More famous than De Aragón is Fray Angelico Chávez, whose book *But Time and Chance* attributes Lamy's prejudices against the native New Mexican clergy to his conversations with the vicar of Galveston, Jean Marie Odin, who had never seen them.[7]

Under the Spanish colonial system, the church had been the focal point of the community for all significant events of social life. According to another historian, George Sanchez, writing in *Forgotten People*:

> Horse races, corridas de gallo [cockfights] and other games, dances, serenades and banquets were the order of the day [during church feast days]. White and Indian friends came from the surrounding area to visit, to trade and to participate in the festivities. During these events, musicians and poets vied with each other in regaling the populace with their offerings. Impromptu songs and poems about important events and persons were recited and dedicated to visitors.[8]

The priesthood offered the only career in which formal education was deemed essential. Because he was often the only educated person for miles in every direction, the priest was sought out by the people to handle every conceivable kind of problem. After 1846, he served as the intermediary between the Hispanic population and the American newcomers, often internalizing the antagonisms the former group held against the latter. Frequently he shared the "fatalism" that afflicted the native New Mexicans in their relationship with the new governmental and legal system that had been thrust upon them. As George Sanchez states, "If anything, successive governmental changes have left him [the Hispanic] poorer than before, the pawn in the clash for power between politicians and between political forces."[9]

Historians Ruth Barber and Edith Agnew have written of the heroic efforts of many Protestant missionaries to forge ahead in the wilderness and spread the fruits of the Presbyterian faith in the late nineteenth century.[10] Their energy and fortitude were certainly inspiring, but they plunged into a social structure whose history and sensibilities they often knew little about. Thus comments such as that made by the wife of Governor Robert Mitchell abound in the literature: "Children grow up here without even the most fundamental training in morals and decency."[11] Struggling as they were against social customs they deplored and religious attitudes they denounced, many well-meaning people ended up causing more harm than good.

Once having reconciled its internal differences, the Catholic Church adopted a defensive attitude toward anything that might upset its monopoly, particularly in the outlying areas away from Albuquerque and Santa Fe. But even in the archdiocesan structure of parish priests, the conservative viewpoint prevailed. A microcosm of Catholic history can be gleaned from Henry Heitz's monograph on St. Vincent de Paul's Parish, Silver City, New Mexico. He notes that "cowboys always managed to be in town when the padre was so as not to miss wedding dances!"[12] The first priest, assigned there in 1874, died after being bitten by a centipede, and thereafter there was a continual turnover of priests who died of poor health and overwork.[13] Perhaps the most famous priest who was assigned to St. Vincent de Paul's was one Father Morin, an Augustinian of awesome energy and resolve. "One can visualize Father Morin standing under the Bell Tower, the rope in one hand, his chronometer in the other and pulling the rope at the exact second of the noon hour. He was never late, he never missed a train in his life. . . . Funerals, baptisms, marriages, masses, every service of the church had its fixed hour and woe to those who were late."[14]

The conservatism forged during the late nineteenth century survived into the twentieth virtually intact. The first half of that century saw the Church involved in a holding action, preserving its citadel of influence, guarding the flock, and persevering with the onerous tasks of school construction and building maintenance. By 1958, eight years after Brother Mathias arrived in New Mexico, the archdiocese of Santa Fe held its first synod since 1893. Clergy were admonished to "exercise the utmost prudence in public places of amusement so as to avoid entirely even the appearance of too much attachment to things of this world."[15] They were not to enter taverns or bars unless performing necessary duties. They could not sue in court without permission and had to take the "oath against Modernism."[16] Women who were indecently dressed or were wearing men's clothing could be denied Holy Communion, "especially if there be scandal or *admiratio populi*."[17] The faithful were warned against joining "condemned, prohibited and disapproved societies," a category that included the Masons, the Knights Templar, Odd Fellows, Knights of Pythias, and the Sons of Temperance.[18] Finally, under the rules for pastoral visitation and confirmation, it was directed that "males will be confirmed first."[19] In short, the Catholic Church in New Mexico still defended traditional bastions, adhered to a strict observance of tradition, and continued to carry the role of moral authority in society. Perhaps more than any other place in the United States, Brother Mathias found in New Mexico a religious climate that paralleled the one in which he had been raised. In addition, he would shortly meet an archbishop whose authority he could both understand and respect.

Brother Mathias's plane landed at the Albuquerque Airport, which boasted an unimposing two-story edifice built in the adobe pueblo style with exposed wooden beams. After the terminals in New York and Chicago, the Albuquerque Airport seemed quaint and charming. When Brother Mathias emerged into the New Mexico sunshine, carrying one little bag and wearing the Roman collar, he was immediately recognized by Father Weber, who had been sent by Father Gerald Fitzgerald to meet him. The two exchanged pleasantries and then started to the car for the trip to Via Coeli. It was hot for September, and Brother Mathias soon took off his jacket.

The road was paved only halfway to Jemez Springs. After the main road that took most traffic on to Cuba forked at the Jemez Springs turnoff, they traveled on dirt roads. The ride took them two hours and led through increasingly wooded country where several Indian pueblos lay, their adobe walls glowing in the late afternoon sunlight. A few little roadside stands offered fried bread for sale. Jemez Springs itself was a village of several dozen structures, and Via Coeli was little more than an assortment of cabins. But the reception given Brother Mathias was worthy of a large, imposing establishment. Father Gerald embraced Brother Mathias and offered, almost from the hour he arrived, to vest him in the gray habit of the Paracletes, with three buttons at the shoulder.[20]

Brother Mathias was introduced to the handful of guests and members of the fledgling order as the man who had "founded the Order of St. John of God."[21] This pious exaggeration was met with some amusement by those acquainted with the order and inspired someone to remark, "Then he must be very old." The laughter was general around the table and Mathias immediately felt at home. After all, he was in the presence of a group that accepted him without question. Moreover, he was under the protection of another son of Ireland, whose aims within the Church's structure were as daring as his own.

Life quickly fell into a routine. The Sisters of the Handmaids of the Precious Blood were located down the road from Via Coeli and assisted with the care of the patients. Brother Mathias would often accompany the Sister who distributed medication on her morning rounds. He became an astute observer of the operation and organization of the facility, served at Mass, and picked apples in the afternoons. In general, he kept himself busy and felt at peace. The atmosphere was energizing and without pressures. The physical surroundings were beautiful. There were tall trees, vistas of low mountains, red earth visible in the cutout sections of the hills, and a mountain stream bordered by grass almost as green as that which grew in Ireland. The starkness of New Mexico he found neither intimidating nor remote, but friendly and full of promise. This was the retreat that he had needed since the time he had left Montreal but had been unable to take. Here he found himself able to relax, laugh, and joke with the people he lived with. Some of the old spirit surfaced, and along with it came the need to be more than a passive part of the institution where he had cast his lot.

He had noticed from the very first that there were problems in the operation of the place, resulting from the mistaken handling of certain situations. There were things that he would have done differently. For example, Father Gerald wanted to have Brothers living together with the priests. This flew in the face of the religious training that Brother Mathias had received with the Brothers of St. John of God. Making such an arrangement succeed required an extraordinary amount of judgment and tact. Due to the category of priests who were residents at Via Coeli, these prerequisites either did not exist, or were in short supply. Friction was constant. Brother Mathias recalls, "I saw some of the problems that were occurring. I would have run it differently, but I kept quiet."[22]

He shared a room with three men, all priests. One had cancer of the larynx, the second was a big Irishman called Kelly who had emotional problems, and the third was a "really smart fellow."[23] The last had just been released from St. Joseph's Hospital and had been living in the streets of Albuquerque where he had caused some minor disturbance. He had been brought to Via Coeli and was busily typing out an explanation of his conduct to send to his superior. Brother Mathias undertook to give him some advice.

> The second or third night I was there, he was typing away until one or two in the morning. I couldn't sleep. He brought it to me to read when he was done and said, "What do you think of that?" I said, "That's rather stupid." He got angry. "What do you mean?" he said. I told him, "Father Gerald called up your Superior and told him what happened and you're writing it all down confirming it. All you have to say is, 'Dear Father, I'm terribly sorry for what happened and I assure you it won't happen again.' "[24]

The man thought for a moment, and then, quite unexpectedly, agreed with him.

Shortly after arriving in New Mexico, Brother Mathias had driven up to Santa Fe to pay his respects to Archbishop Edwin V. Byrne, titular head of the archdiocese and superior of the Servants of the Paraclete in Jemez Springs. The interview proved to be warm and inviting. Brother Mathias recalls, "He was very cordial and open and gave a nice talk to Father Gerald. He told him that we would be working together."[25] The impression that Brother Mathias came away with was that the archbishop was a dynamic and forthright man, one who could be approached, should the need arise, with suggestions or proposals of his own. Already he was thinking in terms of leaving Via Coeli. The "working together" with Father Gerald was not as successful as either might have wished. Perhaps they were both too

Irish, or both too used to managing things without interference. Whatever the cause, Brother Mathias could see that a parting of the ways might become advisable, if it could be done diplomatically and with finesse.

On one of his trips into Albuquerque to pick up residents for Via Coeli at the train station, he also met the vicar-general of Santa Fe, Monsignor José García, pastor of Sacred Heart Parish. It was a brief meeting, but one that impressed Brother Mathias. He admired the sincerity and openness of this pastor, who was destined to play a major part in his future. He was also sent to New Orleans to check out the possibilities of extending a branch facility of Via Coeli to that city. From the first, he had thought the idea unpromising, but at Father Gerald's insistence, he went anyway. There he met with Bishop Joseph Rummel and stayed at St. Patrick's rectory. Brother Mathias saw no real possibilities in attempting a move from Jemez Springs to New Orleans, and reported as much upon his return.[26]

Christmas of 1950 arrived, a difficult time for the residents of Via Coeli. One incident, however, lent humor to the general gloom when a certain priest arrived from Gloucester, Massachusetts, the site of Hammond Hall and Brother Mathias's old stamping ground. He had known the man before and thought inwardly, "Oh, my goodness, watch out!"[27] As it developed, the priest from Gloucester checked into an Albuquerque hotel and then, because Father Gerald was expecting him, decided to take a taxicab out to Jemez Springs, a distance of some seventy miles. When he arrived at Via Coeli late at night, he couldn't pay the cab fare. Father Gerald, incensed by the whole affair, wouldn't take him in and wouldn't pay for the taxi either; so he was carted back to Albuquerque where he landed in jail because he still couldn't pay the fare. In the interim, however, he had left his coat in the Hilton Hotel and inside the coat was sewed the name "Most Reverend Richard J. Cushing." The Hilton Hotel called its attorney, who called Boston. Archbishop Cushing lost no time in getting the message to Albuquerque, "That fellow is a sick man. Get him out of there as quick as you can!"[28] Brother Mathias recalls that these things were "very enlightening, but I kept quiet."[29]

The week after Christmas, Archbishop Byrne came to Via Coeli. He called Brother Mathias aside privately for what was to become a fateful conversation. The gist of the matter soon became clear: Brother Mathias was being asked to move into Albuquerque. Byrne told him, "I want you to go into Albuquerque and start a group of your own."[30] Brother Mathias, at first hesitant, replied at length, "But I have nothing and I know nobody."[31] The archbishop, however, was insistent and told Mathias that it was not true that he knew nobody. He had lots of friends throughout the country. Brother Mathias thought, "I can't rebel now. I'll be on the streets myself."[32] At this point, Father Gerald came into the room and there was a heated discussion. Certain intemperate things were said along the lines of, "I brought him over. . ." and "What right do you have to take him?"[33] Brother Mathias felt acutely uncomfortable, caught as he was in the painful middle of this altercation. He was greatly relieved when the archbishop terminated the interview and rose to leave. His parting instructions to Mathias were, "You get in touch with Father Leary and then get back to me."[34]

As soon as Archbishop Byrne departed, Father Gerald turned to Brother Mathias and told him that he was going to blackmail him: He would get to Father Leary first to warn him, "Beware that Mathias."[35] To his credit, Father Gerald later accepted the transfer with better grace, and consented to work with Brother Mathias and his newly formed group, the Little Brothers of the Good Shepherd. But he always maintained a certain reserve with the Irish Brother who had so precipitously arrived on his doorstep, only to leave just as abruptly.

Father Gerald Fitzgerald remained a friend to the Brothers until his death in 1969, supplying their chapels with priests and advising them on spiritual matters.[36] It was a measure of his forebearance, and that of Brother Mathias, that the two men were later able to resolve their differences.

Brother Mathias left Via Coeli in January, 1951, and went to Albuquerque to establish a house for men on the road. At the time, it was not clear what sort of a facility this would be, or exactly what kind of clientele it would serve. Nor was it clear who had initiated the chain of events that brought him from Jemez Springs to Albuquerque. As mentioned earlier, Archbishop Edwin Byrne had come to Via Coeli the week after Christmas — on December 29, 1950, to be specific — to visit the facility but, more importantly, to see Brother Mathias himself. During the course of their now famous conversation, Archbishop Byrne had told Brother Mathias, "I want you to start a group of your own in Albuquerque. What will you call it?"[37] After things settled down following the squabble between Father Gerald and Archbishop Byrne, Brother Mathias said that one of the purposes of the house would be to establish a place where men could "forget the past, or even forget the future."[38] He responded affirmatively to the request, which may or may not have been a surprise to him.[39]

When one examines the correspondence between Archbishop Byrne and Brother Mathias during the month of December, 1950, some interesting details emerge. The previous week, on December

22, Brother Mathias had written a letter to the archbishop, sent without the knowledge of Father Gerald Fitzgerald, and, presumably without his approval as Mathias's superior. The letter stated, "I do not want in the least to cause any more worry to Father, therefore, I would not like that he be acquainted of my writing you."[40] It continued by relating that he, Brother Mathias, had received to date ninety-five inquiries regarding the work of the Servants of the Paraclete. Then came the pivotal sentence: "A refuge or a House for the aged in Albuquerque would certainly be very advantageous and I know that once in operation it would soon be a success financially."[41] This extraordinary letter continued by quoting from the articles under which the St. John of God order had been incorporated in Los Angeles, almost as if the writer were applying to head a similar organization in New Mexico. He listed as his qualification the ability to set up an institution for ". . . religious education, hospitalization, other charitable and social activities, to further establish and maintain convents, monasteries, novitiates, asylums, hospitals, orphanages, model farms and all activities of a similar nature."[42] It closed with yet another reference to the sensibilities of Father Gerald by saying, "Again, Excellency, I ask that this letter remain with you and no answer to me."[43]

The question of who approached whom about the works of charity in the city of Albuquerque may be immaterial. Certainly it is clear that Brother Mathias and Father Gerald were not in a comfortable working partnership, but rather worked as an uneven, painful set of rivals.[44] With Brother Mathias's past history of being a prime mover and instigator *extraordinaire* of the houses and institutions, it would be logical to assume that he would be restless in Jemez Springs confined to the custodial care of a few priests, just as he had been restless in Ireland confined to Stillorgan. He shared the "empire building" strain that one finds in some other famous Irishmen who have made the United States their home. Such men, however genuine may be their desire for peace, do not in fact seek it at the price of anonymity and boredom.

Moreover, although Brother Mathias may have been the first to approach the archbishop on the subject of going to Albuquerque, there is evidence to suggest that Edwin Byrne was more than receptive to the idea. His nature had been to invite new orders into the archdiocese, including the Servants of the Paraclete and the Handmaidens of the Precious Blood. He was quick to push the fortunes of the new community once it got underway. He was also quick to claim for himself, at least in part, credit for founding the community: "My purpose in starting this Pious Association is to attempt the formation of a Religious Congregation whose work will be among the poor and neglected and abandoned."[45] A few months later, the archbishop was to make a similar reference to the new community by stating that "I established the works of the Good Shepherd."[46]

Similarly, there is little reason to debate which of the two men named the infant association. When Archbishop Byrne asked Brother Mathias during his fateful visit to Jemez Springs, December 29, 1950, "What will you name it?" Brother Mathias eventually told him, "The Little Brothers of the Good Shepherd."[47] However, the word "little" does not appear on anything until late 1953. The congregation was advertised under various names, among them: "Poor Brothers of the Good Shepherd," "Social Service Brothers," and "Good Shepherd Brothers — White Habit."[48] On February 8, 1951, Brother Mathias typed the heading "Brothers of the Good Shepherd — 306 West Iron Avenue" on his letter to the archbishop. In July, the archbishop wrote these instructions to Brother Mathias, "The Brothers of the Good Shepherd is a legal corporation. The name was chosen by the Archbishop."[49]

Brother Mathias had been instructed to go into Albuquerque and look up one Father Leary, a somewhat enigmatic individual who had set up a shrine to the Blessed Sacrament in an old garage. This establishment was located at the corner of Edith Street and New York Boulevard, within walking distance of St. Joseph's Hospital, where the priest regularly took his meals. Brother Mathias lost no time in arranging for a ride into the city to look up Father Leary. He walked the distance from Sacred Heart Church, where his ride had left him, to Father Leary's modest residence, only to find that he was not there. Brother Mathias waited. At length he saw the figure of the priest approaching the house, and he was greeted with the rather uninviting question, "What do you want?" There followed a conversation that must have been unique. Brother Mathias explained his desire to open a house for the transient poor and tried to enlist the support of this priest, whom he had never met before. Father Leary was not impressed. Rather, he treated Brother Mathias to a "big lecture about how nobody bothered with him."[50] Brother Mathias tried to explain that as soon as the Blessed Sacrament Fathers arrived in Albuquerque, which would be in the near future, his little shrine would no longer be needed. Father Leary was even less impressed with this argument. In his report to the archbishop, Brother Mathias related that Father Leary "seemed completely opposed to the proposition. . . . However, after taking the situation from another angle, telling him that he would feel very much disappointed to see his work on the little chapel and the other little building converted into apartments or otherwise, whilst he could very easily take all the articles —

such as altar, tabernacle, etc. — into the house where he is now living and which is his own property, then let his little chapel become the quarters for the men and the Brothers, he was somewhat annoyed that I should even come up with such a proposition."[51]

Brother Mathias returned to Sacred Heart Parish after his abortive interview with the unbendable Father Leary. There the pastor, Monsignor José García, was more hospitable. He offered him the use of two dilapidated structures on Iron Street that had been slated for demolition. Brother Mathias was jubilant, and as the result of his request to Archbishop Byrne for permission to accept the offer, he received this reply on January 11: "Start your apostolate in rooms offered by Monsignor García." It was like telling Moses to undertake the journey to the Promised Land. The two shacks were hardly gifts, but even in their run-down state they were to Brother Mathias the repositories of his dreams. No outward defects they had could tarnish that vision.

In giving permission, however, Archbishop Byrne also sent a request that Brother Mathias clarify his status with the Hospitaller Order of St. John of God. After all, the Irish Brother had only lately appeared rather precipitously in his archdiocese and now that he had taken him under his wing, certain details had to be ironed out. The archbishop's letter requesting this information, however, betrayed the trust that he had already deposited in Brother Mathias when he asked in an almost conspiratorial postscript, "Was there any further reaction of Father Gerald after my departure?"[52]

The Little Brothers of the Good Shepherd were founded in a year of political controversy, and at the start of one of the most difficult periods of the Cold War. On January 19, 1951, the founding date, the *Albuquerque Journal* ran the headline, "General [Douglas MacArthur] Proposes Use of A-Bomb Against China." Warren Austin had addressed the United Nations the previous day and had urged strong action to meet China's "rejection" of the cease-fire appeals. On the local scene, there was an editorial voicing opposition to slot machines in the city's recreational establishments, and ordinary people were going to the movies to see Tyrone Power in *American Guerrilla in the Philippines* or Glenn Ford in *The White Tower*.[53]

The "rooms offered by Monsignor García" were located at Third and Iron Streets, S.W., and it was there that Brother Mathias began his apostolate. His first task was to move a lot of old desks, which had been stored in them, to the basement of the church. He did this with the help of some men waiting outside the union hall across the street. Father Gerald Fitzgerald shortly sent "two fellows that he wanted to get rid of so he pushed them onto me."[54] The first night, a couple of hungry "guests" appeared at the door, referred no doubt by Monsignor García. Brother Mathias served them day-old bread, which had been donated by Chiordi's Bakery, located at First Street and Atlantic Avenue. A kindly neighbor had brought over some bacon drippings so that they might have something with which to flavor the bread. It was a humble meal and a humble beginning.

Difficult days followed. The two shacks were in poor condition, and the weather was cold. Luckily the utilities had not been turned off because the January temperatures often dipped below freezing. Very quickly, however, Brother Mathias reported, "We have ten beds," and then added with some satisfaction, "just as many as the Salvation Army!"[55] The beds had come from the charity of Monsignor García, and from Sister Frances Marie of St. Joseph's Hospital. Brother Mathias recalls that she not only fed him and provided extra food and beds, but also told him that she had met some of his relatives in Europe.[56] A Father Kennedy at the U.S. Air Force base also came up with some extra beds in view of a tacit understanding that he reached with Brother Mathias. "I had to promise to help him with Our Lady of Fátima. He gave me the statue and he gave me the beds."[57] As there were no chairs, the men sat on the beds.

Each morning, Brother Mathias would hike up to St. Joseph's Hospital, a distance of about two miles, in order to collect the used coffee grounds that were discarded by the hospital kitchen staff. Sometimes he would get hot cereal and once he got preserves. Soon there were ten to twelve men depending on him daily for food, shelter, and moral support. He was haunted by the fear that something might happen to him and leave the men without anyone to care for them. It didn't matter that they had been in this condition before his arrival in Albuquerque. They had become his responsibility. Financial support was still almost nonexistent, and he — and they — lived from hand to mouth.

Aside from the candidates supplied by Father Gerald, the first three young men who joined him came as a result of the little ad he had placed in the *Sacred Heart Messenger*. But they did not stay. He was running the operation virtually alone. But, little by little, people began to offer their assistance. Helen Conway, whose husband sold insurance, came by one day and found Brother Mathias washing sheets out by hand in the bathtub. She arranged for a washing machine to be delivered to the refuge.[58] Mrs. Celina Raff, Mrs. Zamora, and Mrs. Wellner (whose husband was the postmaster) helped with the first St. Patrick's Day dinner, an unimposing affair held at Mrs. Zamora's home on March 17. The superintendent of mails, Jim McKinley, mailed one hundred letters for Brother Mathias at a cost of one cent each, provided, of course, that they were not sealed. The letters were appeals for money, and — slowly but steadily — money began to arrive, five and ten dollars at a time. In April, Brother Mathias was able to report to Archbishop Byrne, "I am convinced that it is one of the finest little night refuges in the country." In addition, he reported the astonishing number of three hundred thirty letters of inquiry he had received in response to his little ads, which by this time were being sent all over the country.[59]

Among the letters of inquiry he received was one from the assistant chancellor of Honolulu, expressing great interest in having the Brothers of the Good Shepherd come to Hawaii. It was the first in a long line of requests, some of which Brother Mathias would be able to fill, others of which he would have to refuse, and still others in behalf of which he would strain every nerve to accommodate, only to admit defeat in the end. The irrepressible urge to expand even took the form of thinking in terms of starting a convent of the Sisters of the Good Shepherd. This idea was fueled by a check for $100 that Mother Theodora of that order sent to him in March. He sounded out Archbishop Byrne on the subject, and that cautious prelate responded with tentative approval, adding, "I do not know the size of building necessary, but I suppose we could start off modestly."[60] The same day he received this reply, Brother Mathias fired off a letter to Mother Theodora. After discussing the possibilities of moving to Albuquerque, he asked her, "How do you like the name of Brothers of the Good Shepherd which I myself selected?"[61] The note of pride is obvious. He was back doing what he loved, and it showed.

In February, Brother Mathias had written to Archbishop Edwin Byrne that the refuge was "full to capacity every night," and that "it was only yesterday that a poor man said, 'Gee, the Catholic Church is good to do this for us.' "[62] The same letter mentioned his desire to establish a "group of men who could act as advisors for us. I do hope this is correct."[63] Thus began the men's advisory board. The board would prove to be a major motivating force in establishing the Little Brothers on a firm, practical, and financially sound footing.

Also of concern to Brother Mathias in the flurry of organizing his new group of Brothers were the dual questions of what sort of habit to prescribe for them to wear, and whether the Holy See should be asked to approve the new foundation. With regard to the latter, Archbishop Byrne tactfully responded with a cautionary note on February 20 in which he advised, "Perhaps it is better for us to wait for some time longer before seeking approbation from the Holy See."[64] Again, in April, the question surfaced, this time because a certain Tom Kondrak in Minnesota was anxious to use the words "Brothers of the

Good Shepherd" to apply to his own group of friends. Archbishop Byrne wrote. "We must be careful, Dear Brother Mathias, that he does not steal our Apostolate. If your work is agreeable to him we must first establish solidly our home base in Albuquerque. It would be foolish to spread out before we have one stable center."[65] Again, he urged patience on "seeking approbation from the Holy See and on incorporating."[66] However, by May, he allowed the Brothers to incorporate in order to protect the community from someone who might join it, then leave it and claim compensation. In the archbishop's eyes, incorporation would also protect the community in the future from "lawsuits and dangerous elements."[67]

With respect to the habit, Brother Mathias chose the color white because it was "most sanitary" and would be convenient in case the Brothers were later involved in hospital work.[68] As he wrote to Archbishop Byrne, "One of the young Brothers is able to sew and he is making habits for all five so that perhaps on some future date you will invest us in these habits."[69] In addition, to augment the fledgling community's chapel accessories, a New York Brother donated a tabernacle, chalice, and ciborium, with which the Brothers were able to arrange an altar and to establish a complete regular life of prayer and meditation.[70]

Brother Mathias lost no time in pursuing other matters relative to enlarging and increasing the scope of activities for his infant association. By February 20, he had mailed off the proposed outline of constitutions for the Brotherhood to Archbishop Byrne. By March 18, the names for the first advisory board had been chosen. By April 9, there was a new stamp on all stationary proclaiming the identity and purpose of the organization. By July 26, official stationery — with the logo of the Good Shepherd carrying the lost sheep in his arms — was printed.

Meanwhile, the job of feeding and clothing the poor men who appeared regularly at the door continued. On April 9, Brother Mathias reported that for the month of March, he had given nine hundred twenty-nine nights of shelter to about two hundred men, and had served them stew, bread, and coffee at seven each evening. Clean clothing was also given out, but the men were required to take a bath and to leave their old clothes at the refuge. "In that way they are not disposed to try and sell or give away what they get from us."[71] Brother Mathias continued to insist that his Brothers give personal attention to each "guest" who came to them for sustenance. He wrote to Archbishop Byrne, "One never knows who the poor man is who comes to us for assistance. In this I mean that it is quite possible (since it happened already) that the poor man perhaps in shabby old clothes, torn shoes, etc., could be a priest." [72] He also formed cordial relations with the Albuquerque Police Department and could report with some satisfaction: "It was only last week that the assistant chief of police, a Mr. Doyle, mentioned that 'It is strange that we never call on the police. . . .' " [73] The law officers were being called out for trouble from time to time by other charitable organizations — such as the Salvation Army — but, according to Brother Mathias, "The personal contact that we have with the men seems to have great influence." [74]

The Brothers would arise at 6:00 A.M. and be in chapel by 6:15 for the Office of the Blessed Virgin Mary. At 7:00 A.M., they heard Mass and by eight they were at breakfast. Then, housekeeping activities followed until 11:45, when they were again in chapel. Lunch was served at noon, followed by a period of rest and silence. At 2:00 P.M., Vespers and Compline were chanted. Dinner was served at 5:30, followed by evening prayers at 6:25, the Rosary at seven, and night prayers at nine. In addition to supplying the refuge with food obtained by begging and from donations, the Brothers began to receive surplus commodities from the Albuquerque Department of Public Welfare in July, a fact that greatly eased the difficulties of obtaining staple food items such as flour, butter, and cheese. [75]

From the first, Brother Mathias was called upon to exercise patience and restraint in the handling of candidates for his organization who were either sent to him by Father Gerald in Via Coeli, or materialized at the front door in response to one of his advertisements. In May, Father Gerald offered a bungalow on his property to the Brothers as a place where they might begin a novitiate. Brother Mathias accepted the offer, not without surprise, and on May 18 he sent two Brothers out to clean up and put the facility in order. [76] Brother Mathias and Father Gerald had made their peace. As Brother Mathias recalls, "He had told me to jump in the lake and mind my own business. Well, I didn't jump in the lake but I tried to mind my own business." [77] He and his Brothers continued to pick up priests who arrived in Albuquerque bound for Via Coeli, and transport them to Jemez Springs. Once, they made three such trips in one day, an imposition to say the least, but one that they shouldered without complaint.

Immediately, however, difficulties arose with respect to the relationship the Little Brothers of the Good Shepherd stationed in Jemez Springs were to have with the Servants of the Paraclete already there. Brother Mathias tried to allay fears of potential discord by writing to Archbishop Byrne and saying, "It was only some of the men from Via Coeli who were making the statements that we would be attached again to them" but that he did not let such rumors bother him.[78] By August, the problems had escalated and soon reached the ears of the archbishop from other sources. In September, he wrote to Brother Mathias with direct instructions to recall the Brothers in Jemez Springs. "Upon receipt of this, please phone to the Brothers at Jemez and tell them to prepare the closing of the house there. They should come as soon as possible to Albuquerque. The Cross is appearing on the shield of the Brothers. Be generous and accept suffering. May God send us generous, courageous and long suffering Brothers."[79] The foregoing was penned as a postscript to a letter dealing with the proposed acquisition of property by Brother Mathias on Atlantic Avenue, and was written in the archbishop's own handwriting. Brother Mathias wrote back immediately that the instructions had been obeyed, but that "the others at Jemez Springs have preferred to retire from us and go their way. With such a spirit there is nothing to regret."[80]

Two other disgruntled candidates had earlier left the organization over minor items such as having been asked to do incidental work for the parish or to assist at such jobs as painting.[81] A third, Joseph Duffy, who had been out at the little facility in Jemez Springs, wrote to Archbishop Byrne asking to be considered for the priesthood. He confessed that he had found himself lacking in the "large and peculiar generosity demanded of a Brother."[82]

There were now seven Brothers at the refuge in Albuquerque. To ease their transportation problems, a Brother by the name of Patrick had returned from a visit to the East with his car. In fact, Brother Patrick's car figures in several items of correspondence during this period and appears to have been a major asset to the group. But the living conditions at the refuge were cramped and unsuitable, and Brother Mathias began looking for some other location to which they could move. Several houses were considered at various locations, including Third and Roma Streets, Fourth and Stover Streets, Atlantic Avenue, and Barelas and Hazeldine Streets. In June, he discovered the St. Francis Apartments at Second and Iron Streets, S.W., and reported optimistically to Archbishop Byrne that Mrs. Francis, the owner of the said apartments, might let them go for a reasonable price.[83] Archbishop Byrne was impressed by the description of the property, and urged Brother Mathias to approach Mrs. Francis and suggest the spiritual benefits she might obtain by doing something "pleasing to God and helpful to the soul of her departed husband," namely, letting the Brothers acquire the apartments cheaply.[84] Brother Mathias reported that negotiations were going forward for the acquisition of the property, and that "we are praying and putting medals around."[85]

The best terms that the Brothers could get from the Francis family were to lease the building for a year at $200 a month, with an asking price of $25,000.[86] By this time, Brother Mathias had managed to save $3,000, a not inconsiderable achievement in view of the demands placed upon him by the needs of the refuge. Archbishop Byrne advised him, "If you feel in conscience after prayer and thought that you will be able to carry on indefinitely your grand Apostolate on this property, I herewith grant you the permission you ask."[87]

The advantages of the building at Second and Iron Streets were many. An old brick structure, formerly the residence of the Andrés Romero family, it had been purchased by the Francis family in 1924. Currently it was occupied by boarders. It had a large iron fire escape and was located conveniently close to the railway depot. When Brother Mathias first saw the building, he had peered into one of the unlocked rooms and found that it looked rather awful. Undaunted, he had then brought Father Patrick Keleher, Abner Slone, and Aldo Vaio to see the place. Brother Mathias recalls that Father Keleher remarked to the others when he thought Mathias was out of earshot, "That fellow has great faith or he's cracked."[88] Still, fired by the possibilities, he decided to approach Mrs. Francis with the argument that it would be more convenient for her to deal with only one tenant a month than with seven. Since Mrs. Francis was ill, the negotiations proceeded via her son, to whom Brother Mathias said, "Why doesn't she deal with one tenant instead of knocking on doors every Monday for $20 a week?"[89] With the assistance of attorney James Cooney, who had agreed to advise the men's advisory board, a lease was drawn up for $200 a month for a year, the money to be applied to the purchasing price. The Francis family accepted the lease, and there was much jubilation at the little shacks on Third Street that evening.

Brother Mathias was determined to be in the new facility by October 7, the feast of Our Lady of the Rosary. He enlisted the services of a group of laymen, headed by Joseph Burwinkle, an architect. He persuaded the Francis family to move their tenants to another property they owned in the vicinity. Joe Burwinkle approached a number of building-material businesses he knew of in order to get plaster, lath, and other items donated to the Brothers. Brother Mathias went to the unions, particularly to the plasterers, with the following argument, "When you're on the road you'll have to come to me for a bowl of soup."[90] Impressed by his sincerity, the men agreed to assist in the renovations without charge. The carpenters' union, the metal-lathe workers, and the painters joined the plasterers. When a printer approached Brother Mathias with the complaint that printers had been forgotten in the enterprise, Brother Mathias said, "I did not forget.

117

We are going to have a program printed!"[91] The program was duly provided, free of charge.

One reporter wrote, "Union carpenters, plasterers, lathers, plumbers and common laborers, working under the direction of Harry Bredvad, supervisor for the Lembke-Clough and King construction combine, have already torn the inside of the building apart and are ready to start rebuilding."[92] One volunteer was quoted as saying, "It's going to take a lot of man-hours but we think it's worth it."[93] The same article went on to comment, "Once you've met Brother Mathias, he's hard to get out of your mind. That's apparent by the response shown by Albuquerque firms and union men working on the new refuge home."[94]

The ladies' auxiliary provided the drapes and the curtains, not to mention the bedding and miscellaneous items such as dishes, soap, toilet paper, and old clothing. Due to the combined efforts of the troops he had organized in this extraordinary effort, Brother Mathias was able to achieve his goal of occupancy by October 7. He was invited to speak at a local gathering in October at which he thanked the people of Albuquerque for having made this apostolate possible.

> Thanks to our generous people of Albuquerque, from the little mother who goes through the different markets and stores for food, to the dear family who finds place for all the spare pennies in a glass jar, and the pupils of Saint Vincent's Academy and St. Joseph's Hospital who sacrifice their noon lunch, in a word to all who have come to our assistance. But at the present time to the group of charitably-minded gentlemen who formed the Advisory Board to come to our assistance . . . in getting this newly acquired building on South Second Street repaired and in fit condition to receive both the poor men and the Brothers. Yes, a thousand thanks to all, whose names I have placed in a great book so that they will hear on the great day of recompense, "I was hungry and you gave me to eat. I was homeless and you sheltered me, naked and you clothed me." I know that you will all continue to remain beside us in bringing to a real success this great work begun in such a humble and small way. It is your work. We Brothers are only the Dispensers of your charity.[95]

Aldo Vaio, the first president of the men's advisory board, credits Brother Mathias with far more than simply establishing a refuge for poor men on the road. He first met Brother Mathias at a meeting the latter had called to organize fund raising for the new refuge building. Father Patrick Keleher of Immaculate Conception Parish had asked him to attend the meeting and had told him it was about "some guy and a charity that the Bishop wants.''[96] Vaio recalls that the archbishop "was famous for giving his OK but no money," and so he went to the meeting with some apprehension that it might later involve financial exertions on his part. Brother Mathias took the men, six in all, to see the building he wanted to buy. "He told us it would cost $40,000. He didn't have 40 cents.''[97] Vaio later told his wife, "I've met a man. Either he's lost his balance or he's got more faith in God than anyone else. Any man who meets him — five minutes later he has him.''[98]

The men's advisory board was formed at that meeting and they operated from the beginning with a twofold understanding: anything involving religion would be Brother Mathias's business, but anything having to do with money would be a joint enterprise involving both Brother Mathias and the board. Their first assignment was, as Aldo Vaio had anticipated, to raise money. When the total was down to $17,500 and they thought that they had scraped the bottom of every barrel, Pete Matteucci and Don Woodward said to the members of the board one evening, "Each one of you comes up with $500. If you don't raise it, you're going to get it taken out of your pocket." One week later the money was in. Brother Mathias raised the rest.[99]

But beyond the refuge itself, the biggest contribution that Brother Mathias made to Albuquerque, in Aldo Vaio's view, was to bring diverse groups of people together in a common endeavor. Businessmen in Albuquerque were energized as never before. As Vaio puts it, "This guy had something. He was going to do something good and he wouldn't fail. You just couldn't say no.''[100] People from all walks of life and from all religious persuasions participated. The board included Baptists, Presbyterians, and Jews, working alongside Catholics as well as persons of no particular religious affiliation. There were bankers, lawyers, architects, labor-union members, grocers, furniture-store owners, and motel operators. As Aldo Vaio recalls, "The only thing that counted was Brother Mathias.''[101]

The refuge was dedicated on February 3, 1952. Over fifteen hundred engraved invitations were sent out by the ladies' auxiliary. Brother Mathias had written to Archbishop Byrne in January to suggest that the bishop vest in the Sacred Heart rectory and then "we could come in procession from Sacred Heart to the refuge.''[102] Three days later, he added a luncheon to the program.[103] Seven committees with a total of forty-seven people had worked on the renovation of the refuge building and would be honored at the ceremony. The *Albuquerque Journal* reported that "more than 100 firms donated materials, Central Labor Union donated $500 — one paid day for every volunteered day — W.A. Arias gave the community a refrigerator, and Southern Union Gas donated a stove.''[104] The same article quoted

Monsignor García, pastor of Sacred Heart Parish, as having become "hooked" on Brother Mathias and his plans for serving the poor. The paper further noted that the fifty-four-year-old structure had been built when Second Street still had streetcars and "pressed bricks" had been shipped in by special order. Among its prominent residents had been Arthur G. Wells, later vice-president of the Santa Fe Railroad, and John Fitchcock, later superintendent of Santa Fe Coastlines.

The official program given to visitors at the dedication contained an article entitled "The Strange Wonder of it All," which noted the contributions of the major community groups and individuals who had given of their time and talents to the project.

> Joseph B. Burwinkle, architect, took the chairmanship of the deal, little knowing that from October of one year into February of the next he would be a stranger to family and job as he labored for the Brothers of the Good Shepherd. "Put Paul Peters some place on the top of the list," Joe was saying the other day. "Peters neglected his own business to make the rounds with me. In two days we found the plaster and lath we needed, the materials that would be required." So we wrote Peters' name down, and Francis O'Rourke, and Brian Moynahan, and Aldo Vaio, and Jack Ladd, who met weekly from October to talk over the ways and means along with the long list of committee men who found themselves in some strange wonderful way involved in this work. . . . Let's be modern and call this spreading work of a miracle a chain reaction. One man was touched by the Hand of God and he immediately put his hand out to reach for another. Friend called friend and soon hundreds found themselves involved in the makings of the first refuge for the Brothers of the Good Shepherd that they could call their own.[105]

One of the more amusing stories connected with the activity of renovation concerned Harry Bredvad and the "novena." Bredvad, a non-Catholic, who served as construction superintendent for the project, was told by Brother Patrick, "Oh, 'twill be a wonderful kitchen. We started four days ago making a novena for it." "And where," asked Harry Bredvad, "will you put the novena when it is finished?" On the more serious side, Henry Rivera put a five-dollar check into Joe Burwinkle's hand with the comment, "I was an orphan twenty years ago at St. Anthony Orphanage when you were out there all the time with the Knights of Columbus helping us boys." Fred Azure, who put in long hours plastering, "couldn't tear himself away and came back again and again until his part of the job was in order." W.T.

Wylie reported that he had ridden "the rods" when he was a child and said, "If I hadn't had a helping hand when I needed a meal or a place to sleep, I might have turned to thieving, who knows?" To which Brother Mathias responded, "Ah, Wylie, so now you've repaid the Lord for his guiding hand and who knows how many countless lads will be able to say the same years hence, because of such as you?"[106] "Now it was time for the women to step in. Sheets and blankets were needed, and curtains and window shades. . . . Mrs. Thomas P. Gallagher tries to trace back just how she got involved. Those she called to work with her soon caught the joy and spirit of the work. Within a few short weeks the full quota of sheets for fifty beds was reached, together with a room full of blankets, pillows, and other rooms full of clothing and furniture."[107] The front of the program carried a drawing of a shivering man standing outside the new refuge and saying, "Gee, but it's cold and I haven't eaten for a week." On the other side of the refuge was the same man the next day, striding ahead with a smile on his face and the words "Gee, it's great to be alive!" coming out of his mouth.

Within a week following the gala event, Archbishop Byrne wrote to Brother Mathias cautioning against too much self-congratulation. "It is encouraging to note the warmth of admiration and affection shown the Brothers of the Good Shepherd by all classes of people in Albuquerque," he said, but "let no Brother be deceived by the temptation of vain glory."[108] And within another two weeks, Brother Mathias had his picture in *Time* magazine, wearing a T-shirt and suspenders and grinning in the New Mexican sunshine.

It had been an impressive first year. Not only had the capacity of the old refuge been doubled, but a diverse and talented group of citizens had been mobilized to get it done. The result would greatly enlarge the field of exposure for the Little Brothers of the Good Shepherd. It put their founder squarely in the eye of the public, from whence he has not departed after over thirty years of charitable work. The infant organization had come a long way. It would remain for the following year to flesh out the possibilities of the organization, to acquire a second piece of property, and to begin planning for the novitiate that would anchor the Brotherhood firmly in the institutional structure of the Catholic Church. But as far as the people of Albuquerque were concerned, the Little Brothers were already an institution. They had been welcomed with open arms. In terms of caring for its outcasts and its poor, the city of Albuquerque would never be the same.

8 .... The First Decade

THE FIRST DECADE PRODUCED STEADY — EVEN REMARKABLE — growth in the community of the Little Brothers of the Good Shepherd. Two new facilities were acquired in Albuquerque, and the religious order expanded to Ohio, Louisiana, and Florida. During this time, Brother Mathias kept up a never-ending quest for new members and new projects to meet the needs of the poor. The decade was full of fascinating anecdotes about life in the refuge, the search for new buildings, and the relationships between Brother Mathias, Archbishop Edwin Byrne, and the Albuquerque community.

Work continued apace at the newly acquired refuge on Second and Iron Streets in Albuquerque. Brother Mathias made use of the men standing in line for such inglorious but necessary tasks as excavating the basement with a pick and shovel. Every day, between two and four in the afternoon, he would roll up his sleeves and begin the labor himself. But when the men arrived at five o'clock to be fed, he instructed them, "Come on, get those buckets, come on!"[1] Then they too would begin to haul dirt out of the excavation.

Soon, plumbing problems arose. The sidewalk next to the building was always wet, and Brother Mathias surmised that there must be a broken water pipe somewhere. The plumber whom he called advised him that they would have to dig under the sidewalk and then under the porch to locate the leak. Upset at the probable expense, Brother Mathias decided it would be cheaper to cut the pipe at the meter and run a new line. The plumber agreed and did as instructed. When the bill arrived for his services, Brother Mathias found it excessive. "I showed him my new stationery with all the names of the big men on the board in the margin. I told him if he didn't rectify the bill, I would raise a holy show with those men! He took a zero off the bill."[2]

Gradually, the facility took shape. In May, the *Albuquerque Journal* carried an article entitled "Refuge for Transients Gets Big Food Freezer." Readers learned that a one-thousand-pound-capacity freezer had been donated, and that Brother Mathias, head of the order, had conducted a committee of friends through his kitchen and storage rooms Friday night to display both the efficiency of the freezer and his food coordination plan.[3] The report observed that "already stored are donated fish, leftovers from a church benefit, and soup stock made from bones donated by a local grocery." In addition, the

122

refuge had acquired a flock of chickens that were being "farmed out to a friend."[4]

In the same month, Brother Enda Farrell, a nineteen-year veteran of the St. John of God order, arrived as the third Brother.[5] Brother Mathias also had two ladies and one man who were "a great deal too old" seeking admission to the community. He suggested to Archbishop Byrne that a new religious order be organized to accommodate those who did not fit in with his. It might be called the Helpers of the Holy Souls, modeled after a group he had known in Los Angeles.[6] Archbishop Byrne was intrigued at the prospect and wrote back asking, "Do they also teach?"[7]

By July, the refuge had assisted over two thousand needy men and was garnering praise from all segments of the Albuquerque community. One restaurant owner was ecstatic over the fact that he could call the refuge day and night and get a dishwasher.[8] Men who had been assisted by the Brothers began to write letters of gratitude. One such letter was received from a young man with a pregnant wife. It read, "I'll never forget Brother Mathias. No questions were asked. I was fed, my wife got a place to sleep and a job was given me. Any wonder word was passed along about the wonderful place you have here?"[9]

On Sunday, July 20, 1952, the archbishop's letter in praise of the work of the Little Brothers was read from all pulpits in the archdiocese. The Columbian Squires — a young Catholic men's group sponsored by the Knights of Columbus — handed out leaflets and pledge cards to aid the one-dollar-a-month club. The one-dollar-a-month club had been organized earlier in the year by Brother Mathias in order to pay rent for the refuge. It soon had enough members not only to pay the rent but also to handle the utility payments.

By September, enough money had been raised by the men's advisory board through its various activities to purchase the refuge building. The *Albuquerque Journal* reported the big event in its article entitled "Good Shepherd Brothers Purchase Refuge Building," and ran a photograph that carried the caption "Aldo Vaio, chairman of the Board of Trustees, presents the money contributed by community backing as Brother Mathias Barrett beams over the proceedings."[10] The total cost of the structure was $30,000, and the Brothers had raised the $12,400 needed as down payment. Over $20,000 in renovation costs had already been sunk into the enterprise.[11]

Archbishop Byrne continued to oversee the Brotherhood with paternal solicitude and a critical eye. In March, he wrote to Brother Mathias, "I thought it would be better for you not to appear in photographs without the habit."[12] The archbishop also expressed his concern over the suitability of candidates that were being accepted by the Brothers. He was also occasionally annoyed by the number of activities Brother Mathias began without his knowledge. As he wrote in March, "It seems to me that it is more prudent for you to treat with me concerning all new plans before treating with anyone else."[13] Byrne became especially worried over Brother Mathias's penchant for committing himself to real estate deals without first consulting his superior.

Brother Mathias, for his part, made judicious use of the archbishop's prestige to furnish publicity for his group and its activities. In connection with the erection of the Stations of the Cross in the chapel of the refuge, for example, Brother Mathias suggested that the press could take a photograph at the same time of Byrne "unveiling a large painting of the Good Shepherd."[14] He also maneuvered his prelate into writing letters of gratitude to the various members of the men's advisory board, both to thank them for their efforts and to remind them that attendance at meetings was expected.[15]

By July, 1952, Brother Mathias was already thinking in terms of another building. He wrote to Archbishop Byrne that he had spoken to Pete McCanna to keep an eye out to see what he could find, stressing that anything was better than nothing.[16] The need for another place lay with the fact that premature contact with the "knights of the road" often proved to be a jarring experience for the young candidates trying out life as a Brother. Brother Mathias felt that if they could have a period of training before being thrust into the stark surroundings at the refuge they might be better fortified to survive. "I find that many of the candidates are liable to either go too far or not sufficient with the men; it takes a training. We well recall the Retreat Master's remarks which are somewhat to the point, 'It takes a very noble mind to see the beautiful butterfly in that caterpillar.' "[17]

The first that Archbishop Byrne heard of the proposed training site came in a letter he got from Brother Mathias in early August. In it Brother Mathias reported that he had found a "little place," an old adobe house on La Vega Road. It lacked running water, but, he added optimistically, it came with gas and electricity, and it was near San José Mission Chapel.[18] This location was soon abandoned, however, in favor of a new discovery: a chicken coop on Guadalupe Trail in the little north Albuquerque community of Alameda. Archbishop Byrne encouraged Brother Mathias to pursue the idea but not to go into debt over it. Armed with this permission, Brother Mathias answered the ad in the *Albuquerque Journal* that has since passed into the legends of the Brotherhood. It read, "2 1/2 acres — large modern home, large chicken house, irrigation. Small down payment. Box 145,

Guadalupe Trail, Alameda, N.M."[19] Many of the Brothers who later came to Albuquerque did so in response to Brother Mathias's recruiting ads to come and join him in the "chicken coop." The property was listed at $9,500, with a $500 down payment and costs of $100 per month.[20] It was not long before work began in this new acquisition and Brother Mathias happily installed Father Arthur Gagnon, an arthritic, as resident priest with his own oratory. He added that this new priest was "willing to pay expenses for care, could say Mass and has a marvelous appetite. All he needs is a special diet."[21]

The materials to renovate the Alameda facility came from the demolition of the old historic "shack" on Third Street where the community had begun its days supplying day-old bread, coffee from used coffee grounds, and bacon drippings to whoever rang the doorbell. No sooner had Alameda been acquired, however, than Brother Mathias was writing to Archbishop Byrne with still another new project, this one involving the care of epileptics.[22]

Brother Kevin Carr's primary responsibility was to check in the men who would be spending the night in the refuge dormitory. He set up his table near the front door and took careful notes in a precise hand in the refuge record book. The men were asked their name, age, and where they were from. Under "remarks," Brother Kevin penned his own observations of each individual. Some of them read like sentence fragments from a novel on Depression-era America. Typical of Kevin's entries from the registration book for June 22, 1952, to March 20, 1953, were: " 'working as a salesman' . . . 'looks like an alcoholic' . . . 'enuresis case' . . . 'wears moustache' . . . 'flagpole painter' . . . 'looking for work' . . . 'has tremors of hands' . . . 'homeless' . . . 'feet had blisters, needed dressings' . . . 'brought here by police. Head badly cut' . . . 'deaf' . . . 'mentally unbalanced?' . . . 'had one lung removed'. . . ."[23] Kevin was also in charge of checking the men for concealed bottles of booze, and he became an expert in the art of finding even the most cleverly hidden contraband. On two famous occasions, however, he missed. Once, he overlooked a bottle that a man had stashed above his belt in the middle of his back. On the other occasion, he missed finding the bottle because the man had hidden it in his coat and had first laid the coat down before submitting to inspection.[24]

Another story told about Brother Kevin grew out of the reciprocal understanding that Brother Mathias had with Father Gerald Fitzgerald in Jemez Springs. Whenever a priest would arrive in Albuquerque headed for Via Coeli, Brother Mathias would arrange transportation for him. Usually the transportation was supplied by Brother Kevin. Once, Kevin was sent down to meet the train on which one such priest was due to arrive. Kevin walked along the platform next to the train looking for his man. When he saw a distinguished clergyman in a Roman collar, he went up and took the man's arm saying, "Let's go." "What do you mean?" the man replied. "I'm the Bishop of Davenport." "That's what they all say," said Kevin flatly. In this case, however, it happened to be the truth. Brother Mathias recalls that "he came back to me wild, Kevin did. I said, 'I didn't tell you to pick up a bishop!' "[25]

Brother Mathias also remembers another "guest" who caused more than passing trouble for the Brothers. He happened to be an attorney from San Diego who was a friend of a member of the men's advisory board. The board member called up Brother Mathias for help when the man in question began drinking heavily and seemed to be in danger of setting fire to his motel room. He arrived at the refuge with a big bottle, which Brother Mathias skillfully removed by following him up the stairs and taking it out of his pocket.

> I gave him a big bowl of soup and put him to bed in the dormitory. . . . About 2 A.M. he was in a bad way. So I gave him a little drink. Then again at 3, and at 5. By 7 A.M. the bottle was empty. At 11 A.M. he went into the bathroom and I said to myself, "Anyhow, he's alive." I didn't hear another sound. At 5 P.M. I came up and the bed was empty. How did he get out? At 6:15 I got a call from the Assistant Chief of Police who said, "I have one of your men down here." So I went down. He released him to me. There had been a ladder on the wall and he told me he thought I had left the ladder there for him to get out. I said, "You know very well I didn't do that. An attorney like you. Who are you trying to fool?"[26]

Another incident involved an Irish priest with a clubfoot who came into town from Via Coeli. He went to the refuge, and Brother Francis told him, "I think Brother Mathias is out of town," knowing that Brother Mathias did not want to be bothered with this particular individual. As Brother Mathias recalls:

> He had his belongings in a shopping bag and he looked like the biggest unfortunate on the road. He went out to Coors Road walking and the State Police car came and gave him a lift. There was a little radio on the back seat. Instead of turning to the left, they turned to the right and ended up at the retreat house belonging to the Dominican Sisters. He was there all day. In the evening the Sisters called me and said, "We'll have to take him out of here." So I went down and walked in. He said, "Mathias, you spied me partying." "Let's go," I told him. I put his belongings in the car, took him home, and put him in his room. Next morning the police

came around. "We helped a man yesterday on the road and we understand he's here now. He has our little transistor radio." So I went up to his room and confronted him. "Aside from what else you are, you're a thief!" I said. "Mathias, what are you talking about?" "Look at that [the police transistor radio]! That's not yours." He said, "That was here when I came in."[27]

Brother Mathias still corresponds with this interesting character, who has since retired to San Francisco where he helps out in old people's homes. Mathias predicts that the two of them will meet again, if not in this life, then in the next, and "that's when we'll have some fun in heaven."[28]

Brother Mathias has spent his life dealing with alcoholism as it has affected people on the streets of every city where he has lived. Albuquerque was (and still is), in this respect, no different from other metropolitan areas. Once, he met a man on First Street who was a public accountant and whose wife was a nurse. He recalls that the man "went very quickly down the drain," another victim of alcoholism. The man insisted that he needed a job washing dishes, but Brother Mathias told him that washing dishes wasn't for him. Then when the man asked if he could stay the night in the refuge, Mathias told him he could. Later, when he arrived, and Brother Kevin frisked him, he was carrying two small bottles of booze in his pocket.

On another occasion, a cook for the Alvarado Hotel had been thrown out of the house by his wife just after Christmas for getting drunk. Brother Mathias called the wife on the telephone and tried to get her to forgive him and take him back. She was adamant in her refusal and told Brother Mathias, "I don't want to have any more to do with him." So Brother Mathias sent the man up to the chapel to pray. In the meantime, Mathias went out and bought some candy and wrapped it. He also got a calendar and circled the day's date. Then he called up the man's wife again. This time she relented. With the calendar tucked under his arm, Mathias went up to the chapel where he told the weeping man he could go home, but to take the calendar with him and whenever he felt like drinking to "look at that calendar!"[29]

Also, that Christmas Eve, the kitchen sink had stopped up and Brother Mathias couldn't find a plumber anywhere; so, taking a sledgehammer and putting a hole in the drainpipe, he unplugged the drain with a wire. Then he patched the hole with a piece of tire and some bandages. The patch held for months.

As Easter approached, the refuge was planning for the men a dinner that included ham and sweet potatoes. Brother Mathias asked for volunteers to cook potatoes. Meanwhile, he got a call around nine o'clock at night from a man at the Hilton Hotel who had no money. The doorbell rang around 11:00 P.M., and Mathias opened the door to two men. He fed them, and since there was only one bed available, he told one to sleep on the floor, and then went back to bed himself. At midnight, the doorbell rang again. This time it was the man who had called from the Hilton Hotel. So Brother Mathias bedded him down on the floor also. When morning arrived, he fed the men breakfast and then departed for the Veterans Hospital to sing Mass for a Father McHugh. He left the potatoes to cook in the pressure cooker. When he came back to the refuge, however, he met an astonishing sight: The pressure cooker had blown up and potatoes were plastered all over the ceiling. The man who had been washing dishes at the sink wasn't hurt, but the stove was ruined and the window had been blown out. The men he had taken in the night before couldn't do enough for him. Somehow they got Easter dinner on the table. The ham was already cooked, but the rest of the dinner was made up of "radishes and other things."[30]

During 1953, the stove was replaced, a second-floor bathroom was improved, and the ladies' auxiliary covered the dining-room tables with linoleum. Mrs. Celina Raff gave screens for the refuge windows and made possible the rewiring of the facility.[31] In July of that year, Brother Mathias wrote an ebullient letter to Archbishop Byrne over the dedication ceremony planned for the original eight Brothers in September, at which time they would take their final vows. The Brothers were Patrick, Enda, Kevin, John, James, Matthew, Eugene, and, of course, Mathias himself. "I do feel that our group is called on to render great services to the Church all over the world," he noted. "Please God and His Blessed Mother . . . there should be no limitation to what we should do."[32]

That fall, he wrote the archbishop that six rooms for the Brothers had been constructed out of the old chicken barn in Alameda. The facility had been given the gift of a heating system, and now Brother Mathias was looking for some plumbers to install it, praying, "Please God and His Blessed Mother some generous person will turn up in due time."[33] He also reported that he had numerous convicts writing to him and that he was answering the letters with the consolation that they, "by their example and spirit of resignation," could be apostles in prison.[34]

The early months of 1954 were taken up with internal concerns. Both Brothers Patrick and Enda had decided to leave the order, and their departure was a cause of grief for both Brother Mathias and Archbishop Byrne. In March, Brother Mathias had written to Archbishop Byrne concerning his fears for Brother Patrick after his trip to California with a certain Father Murphy, "on account of the manner in which things turned out."[35] The trip had been exceedingly difficult for Brother Patrick because of the personality of the priest, and since his return, there had been much argument. Shortly thereafter, Brother Patrick announced his intention to leave the order. Archbishop Byrne wrote to ask if there was anyhing that could be done to repair the breach and hold on to Brother Enda.[36] Neither Brother had told Brother Mathias of his intentions. He surmised that part of the difficulty lay with the fact that Brother Patrick did not like the secular institute form of organization.[37] After departing, Patrick evidently had second thoughts, and returned on St. Patrick's Day amid much rejoicing. But he left again in July. At that time, he wrote a simple letter to the archbishop stating that "the Brothers of the Good Shepherd is not my vocation."[38]

Also, during the first months of 1954, the project of visiting the county jail was undertaken and pursued with enthusiasm by Brother Mathias. The Brothers would visit inmates one day during the week with "little comforts" such as soap, stationary, and pious literature, and then return on Sunday to say the Rosary and to offer "a little encouragement in a spiritual manner."[39]

The "Report to Benefactors" for April asked for more clothing and reported that 2,853 meals, 421 nights' lodging, and 149 items of clothing had been distributed in one month alone. In May, Daniel Donahue sent $5,000 to Archbishop Byrne for Brother Mathias, and in June, Brother John (who had complained of "too much spirituality" at the retreats) went for a week to the mountains with the Sacred Heart Boy Scouts.[40] There were now seven Brothers in Alameda and six at the refuge. Brother Mathias was again faced with housing problems and tried to buy an eight-room surplus building from Los Alamos "very cheaply," but "Father Gerald found out about it and got it first." He consoled himself with the observation that it was "all for the Church."[41]

The July issue of *The Shepherd's Call* was full of news about the activities of the Brothers at the refuge and at Villa Maria. The issue included poems such as "Be the Boy They Don't Meet Every Day" and "Sweet Charity," both by Danny Cavanaugh; an invitation to "you dear ladies" to join the ladies' auxiliary; and a form for wills because, "You can't take it with you. . . . That we know must surely be true if we think of money left in vaults, safety boxes," etc.

In early August, Brother Mathias appeared before the city commissioners in an effort to get a reduction on the refuge's water bill and gave this account to Archbishop Byrne: "At that particular meeting the Meeting Hall was filled to capacity with people from all over the city with their problems. I stood up to ask a reduction of 50% on our Water Bill and all in the audience shouted out 'No, no, give him 100% reduction.' So Mr. Tingley said, 'Brother himself should know what he is asking for and let us be directed by that.' Of course, I renewed my request for 50% as I feared that some of the Commissioners might be of the opinion that something was arranged beforehand with those people. I got the 50% reduction and the guarantee that if there was too much of a burden on me I could come before them again. All this made me happy especially to know that we have the sincere sympathy of the people in all [our endeavors]."[42]

In December, the resident priest at Villa Maria in Alameda left in a huff and returned to Via Coeli. In an angry letter to Archbishop Byrne the priest, a Father Pochily, complained that Brother Mathias had not provided him with proper candles or wine for his services, and that he had to borrow these supplies from the Alameda parish. He accused Brother Mathias of buying candles from the five-and-ten store and wine from drugstores. He told his superior, "They aren't that poor. It is a matter of conscience to me and I will not yield."[43] Archbishop Byrne sent the letter on to Brother Mathias with a note in the margin that read, "Please tell me if what is stated here is true, namely that you do not use proper wine and candles, etc."[44] Brother Mathias wrote to assure the archbishop that the letter was full of misinformation, and that "this all proves my statement some months ago, 'Father [Pochily] is a sick man,' when our little brothers complained of Father's ways."[45] The Mass wine came from the Christian Brothers and the company of Will and Baumer had always furnished candles and sanctuary lights free of charge.[46]

Brother Mathias wrote an open letter to the Albuquerque community in *The Shepherd's Call* at the end of the year, in which he gave his Brothers this tribute: "While all people were fearing the ravages of Communism, a little band of laymen were striving to keep together and live off public charity, and at the same time caring for the needy and abandoned men — 'Our own displaced persons' — without distinction of race, color, or creed. . . . It is a group of Brothers who devote their lives for the welfare of their fellow men, even at the risk of their own lives."[47]

As 1955 began, things continued to progress at the refuge and at Villa Maria, with a few hitches here and there. One continual difficulty experienced by the Brothers was the problem of keeping priests to staff two chapels. Those sent from Via Coeli were often in poor health or unsuitable for extensive service. For example, one Father Schneider, who had been with the Brothers for two years, began to suffer severe health problems in May. Brother Mathias wrote to Archbishop Byrne:

> I just wish to inform you that for some time now poor Father Schneider's health, especially his mental condition, seems to be deteriorating considerably. Each day he discovers something new wrong with him. He goes to see his Doctor almost every other day. Some days he tells me early in the morning that he cannot say Holy Mass but I encourage him to say Mass. Other days when he meets a Brother he tells him that he is not able, so then I cannot interfere as he remains in bed. . . . In the past he used to pass almost whole days in the Chapel, but of late he has given up that pious practice also. I am sure with the help of God and His Blessed Mother he will snap out of this again, but I just wanted Your Excellency to know how he is.[48]

The annual report of the Good Shepherd Refuge for 1954 listed 53,369 complete hot meals served, 5,774 nights of shelter given, 1,440 items of clothing issued, and 213 families assisted. The report noted, "While this is not a comparison report, an interesting item to note is the number of meals served in 1952 totaled 16,606, while the number for 1954 is 53,369."[49]

Brother Mathias was now pursuing a new objective, namely, a home for the aged and chronically ill. He had been elected secretary of the New Mexico Association of Nursing Homes and had discovered that Albuquerque did not have a Catholic home for the aged. In a letter to Archbishop Byrne, he reported, "I find that in all those who run these nursing homes" there are no Catholics among their staff members; therefore, "we should study some means of doing something in that direction."[50] Assuring the archbishop (who was always a little cautious about beginning new projects) that the addition to the refuge would be finished soon, he continued, "And then we will try to have a meeting of the men's advisory board for they have not been active for some time."[51] The idea was obviously dear to Brother Mathias's heart, and he felt it would also galvanize the men's board to renewed activity. As predicted, the archbishop was not enthused by the idea of a home for the aged. He wrote to Brother Mathias, "As I told you in a previous letter, I do not think it is prudent for you to work on two objectives of the novitiate proper and of the home for the aged."[52] In his view, the establishment of a novitiate, representing as it did a stabilizing force in the life of the community, was by far the higher priority.

Archbishop Byrne was also concerned about the status of the Little Brothers of the Good Shepherd and he hoped to organize them into a secular institute.[53] Brother Mathias had never warmed to the prospect but did not want to appear to be in opposition to the wishes of his superior. Thus, the two men carried on a peculiarly uneven correspondence on the subject. When Brothers Patrick and Enda left the Brotherhood, Brother Mathias had informed the archbishop that their reason was, in part, due to a resistance to the idea of the secular institute. At the time, Byrne had replied, "If Brothers Patrick and Enda did not favor the idea of the Secular Institute, why did they not speak to me about it?"[54]

In July, 1955, Archbishop Byrne wrote to Brother Mathias that he had met with one Father Sigstein who had informed him that "you [Brother Mathias] don't take kindly to my advice for a Secular Institute of Little Brothers of the Good Shepherd."[55] (Father Sigstein was then working with the Brothers to set up the novitiate program.) He reminded Brother Mathias that when he, Archbishop Byrne, had been in Rome, the Sacred Congregation for Religious and Secular Institutes (as it is now called) had indicated that this was the proper form of organization for the order. Moreover, he expressed his disapproval of Brother Mathias's premature preparation of new constitutions. "Please desist from doing anything in regard to the Constitutions. The copies you are sending out have not my approval. You seem to have the custom of doing things and then advising me after they are done. This is not the proper way to act."[56] Apparently, the archbishop and Father Sigstein had discussed the situation and were agreed that there should be no further extension of Brothers to new foundations. "Be patient and do not push this matter too quickly."[57] In a moment of exasperation, he wrote Brother Mathias, "If you disobey, the work will die here."[58] Clearly, this was an issue on which Byrne would tolerate no opposition.

The renovation of the chicken coop in Alameda, which had been named Villa Maria, also proceeded apace in 1955. In January, *The Shepherd's Call* issued an appeal to the Albuquerque community to "help us complete this building," accompanied by an idealized drawing of the facility. Readers were called upon to assist the Brothers so that "it will look like the above drawing."[59] "Will you buy a cement block, a bag of cement, a pane of glass, a keg of nails, a piece of lumber, or even a brick to help us realize this project?"[60] Readers were reminded that the first remodeling of Alameda had been undertaken in December, 1952, led by Brother Mathias "in black trousers, T-shirt and suspenders." One Brother, who had borrowed a truck in those days to haul materials, quoted the owner of the truck as having said, "It's no use refusing him. When you say 'no' at the front door, he just returns again through the back door."[61] In response to the appeals that appeared in *The Shepherd's Call*, the Brothers received a typewriter from an Albuquerque city official, and a good washing machine from "another kind and charitable Albuquerquean."

Letters of gratitude from the "guests" of the refuge illustrate the kind of impact the Brothers were making on the people they directly served. One, from a man who signed himself "T.K., Missouri," gave the following account of his stay with the Brothers: "I stayed with you a few days when I first came to Albuquerque and you were so kind to me, without knowing anything about me, and without asking any questions. When you put me on my feet I went to work cooking. Two of the Brothers will remember they used to drive past First and Central when I was standing on the corner waiting for my ride to work and holler at me."[62] Another testimonial, from "Leo" to Brother Patrick, said, "Webster in his entirety could never express my sincere thanks."[63] Enclosed was a donation of $5 and the promise of more to come. "I only wish it could be a 50 instead of a 5."[64]

On one occasion, a Brother found a man named Jim sitting on the refuge steps with a plaster cast on his hand. The man asked the Brother if he could tell him where to go to get it removed. "Hop in the car," said the Brother, "and we'll see if the hospital can help us." Due to delays at the hospital, Jim wandered off by himself and had the cast cut off at a blacksmith shop. Then he proceeded to the refuge, showered, got a clean set of clothes, and reported to the Army induction center. The Brothers later got a letter from him that read:

> Sorry I haven't written sooner, but it's pretty hectic going into the Army. I had a swell trip from Albuquerque to here on the train. . . . I am often praying for you and all the Little Brothers. You certainly are doing a tiring and thankless job as far as most people may go, but for me, Brother, it was a blessing. When I wandered into the Refuge broke, hungry and very much alone, your own sincere friendship and interest struck me in a way that has led me back to hope.[65]

Brother Mathias also received an unexpected commendation from Father Gerald Fitzgerald in a letter that the latter sent to Archbishop Byrne. Father Gerald wrote, "It gives me great satisfaction to make the following comment. . . . If Your Excellency has a truly holy Religious in the Spirit of St. Vincent de Paul under your jurisdiction, that man is the venerable Brother Mathias."[66] He referred to the "grandeur of Brother Mathias's apostolate that makes sour soup and stale bread acceptable to lips that have been touched by the caress of Divine caritas [charity]."[67]

In December, the Little Brothers received a Hill-Burton grant from the federal government in the amount of $50,000, for a three-year period, on condition that the amount be matched. Archbishop Byrne wrote to Brother Mathias his congratulations but appended the comment, "Now you will have to be careful that the money is spent in accordance with the grant, otherwise you will get in trouble. . . . Already one of the newspapers is critical of the grant to you."[68] Brother Mathias wrote back that he had enlisted the support of the men's advisory board to match the funds, and then slipped in the comment that "perhaps Almighty God wishes that we consider the property on Thirteenth Street which is a very fine property and . . . [has plenty of] privacy."[69] However, after every avenue had been explored for the raising of the needed matching funds without success, Brother Mathias had to give up the grant. The New Mexico Department of Public Health sent him a letter acknowledging that fact, and noted that the application would remain on file for future action.[70]

Daniel Donohue turned out to be the guardian angel of the Good Shepherd Novitiate. Brother Mathias wrote to him about needing a place to establish the facility, and he came to Albuquerque. The two men went to see the house that was for sale on Thirteenth Street. Brother Mathias recalls having said to Donohue, "I want no more old shacks."[71] It was a bad day. The wind was blowing, and tumbleweeds careened down Mountain Road. The house was vacant, and Brother Mathias assisted Donohue in climbing in by an unlocked window. Although the premises were dirty, the place appeared to have real possibilities, so Brother Mathias called up the real estate agent. By a remarkable coincidence, the property was owned by a Catholic newspaperman named Paul Bell, and the mortgage was held by none other than Archbishop Byrne. Brother Mathias recalls that he wrote to the chancellory and was told, "Mind your own business." "That's what I'm doing," was his reply.[72] Later, the archbishop came down with the local sheriff, John Flasca, and an insurance agent to discuss the deal. Brother Mathias insisted on also getting the vacant land extending back to Fourteenth Street. The archbishop was annoyed. Eventually, however, he saw the inevitability of the transfer, and both the house and the land passed into the hands of the Little Brothers.

Brother Mathias was still not satisfied. Next door to his property on Thirteenth Street was a rooming house that had residents of questionable character. They ran their television sets until the early hours of the morning, and then cooked bacon and eggs, sending the smell — and the smoke — all over the neighborhood. Brother Mathias went to the archbishop about acquiring that property also. According to Mathias, the response he got when he requested permission to buy the rooming house was, "Oh, you never stop! You never end!"[73] Brother

Mathias replied, "But we must have peace and quiet, Your Excellency."[74] The issue would surface again.

Daniel Donohue assisted with the renovation costs of the new acquisition on Thirteenth Street. He sent a two-thousand-dollar check to Archbishop Byrne for the Brothers in January, 1956. His letter accompanying the money, and explaining the routing of it through the archbishop's office, said, "My reason for imposing on Your Excellency is to sort of keep Brother 'in tow.' I feel if these things come to him per his Ordinary he will be more inclined to go slow with things. I still get after him about taking things slowly and to be very cautious as to whom he admits into the community."[75] Brother Mathias put the money to use for work on the chapel. He soon received another grant of $5,000, with an additional $5,000 arriving in May; the total estimate for the chapel was $7,946, with $3,765 for the kitchen remodeling.[76] On May 7, Brother Mathias informed his superior that "Daniel is shipping the altar in a few weeks, and other pieces of furniture are on their way."[77] In August, the benches arrived and were set up in the chapel. The finished chapel was a monument to the generosity of Donohue but also to the vision of Brother Mathias. It stands today as a beautiful reminder of the spirit that animates both men.

In August, the issue of the secular institute became a bone of contention again. Archbishop Byrne informed Brother Mathias that he was forming the institute according to the wishes of the Sacred Congregation of Religious (as it was then known). He reminded him, "If the Little Brothers begin their life with disobedience, the blessing of God will not be upon them." In closing he asked the Holy Spirit "to give all of us the grace of docility. . . ."[78]

By October, Brother Mathias was complaining about the delays in achieving the status that the archbishop was so resolved they should receive.

> I am wondering where we are with the constitutions as there seems much unrest here and always questioning me as to our status, etc. . . . So I just tell the Brothers we are observing the Rule of St. Augustine and when they live according to that rule they have nothing to complain about. . . . Father, it is now close to six years that we have been established and I hope and pray that we will have some definite news soon. Brother Francis says that the new candidates or prospective candidates have a right to know our status and where we are aiming.[79]

Again in December, he wrote his superior: "In all Brother Kevin's letters he asks me what we are doing for the Constitutions, etc. He is all out for the Secular Institute as he sees that in the work both at the

Refuge here and in Columbus it takes that type. . . . I would like now to be able to give him some definite news in my letter to him for the New Year."[80] Archbishop Byrne responded in a brief letter at Christmas with, "Constitutions with final corrections being prepared for the Holy See."[81]

Along with these irksome matters of organization was the equally difficult task of obtaining a priest to serve the novitiate. In August, it appeared that one Father Moylan might come from Via Coeli to be novice-master. By October, Brother Mathias was writing that "some of the young candidates at the Novitiate left us during the past week as they thought the work would be too hard for them" and that the spiritual director was not expected soon.[82] By November, Brother Mathias was at his wit's end. "I have by now exhausted all possible means for securing a priest for the Novitiate."[83] It appeared that Father Schneider, who was serving the needs of the refuge, might have to be commandeered into also serving the novitiate. Then, in December, Father Gerald Fitzgerald proposed a certain Father George, but Brother Mathias was not impressed with his qualifications.[84] All in all, it was a dilemma. By June of the following year, Father Schneider was still saying Mass at both places, but Brother Mathias could finally report, "Father Gerald has finally acceded to my repeated requests for Father Sheridan's presence at the Novitiate. God willing, it should open officially very, very soon."[85] On June 20, he wrote triumphantly to Archbishop Byrne, "Father Sheridan has arrived!"[86]

In 1957, Brother Mathias became ill. It began with a bout of intestinal flu in January. Even so, he was still buzzing with projects, including becoming a distributor of Lourdes water in the Southwest, having the archbishop pose in front of a pickup truck to aid the St. Vincent de Paul Society, and having the ladies' auxiliary incorporated so that they could "negotiate with the Old Ladies Home."[87] By February, however, he found himself in the hospital, where he remained for a month. The cause apparently was some medicine he had been given for a cold in January that had adversely affected his liver. "It could happen in one case out of a thousand and it happened to me," he observed.[88] Archbishop Byrne wrote a concerned note, and advised him to "enjoy St. Patrick's Day but do not eat too much corned beef and cabbage." He added, "Much is due to your prayer and exemplary life. May the Lord preserve you for many years."[89]

As soon as he recovered, Brother Mathias renewed the discussions over the issue of the home for the aged with his reluctant prelate. In April, he wrote ebulliently to the latter, saying: "I have been informed unofficially that the two apartment houses next to the Novitiate may be on the market soon. . . . I do not wish to make any move without the permission from Your Excellency. . . . I did, however, consult Mr. Hugh Graham, President of the Men's Advisory Board, and he also asked me to see Mr. Dickinson at McCannas to get the evaluation."[90] Archbishop Byrne shot back a reply: "I doubt that this is the proper time to start a home for the aged. . . . It is more important to get a good priest for the Novitiate. Until it is functioning, we will lose good candidates."[91] But Brother Mathias was not daunted. Reporting on his efforts to find such a priest, he added, "With regards to the property adjacent to the Novitiate on 13th Street which I mentioned for a home for the aged, it was primarily not to lose the opportunity of this valuable property at such a reasonable price. It may get into the hands of undesirable people."[92] He suggested that when the archbishop was in the vicinity he might come see it; Byrne was adamant about rejecting the whole idea. "As I told you over the phone, the urgent need of the Little Brothers is the opening of the Novitiate. All Brothers should enter it, including Kevin. Let him close the work of the Brothers in a prudent way and report to Albuquerque."[93] This last reference was a direct threat to the continued existence of the Brother Martin Home in Columbus. Here the matter rested. In July, Brother Mathias went back to Ireland for a visit and a rest. It was a trip that was quite clearly needed. He was exhausted.

Although Father Sheridan had indeed arrived in June, amid much fanfare, to serve as novice-master, problems soon arose with his appointment. He was not happy, and he missed the companionship of other priests. Brother Mathias avoided visiting him "so as not to aggravate him," but by September, Father Sheridan was back at Via Coeli and the novitiate was back in the same predicament.[94] Archbishop Byrne finally solved the dilemma by appointing Brother Mathias to the post of prefect with the task of training his own aspirants. In his letter to advise him of this appointment, Byrne noted that the decision had taken "much thought," but that "I have reached the decision to entrust you with this delicate task."[95]

The remainder of the decade saw the Brothers branch out to cooperate with various other agencies in the city of Albuquerque concerned with the poor, including the St. Vincent de Paul Society, Catholic Charities, Travelers' Aid, the Department of Public Welfare, Alcoholics Anonymous, the Juvenile Detention Home, and the city and county jails. Accompanying these efforts was a recruiting leaflet that showed Christ pointing with one hand, the other resting on the shoulder of a young man, saying, "The Harvest is great. . . . Are you willing to help Me save the world?" It appeared as if the Little Brothers were on their way to doing just that. In 1957, the refuge served 58,000 meals, provided 6,500 nights of shelter, and 3,000 pieces of clothing. In the annual report for that year, the following was stamped on the margin, "The Way to be happiest is to dedicate your life to God and His poor with the Little Brothers of the Good Shepherd."[96]

By July, the refuge was in need of a new roof, and Brother Mathias made a public appeal through the newspapers, netting about $800 to pay for it.[97] He was also back on the delicate subject of a home for the aged, and slipped a newsclipping into his letter to Archbishop Byrne describing the Phoenix facility run by the Little Sisters of the Poor, which accommodated one hundred seventy-two persons and was graced with an "early American light green roof."[98] Archbishop Byrne made no response to this hint.

Then a second major health crisis arose for Brother Mathias with the discovery, after a five-hour examination, that he was suffering from glaucoma in his right eye. The prognosis was grim. The doctor's report read, "It is very serious and you could probably lose your sight."[99] Archbishop Byrne wrote immediately and told Brother Mathias that this cross was being sent for his sanctification and for the success of the apostolate, that he should accept the divine will and "then do all you can to cure the trouble with faithful obedience to the doctor."[100] Almost at the same time came the offer from Daniel Donohue in Los Angeles to pay for Brother Mathias to go there for surgery and treatment. Mathias protested that money should not be spent on him, and followed this statement of resistance with an unusually newsy letter filled with projects: notes on prospective candidates, conferences for aspirants, retreats for Brothers, stipends to pay off the refuge ("we only owe $3,000"), additions to the refuge, more salvage stores, more county jail Masses, and, of course, "the venerable Home for the Aged."[101] He delayed undergoing surgery for a month. Archbishop Byrne ignored all the items listed in the aforementioned letter and came directly to the point: "The sooner you go the better."[102]

Having been prevailed upon by practically everyone, Brother Mathias gave in and flew to St. Vincent's Hospital in California, where he put himself under the care of Dr. Irvine. He reported in his letter home, "Of course I am praying, the more and more especially to Our Lady of Lourdes. . . . In fact the nurse at the Doctor's office asked me the second day to whom I was praying as the result already was very encouraging."[103] He was home within weeks. He returned to Los Angeles and underwent an operation on November 21. He was home by Christmas, in order to "spend Christmas with my own, the poor unfortunates on the road."[104]

Meanwhile, the slow wheels of bureaucracy were moving toward a clarification of the status of the Brotherhood. A letter from the procurator general of the Sacred Congregation of Religious was received, asking for a historical sketch of the foundation of the community, a biographical sketch of the founder, and whether "extraordinary facts such as visions, prophesies, and so on, were verified in the foundation of the Community."[105] Brother Mathias prepared the documents requested and Archbishop Byrne had them translated into Italian for transmission to Rome. "No extraordinary facts" were noted, but the financial statement was in itself impressive. The refuge was then valued at $60,000, the novitiate on Thirteenth Street at $26,000, and Villa Maria in Alameda at $9,000. The community was only $17,500 in debt for all the above possessions.[106]

The Little Brothers of the Good Shepherd ended the decade with houses not only in Albuquerque — where the refuge, the novitiate, and Villa Maria were located — but also in Columbus, Ohio; New Orleans, Louisiana; and Miami, Florida. Moreover, negotiations were underway in 1960 to establish the first foundation in Canada. These new houses will be discussed in the following chapter. It was an impressive record of achievement. But, compared to where the order was going in terms of growth and expansion, it was only a beginning.

St. Stephen's School, run by the De La Salle Brothers, in Waterford, Ireland, where Maurice Barrett entered at the age of four and attended until he was sixteen.

Maurice Barrett (center) with his father, Tom (left), and John, his older brother.

Brother Mathias as a Hospitaller Brother of St. John of God, Stillorgan, Ireland, 1917.

Kitchen-refectory at the Canadian birthplace of the Hospitaller Order of St. John of God on the Rue Saint-Paul in Montreal in 1929. At left (standing in back) is Brother Mathias; also standing in back (second from right) is Brother Macaire Poitras.

Interior view of the chapel at Our Lady of Mercy Shelter in March, 1929. Left to right: Brothers Laurent Cosgrove, Macaire Poitras, Mathias, Paul-Marie Winterhalter, and Achille Godin.

Brother Mathias (center, back row) and Brother Léonard Mondat (standing at right) pose with some young vacationers in the summer of 1931.

Brother Mathias (center) talking with a couple of workers during renovation work at the first shelter of Hospitallers in the early 1930s.

Members of the Canadian community gather on the occasion of a visit by Brother Raymond Brender, counselor general, and Brother Donatien Corabeuf, provincial for France, in July, 1932. Brother Mathias is seated on the end at right.

In 1934, Brother Mathias (third from left, front row) was named superior of Our Lady of Mercy Hospital on Boulevard Gouin in Montreal. Here we see members of the administrative council, the women's committee, benefactors, and almoners posing with religious personnel at the main entrance.

In 1939, Rome announced the foundation of a general delegation for Canada. From left to right: Brothers William Gagnon, Judicael Maréchaux, Mathias, Dorothée Normandeau, and Laurent (Exupère) Vien, who made up this body.

Brother Mathias is shown on November 21, 1936, celebrating the fifteenth anniversary of his religious profession in the Hospitaller Order of St. John of God.

Brother Mathias (right) with his father, Tom, in Ireland, in the 1930s.

Brother Mathias (center) with his brother John and sister Mary.

Brother Mathias (left) with Cardinal Richard Cushing of Boston,
in 1948.

Brother Mathias at the entrance of the first Good Shepherd Refuge, Albuquerque,
in 1951.

The men's advisory board during a meeting in 1954. Seated (left to right) are Ben Raskov, Ernest Love, and Maurice Maguire. Behind them (same order) are Cliff Minor, Brother Mathias, and Pete Mateucci.

Aldo Vaio, first president of the men's advisory board, Albuquerque, in 1951.

Brother Mathias relaxing on the porch of the Good Shepherd Refuge in Albuquerque.

Brother Mathias poses formally for the photographer in the 1950s.

Archbishop Edwin V. Byrne of Santa Fe with the first group of Little Brothers of the Good Shepherd following the group's profession in a special ceremony in the archbishop's chapel on August 6, 1959. Left to right: Brother James Keily, Brother Kevin Carr, Brother Mathias, the archbishop, Brother Camillus Harbinson, and Brother Francis Abraham.

Brother Mathias in the garden of
the motherhouse in 1970.

Brother Mathias (right) with
Brother Francis Abraham in 1965.

Bishop Joseph Imesch of Joliet (right), with Brother Mathias (seated) and Brother Camillus Harbinson during the November, 1983, second general chapter.

Brother Mathias with Judge Thomas Mescall's children, Regina and Thomas J. Mescall II.

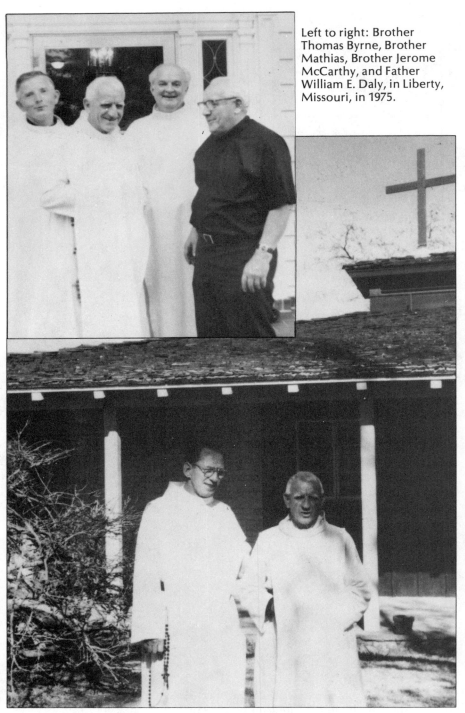

Left to right: Brother Thomas Byrne, Brother Mathias, Brother Jerome McCarthy, and Father William E. Daly, in Liberty, Missouri, in 1975.

Brother Mathias (right) and his successor, Brother Camillus Harbinson.

Brother Mathias enjoying a moment of relaxation.

9 .... Expansion

*IN 1953, A PRIEST CAME THROUGH ALBUQUERQUE FROM COLUM-*bus, Ohio, on his way to Via Coeli at Jemez Springs. He was, according to Brother Mathias, "a big problem." At Via Coeli, he behaved as if he were "holier than thou," and Father Gerald Fitzgerald kicked him out. He landed back with Brother Mathias at the refuge. Brother Mathias later received a letter of gratitude from the chancellor of Columbus, thanking him for the care he had given this priest, and inviting the Brothers to Columbus. Brother Mathias referred the matter to Archbishop Byrne, who then called him and said, "Go and see what you can do for Bishop [Michael J.] Ready."[1] Thus began the extraordinary expansion of the Little Brothers of the Good Shepherd from Albuquerque to seventeen cities and three foreign countries. Certainly, no one at the time could have predicted the outcome of this visit that Brother Mathias, in accord with the wishes of his superiors, duly made.

The Brother Martin Home for severely crippled young men in Columbus had come into existence four years earlier as the result of the efforts of Dr. William Mitchell. It was his conviction that "it is better to light one candle than to curse the darkness."[2] The home cared for boys over eighteen, most in their late twenties, the majority of whom were victims of cerebral palsy. Funds were forthcoming from public welfare — which accounted for one third of the costs — and private money, which was not solicited, since "the few times when it was, caused such embarrassment the practice was dropped."[3]

The tireless Dr. Mitchell spent his evenings and weekends with the boys in the home. This began to put considerable strain on both his health and family life. As Brother Kevin recalls, "Dr. Mitchell had a wonderful wife. She said, 'You are doing three things: medical practice, boys' home and a family. You can take care of any two but not three. So you had better decide what you're going to do and drop one.' "[4] The doctor met with Bishop Ready and the chancellor to discuss what could be done. The bishop entered the conversation by recalling the "big problem" whom he had shipped out to New Mexico. Since then, he confided, "This is the first six months I've had no trouble from him. If Brother Mathias can take care of him, maybe he can do more than that."[5] Brother Kevin remembers that when Bishop

Ready wrote to Brother Mathias, the latter did not want to have anything to do with the Brother Martin Home. But he, Kevin, urged him to "try it and see what happens. Maybe some good will come of it."[6]

So Brother Mathias went to Columbus. He soon discovered that the Brother Martin Home was too small to even offer accommodations for the Brothers. So he made some inquiries on his own. Appearing at dinner, he was accosted by Bishop Ready, who said, "Brother, you weren't here for lunch! And you are my guest."[7] Brother Mathias told him that he had been measuring the distance between the Brother Martin Home and the nearest church. The bishop made the connection and said, "Splendid! The Brothers can be put up in the rectory."[8]

On September 23, 1954, the Little Brothers of the Good Shepherd assumed the operation of the Brother Martin Home. But the Brother who was sent from Albuquerque to be in charge wrote a letter at the end of the first week saying that he did not want to remain. Columbus was a bigoted place, and he wanted to close the establishment and come home. Brother Mathias asked Brother Kevin what he thought of the matter, and Kevin said, "He's not really given it a chance. He's been there less than a week." Brother Mathias looked Kevin in the eye and said, "You got me into this by advising me to try it. Now you go down there and see what you can do."[9] So Kevin went to Columbus. He reported that he thought it was a fine place. "Good," said Brother Mathias. "You stay there."[10]

The fortitude and endurance Brother Kevin exhibited throughout difficulties that followed can only be described as remarkable. His letters to Brother Mathias were written at least once a week, and sometimes every day. They reveal the overwhelming trials he faced. The letters can be quite moving. The following excerpts are from the letters of 1955:

> Brother J. finds it hard to get up in the morning. Now and then I have difficulty myself. Our hours are long and we have these boys with us all day with their cares and requirements. . . .They have their radios blaring away all day long and all evening. . . . The Brother who thinks only of his own comfort will not last here. . . . I wash, dress, feed, take them to the bathroom. There are some repulsive features. . . . I feed the one on the left with my left hand and the one on the right with my right hand and also do my own eating along with waiting on the table which has eight places. . . . I am praying that the Good Shepherd will call some laborers for our little acre of his vast vineyard.[11]

The Brothers soon were able to acquire the home next door for their own use. In November, Kevin reported that there were problems having two houses because "I can't sleep at both." The same letter advised Brother Mathias not to open up a nursing home until the order was more firmly established. With gentle humor he added, "Your first concern should and must be to develop more brothers or you will not need to consider a nursing home at all, except for yourself and perhaps me."[12]

Meanwhile, the board of directors of the home had been discussing plans for turning over the property to the diocese. Brother Kevin was skeptical about the transfer and wrote to Brother Mathias about problems that similar homes had encountered. He gave as an example a home for the aged that was turned over to the Carmelite Sisters "together with a bill for $180,000. The Superior had to go into the kitchen and become the cook."[13] The financial situation at the Brother Martin Home was, happily, somewhat brighter. At the end of the first year of operation, Brother Kevin could report a balance of $4,681.35 for 1955. However, over $9,000 of the funds had been donated by Dr. Mitchell's sale of stock. "Without his contribution we would be $4,369.92 in the hole."[14]

About the same time, problems began to occur with Dr. Mitchell. Brother Kevin had to defend the transfer of Brother Joseph away from the home against the doctor's charges that the Brother Martin Home was a "stepchild" for the Brothers and that Brother Mathias was "interested only in refuges."[15] The board decided it would be "foolish to turn over their property they had worked hard to build only to find that perhaps in a few months the Brothers of the Good Shepherd might be only two old men, Brother Mathias and Brother Kevin."[16] Kevin confided to Mathias, "Dr. Mitchell is a quick-tempered, tempestuous man and somewhat like you are: impatient to get things done and done right."[17]

The doctor became increasingly unhappy over what he called inadequacies in the operation of the home. He wrote a four-page letter of bitter complaint to Brother Mathias. It began, "I am well aware of your difficult situation. You cannot make men join and you cannot make them stay. Without a full novitiate they must be sent out before they are tried. Apparently you had to send men who had no taste for this type of work. Not everyone can stand it."[18] He criticized Brother Mathias for opening up other houses "while Brother Martin Home was hanging on by the skin of its teeth." However, he had nothing but praise for Brother Kevin's legendary eighteen-hour days.[19]

Brother Mathias recalls that "something happened with the doctor. I never went to the depths of that thing. It didn't bother me."[20] But the reply he sent to the doctor's four-page letter was a minor masterpiece: "No doubt you also had times after you started the

159

home there when things went badly without any fault of yours. There may have been times when you were almost at the point of giving up such a worthy effort, but you persevered and carried on for the love of God. That is the same problem that I must struggle with."[21] He appealed to Dr. Mitchell's faith and patience. He addressed the doctor's complaints and then disarmed them with, "I have given over forty years of my life to this [that is, helping the poor] without regret." He attributed the stumbling blocks to "satanic influences." The letter closed with the assurance that "between us there is no difference in principle."[22]

Meanwhile, Bishop Ready, whose health was failing, went to Florida for a rest. The chancellor put a copy of Dr. Mitchell's letter on the bishop's desk, and upon the latter's return, he wrote immediately to Brother Mathias, referring to Dr. Mitchell's "unbelievably bad taste letter to you," and praising Mathias's reply as "edified by its wisdom and charity." He went on to express the opinion that "the work of the Brothers seems little appreciated except that they are the hired servants of the board." He suggested that it might be too difficult for the Brothers of the Good Shepherd to continue the effort. However, "Brother Kevin has been magnificent."[23]

Brother Mathias recalls this situation with some humor. "That was a challenge, wasn't it?"[24] When Bishop Ready died and Archbishop Byrne got the news, he promptly fired off a letter to Brother Mathias that said, "Now is the time to pull out of Columbus."[25] So Brother Mathias called up the chancellor with the news, "What the Bishop [that is, Archbishop Byrne] says is an order." At the same time, he also tried to reason with Byrne to the effect that "in all charity we cannot . . . [abandon] those thirty boys" at the home. In the end, he executed the order by transferring Brother Kevin back to Albuquerque. "But," he recalls with some relish, "I put another Brother in his place!"[26] The Brother was Camillus.

Brother Camillus had difficulties adjusting to the work with the crippled residents similar to those that Kevin had earlier encountered. He also wrote weekly letters to Brother Mathias that give a day-to-day view of the operation of the home. His first letter admitted that he had been eating with "these poor young men and pretending to enjoy it," while in fact "I have been sick to my stomach every time I sat down to table."[27] He had misgivings about the work that was "absolutely and entirely different in every way from the work in New Orleans."[28] But, nevertheless, he plunged in with fortitude and resolve. Subsequent letters found him painting, planting a garden, having a scuffle with a helper who was hauled off by police, experiencing difficulties with a young, immature postulant, trying to finance the purchase of a piece of property in Granville and asking such nuts-and-bolts questions as, "Have the shower cabinets arrived yet?" Earlier, in a dark hour, Kevin had fallen back on his faith. Referring to Christ in a despairing letter to Brother Mathias he had said, "He was not a quitter on me, how can I be a quitter on Him?"[29] Brother Camillus likewise was forced to call on spiritual resources to make it through the day. One time he reported getting very little bread from the stores. He lit a vigil light before a tiny statue of the Infant of Prague "promising to buy a much larger statue if He brought home the bread." The day after, they were given two hundred loaves. "I am just dumbfounded," he wrote Brother Mathias, "I guess I'd better get busy and buy that statue!"[30]

By 1962, the home was renamed St. Martin's Home, following the canonization of Blessed Martin de Porres. The "St. Martin's Chatter" newsletter reported that at the Halloween party every boy dressed as a prisoner and they all went as "Brother Martin's Hoodlums." One resident accidentally fell through the wall in the laundry room, but the damage was minimal.[31]

One indication of the impact the Brothers were having in Columbus can be seen from a letter to Brother Lawrence from Wilber L. Shull, judge of the municipal court, in 1964. The judge praised the work of the Brothers and asserted, "As I have said many times, I believe that the only answer to Communism, alcoholism, juvenile delinquency and the breakdown of the moral fiber of the average citizen, is a return to God. . . . Unless there is a return to God by our great nation, I am afraid we are going down the sewer."[32]

In 1969, the Brothers and the residents of St. Martin's Home transferred their operations to Mount Aloysius, New Lexington, Ohio. The order had acquired a magnificent old academy for girls, which was remodeled for the use of the handicapped young men. A former Western Electric executive, Vincent B. Lane, was a major benefactor in making the move possible from Columbus to the small southern Ohio community.[33] The formal opening was celebrated on November 1, 1969, and Brother Michael Carlyle became the director.

Brother Mathias also moved part of the Columbus operation to Wakefield, Ohio, and later to Momence, Illinois. The Wakefield move came about due to his concern that smaller boys should not be housed with young men in the same environment. After some searching, he located a place on ten acres that had been constructed as a school for the children of atomic workers. By the time the school was completed, the workers had moved away and the state was going to buy it for the sum of $65,000, a remarkable price considering the original cost of the facility had been $800,000.[34] Soon word got out that the

Brothers were interested in acquiring the property. Brother Mathias recalls, "I got all kinds of calls saying, 'You're going to cause trouble.' " Wakefield was in the Bible Belt, near Kentucky. The parish priest from the nearby town of Waverly called up and told him, "You shouldn't come down here at all." Brother Mathias retorted, "What do you mean? I'll go where I like."[35]

A public meeting was held on the proposed facility. Brother Mathias had brought photographs of the Brothers at work including some of the refuge in Albuquerque. He recalls a conversation with an old farmer that began when the latter accosted him with, "You're Catholic." Brother Mathias replied, "Yes, Roman Catholic, but we have 99% of your kind to take care of tonight." The farmer reflected for a moment and then said, "Well, there's 99% of my kind out on the road, and here's one for you. You're all right."[36] Someone else asked, "How do you get on with the people in the surrounding area?" Brother Mathias replied, "The door's always open. We've got nothing to hide." Gradually, the fears of the residents were allayed. The meeting proceeded, and the offer of $65,000 was made, and accepted. Brother Mathias had not even seen the place. He remembers, "When I saw it I thought, 'My God, and I didn't even take a Finn.' No one gave me anything. It was beautiful." He reported his success to the bishop of Columbus, Clarence Issenman (Bishop Ready's successor), who congratulated him and gave him a check for $65,000.[37] The bishop said, "We'll call it St. Mathias Manor." "We will not!" responded Brother Mathias. "We'll call it Clarence Manor." The bishop declined the honor. The issue was resolved quite amiably by the decision to call it "Good Shepherd Manor."[38]

On April 12, 1964, there was an open house and formal dedication of Good Shepherd Manor, Wakefield, which was attended by over one thousand local and out-of-state guests. The visitors toured the facility and viewed "bright cheerful dormitories with sturdy furnishings, spacious dining room, well equipped gymnasium, infirmary, laundry, boiler room and kitchen, and a simply decorated chapel."[39] In 1965, the Chillicothe Exchange Club helped the Brothers build a swimming pool, 60 feet long and 20 to 40 feet wide, which proved to be a boon to both staff and residents alike. "When the sun goes down and the boys are in bed and asleep, the Brothers take their turn in the pool for a relaxing swim before retiring."[40]

Brother Camillus was appointed director of the facility, and, for awhile, things went smoothly. Then, in June, 1967, he wrote an amazing letter to Brother Mathias. It recounted his efforts to raise funds for the faculty house, obtain an architect, approve plans, and incorporate the "changes that you and Brother Kevin suggested."

I am startled that you suggest "not to start construction" at Wakefield. At this late hour such a statement is truly most disturbing. You have urged me *constantly* for well over three years to get the Faculty House under way. I have acted according to your instructions. . . . Contracts have not been signed, but I have assured the Architect that the contract *will* be signed. He has already arranged his schedule accordingly. . . . All is now in readiness and *we must proceed.*[41]

Brother Camillus, however, deferred to Brother Mathias's position as head of the community, pointing out: "As you well know, all that I write is done so with all due respect to your office and authority, all that has been done has been accomplished with your complete knowledge for the glory of God and our community."[42] Clearly, Brother Mathias's desire to see the plans altered to include more facilities for residents had come at an inopportune time. Brother Camillus went ahead with the plans as already formulated, but a rift had occurred that would widen with the passage of time.

At the same time that the Brothers were struggling to make a go of the operation in Columbus, Brother Mathias was branching out to a third city, New Orleans. Archbishop Byrne got a letter of inquiry from Bishop Joseph F. Rummel of New Orleans and went to Albuquerque in October of 1954 to ask Brother Mathias to "go and see what you could do for Bishop Rummel in New Orleans." Brother Mathias recalls that upon his arrival he tried to get a room at several hotels. Because Mardi Gras was being celebrated, all the hotels he tried were full. "So I went to the church, St. Patrick's, and knocked on the door, with my little talk prepared. Here came this very distinguished Monsignor Bejou. He said, 'You're Brother Mathias!' I said, 'I am?' Then I told him I'd been to the St. Charles Hotel and there was no room. He said, 'Oh, yes, there is room. The reservation.' Then he said, 'A delegation went up to meet you at the plane.' I said that I had come on a train. So he called them up and they came right away. We went to the hotel and they had a push-cart with a little supper. 'This is Southern hospitality,' they said."[43]

The three-room suite he occupied had been relinquished by Mayor de Lesseps S. Morrison of New Orleans, owing to the great difficulty of getting accommodations during Mardi Gras. Brother Mathias was uncomfortable in the lavish surroundings. The next day he left the key at the desk and told them that he wasn't coming back. When he reported this to Monsignor Bejou, the latter asked him what had happened. "Nothing happened. But I'm not going to stay there, that's all." Then he said, "Next door at that old building there I think

163

there's a rooming house." The "old building" was the structure being proposed as the refuge by the St. Vincent de Paul Society. The rooming house was run by a certain Annie Staggers, a woman of determination and ingenuity who rented him a room for $10 a week. When he walked into the lobby of Annie Staggers's place for the first time, an old longshoreman who couldn't stand up greeted him with the words, "Father, there's no holy water here." Brother Mathias looked at him and said, "You have it in you."[44]

The next day there was a meeting at the bishop's residence during which it was decided that the refuge would be staffed by the Brothers of the Good Shepherd, administered by the St. Vincent de Paul Society, and supported by the bishop, who donated $25,000 on the spot to pay for renovations. It would be called Ozanam Inn. Brother Mathias reported back to Archbishop Byrne that the "building is most appropriate," the St. Vincent de Paul Society will "handle all expenses," and that the latter were a "fine group of laymen."[45]

Since there was to be a meeting in Chicago for religious orders that Brother Mathias could not attend, he sent a telegram to Brother Kevin in Columbus telling him to go in his place. By mistake, instead of putting "Chicago" in the telegram he put "New Orleans." Brother Kevin called from the railroad station. A surprised Mathias demanded to know, "Who brought you here?" "You did," said Kevin. The two of them proceeded to a coffee shop and Brother Mathias gave Kevin the key to his room at Annie Staggers's place. Then he took the train himself back to Albuquerque. Brother Kevin, later expressing mild annoyance over this whole affair, told Brother Mathias: "When I left here for New Orleans, I received nothing, so I had to pay my very own way, plus what it cost me to live in New Orleans. . . . That used up the $70 I had left from Christmas presents. When you send me a letter to go someplace again to serve you, include the fare."[46]

Upon Archbishop Rummel's death, Archbishop John P. Cody took his place in New Orleans. The new prelate visited the refuge and didn't approve of the conditions. He ordered that it be closed down. Brother Mathias was called and told of the situation, and that Archbishop Cody had changed his mind and decided to put in a sprinkler system in the old building. That did not satisfy Brother Mathias, who made an appointment to see the archbishop. Brother Mathias recalls, "I went on a Saturday. I wanted to see Monsignor Bejou just to torment him." The day of the meeting with Cody arrived, and before the latter got in a word, Mathias jumped in with, "Excellency, what we need is the house next door." The archbishop looked at him and said, "Well, go and get it." Clearly, the question of money had not come up. When Brother Mathias suggested that the archdiocese should buy the Druid's Inn, which had been turned into a low-grade movie theater and was again vacant, he ran up against resistance. He recalls, "I said, 'It's a disgrace to the Catholic Church. It's a disgrace to society. If you build sprinklers you will be spending other people's money uselessly. . . . We've been here for the last twelve years and we have never had problems with the colored. Now you go ahead and do what you like.' He called in the St. Vincent de Paul people and told them, 'Get the house next door.' "[47]

Among those impressed with the establishment of Ozanam Inn in New Orleans was Archbishop Byrne, who, in March, 1955, wrote to Brother Mathias (who was then back in Albuquerque), "Maybe New Orleans would be a better place for the main center of the Little Brothers of the Good Shepherd. It has advantages over Albuquerque. Going there would not offend me. You need to consider it."[48] Brother Mathias answered this offer quickly, stating, "We have a perfect organization here in Albuquerque and Alameda . . . and that is what is needed."[49]

In 1960, Ozanam Inn celebrated its first five years of existence with an open house. Brother John Hurley, the director, noted that the inn had fed 379,246 men, housed 74,502, distributed 23,766 articles of clothing, and assisted 816 needy families in that time. He also noted that "it takes six days a week of begging to keep the Inn adequately supplied with food."[50] Mayor Morrison of New Orleans was duly impressed. "I notice you have supplied more than 5,000 hot meals per month and given shelter to approximately 2,500 of our less fortunate citizens per month, all at no cost to the City of New Orleans," he wrote in a letter of congratulations.[51]

Nineteen-sixty was also the year that Camillus House was established in Miami, Florida. The sequence of events that led to this new foundation was unique. But the role of Brother Mathias in forging ahead despite obstacles to realize this new vision in concrete terms was the same. It transpired that a certain Monsignor Patrick Barry of Miami Beach was celebrating his golden jubilee, and Brother Mathias sent his customary congratulations along with his "little flyers" of information on the work of the Good Shepherd Brothers. Then, a Father Flynn, returning from an unsuccessful stint at learning Spanish, happened to mention that "something should be done about the poor in the Tenderloin District." Monsignor Barry rummaged through his desk and produced the little flyers that had arrived from Albuquerque and said, "I have just the men."[52]

The archbishop of Miami, Coleman F. Carroll, wrote to Brother Mathias, "What are your requirements?" Brother Mathias wrote back, "When I see you, I'll let you know."[53] He arrived in Miami after some delay on the train, "not knowing any more about it than the man in the moon." After looking up a church near the station to attend Mass, he went into a restaurant for a cup of coffee. It became immediately clear what not knowing about Miami meant. There was an obvious separation of the races. Blacks sat in one section of the restaurant and whites in another. Brother Mathias stood there trying to decide what to do. He thought, "I could sit with the Whites and be a coward, or I could sit with the Blacks and cause trouble." After some indecision, he turned around and left the place. Under the circumstances, he later recalled, "It was better to forget the coffee."[54]

He arranged an interview with Archbishop Carroll, who arrived wearing a straw hat and inquired, "What brought you here?" Brother Mathias reminded him, "I've come to take care of the poor." Whereupon, the archbishop told him, "We have no money." That rather inauspicious beginning marked the start of a lonely week for Brother Mathias. He stayed at a Jesuit rectory and walked the streets by himself looking for a suitable place to start the refuge. He found an old bungalow on Eighth Street and rented it for $55 a month. The first night he slept on the floor, listening to the sounds of the city around him. They were not reassuring. There was the noise of a Cuban wedding on one side that lasted far into the night, and the intermittent arguments of some Chinese men on the other. Brother Mathias hardly slept for fear someone would think the bungalow was uninhabited and try to get in.

The following day he got the telephone hooked up and the utilities turned on, all in the name of the archbishop as the guarantor of payment. The St. Vincent de Paul Society store provided the refrigerator, stove, beds, and chairs. A donation of cornflakes and milk provided the first meal. Brother Mathias then called Brother Camillus with instructions to send a Brother to take care of the place. The man who was sent stayed less than twenty-four hours. But then Brother David Keane arrived, stepped in, and took over the responsibility. The staples remained coffee, doughnuts, and sandwiches. Brother Mathias wrote to several neighboring parishes to inform them "what I was up to and what I intended."[55]

After several weeks, a bigger facility at 726 N.E. First Avenue was located for $30,000. The archbishop, whose mind had been changed by what he had seen happening in the bungalow, found the money. The owners, Mr. and Mrs. Joseph Rendinell, were most cooperative. Brother Mathias reported, "Mr. Rendinell has been our backyard neighbor since the beginning and he took an interest in our work when he saw the men line up twice a day for meals."[56] A secluded driveway in the rear of the new building enabled the men to line up without being seen by street traffic. "We were always looking out for the men," said Brother Mathias.[57]

Brother David Keane, director of Camillus House, described its operations: "About 20 percent of the soup line at Camillus House are Cuban refugees, who are directed here for their first meal in the United States by the Dominican Sisters at the Jesu Latin Catholic Center. They are provided with a night's lodging in small, off-beat hotels . . . for as little as 60 cents per night. . . . We have never really run out of food, but sometimes the stew gets a little thin. We can calibrate the line, just as one calibrates the trajectory of a shell, and measure our footage accordingly. There are 40 people from the door to the sidewalk, and 80 people back to that soft drink sign."[58]

One of the welcome effects of the opening of Camillus House from the standpoint of the city police department was the drop in petty crimes in the area. The *Miami Voice* ran an article on the subject headlined "Cops on the Beat Praise Camillus [House] as Crime Stopper."[59] Brother David put it this way: "One of the purposes of the Brothers of the Good Shepherd is sin prevention. That may be a bit different from crime prevention, but not that different."[60]

In the first three years of operation, some 570,000 people passed through Camillus House. Christmas dinner was served to 1,439 people, who waited patiently outside with "lined and hungry faces."[61] In 1965, Brother Victor became the director of Camillus House. He undertook necessary renovations, namely, the installation of steel sinks, a sanitizer, two stoves, a new refrigerator, steel worktables, fluorescent lights, a terrazzo floor, a new ceiling in the dining room, and a new roof. During the five weeks the kitchen was closed, fifteen thousand sandwiches were served to the men outside.[62]

One of the people who visited Ozanam Inn in New Orleans with more than casual interest was Father Anthony J. O'Neill of St. John the Evangelist Church, Philadelphia. For years, he had been giving out three hundred to four hundred sandwiches a day to vagrants outside his church. After visiting Ozanam Inn, he was inspired to get a similar facility in Philadelphia. With his own resources, he bought a three-story former printing establishment and installed heavy-duty kitchen and laundry equipment.[63] He got in touch with Brother Mathias to arrange for the Little Brothers to staff the facility, and in November, 1962, Brother Mathias sent Brother John Hurley to see what could be done.

In August of 1963, the *Catholic Standard and Times* of Philadelphia noted the Brothers would be "bringing a new concept to the old style gospel mission house." Not only would the hospice provide basic necessities, but, according to Brother John, "The purpose of the

167

shelter is solely spiritual. We are only interested in the salvation of men's souls. . . . However, we do not intend to shove spirituality and religion down the men's throats."[64] Among the volunteers in the new refuge was Jim Folse, who rose from skid row in New Orleans and "came here on his own accord to return a favor to the Brothers."[65]

The formal opening of St. John's Hospice in Philadelphia was held on September 7, 1963. Cardinal John Krol, archbishop of Philadelphia, officiated, and hundreds of citizens from all walks of life attended. Visitors to the open house that followed were impressed with the laundry facilities which ran during the night while the men slept. Brother John explained: "We believe clean clothes will lift the morale of the men. Some of them go for months without a change. If a person lives in filth or squalor, he loses the ambition, will and desire even to attempt a comeback."[66]

By the end of the first year, St. John's Hospice had served over 245,725 hot meals, provided shelter for 11,809 men, distributed 21,962 articles of clothing, and assisted 92 families.[67] The *Shepherd's Call* noted that in the food line "over 4,000 slices of bread alone are consumed on a daily basis by the derelicts."[68]

During the 1970s, the Philadelphia newspapers ran a series of articles designed to sensitize the city's majority to the plight of the poor among them. According to the *Philadelphia Daily News*, one arrest cost $50, amounting to a city total of $1.7 million a year. To the extent that the Brothers took in potential criminals and cared for them, the city was spared that much expense.[69] The *Philadelphia Inquirer* followed the saga of a man who lived on one of the city's major bridges in a cardboard lean-to. "He says he finds the whole 20th Century difficult. He roams the streets looking for treasures — a protractor to measure the angles of the moon. He sleeps on bald tires, a board and a rug. He eats at St. John's Hospice."[70]

In 1979, the *Philadelphia Daily News* sent a reporter to stand in line at the hospice. He described the "sullen brooding men in heavy coats and scarves." One man had his pants tucked up into his boots where they were held by plastic bags wrapped around his lower legs. The reporter noted with some humor that Brother Stanley stood six feet three inches, "which makes him one of the bigger Little Brothers."[71] In discussing the depths reached by some of the men — standing in line, being served, eating in silence, leaving — he concluded, "What it comes down to for almost all of them is that someone who should have loved them didn't."[72]

The city of Philadelphia gave serious consideration to wiping out skid row in the 1970s. One proposal put forth was to give the residents of skid row moving expenses. One critic attacked the plan by asking,

"What is going to happen when you give $220 moving expense to a Skid Row wino who doesn't have anything more than a toothbrush and an old copy of Life Magazine?"[73] It was a time when every conceivable minority was demanding its due from the federal government. Ira Shandler of the city's center for alcoholic treatment asked, "But do you think these guys are going to raise up a shaky fist and start shouting, 'Skid Power'? "[74] Other observers noted that stamping out skid row in one place would only cause it to surface somewhere else. Brother Mark, now the director of St. John's Hospice, contributed to the debate quite simply. While viewing the sleeping men in the dormitory he commented, "Look, it's early but they're all in bed. They look like little children." The reporter standing with him in the darkened room said, "They are."[75]

The last major expansion of the order to a city in the U.S. got underway in 1965 in Kansas City, Missouri. Brother Mathias was feeling the crunch. A corporation to assist in the care of the severely handicapped had been organized nine years earlier.[76] The group had purchased a piece of income property near downtown Kansas City that was then sold and resulted in funds to augment the corporation account. Through the years, they had contacted various religious orders asking them to establish a custodial home but were unsuccessful. Brother Mathias received a letter from the vice-president of the organization on December 1, 1965, inviting the Little Brothers to come to Kansas City for this purpose. "We have hundreds of parents waiting to help you. We offer you all the resources at our command, most of which are waiting for the opportunity to be utilized."[77] Other letters followed. Brother Mathias answered, "I fully understand your anxiety . . . but with so many irons in the fire and with so little time for all, I hesitated to write. . . ."[78] He told the group that he would try to staff a place but that the corporation should first "approach His Excellency Your Beloved Bishop." Moreover, they should not "get too anxious or nervous if you do not hear from him at once because it is possible that he could be investigating and seeking information without consulting you."[79]

In July, 1966, Brother Mathias wrote to request an appointment with Charles H. Helmsing, bishop of Kansas City. "I should say at this time that I do not know what your Excellency wishes, so I have not taken this matter up at all with our own Archbishop."[80] The two men met the following month. The corporation took Brother Mathias to look at the Queen of the World Hospital, which was vacant and in need of renovation. During the visit Mathias tripped over a sandbag and tore his pants. Luckily his coat covered the affected area as long as he kept the coat on. Later that day he was asked by a member of the group, "What would you like for lunch?" He replied, "Six or seven pins!" Someone said, "Take off your coat, Brother." He answered, "I can't."[81]

It was obvious that the hospital was too big. One worry would simply be how to heat the place. Bishop Helmsing assured Brother Mathias that heat would be "our contribution."[82] Ultimately, the old section of the hospital was pulled down. A frame building across the road was given to the corporation for a girls' home. This was named Our Lady's Manor and was later staffed by the Benedictine Sisters. It so happened that two of the contractors working on the renovation of the hospital and of the girls' home had handicapped daughters. They told Brother Mathias, "You give to the sisters and we'll forget the debt."[83]

In January, 1967, Brother Mathias finally informed Archbishop James P. Davis (Archbishop Byrne's successor) of his negotiations with the corporation and the bishop of Kansas City. He hastened to assure him, "There is absolutely no financial obligation on the part of the Little Brothers of the Good Shepherd and it would start very small, by feeling our way along first."[84] Whatever his private thoughts may have been to be informed at this late date, Archbishop Davis gave his permission to proceed.[85]

By October of that year, the Brothers were "on the job" at Good Shepherd Manor in Kansas City. Brother Damien Prabel was the first director. With a staff of four Brothers, the home accepted twenty-two severely handicapped young men. Shortly thereafter, the former laundry building of the hospital and the former convent were remodeled to provide for twenty additional residents and for recreation.[86] The Good Shepherd Manor guild, an organization of women dedicated to support the manor primarily through fund raising, was organized on October 31, 1968. Within four years it had one hundred eighty members.[87]

When, in 1978, the residents and staff members of the manor said good-bye to Brother Jerome McCarthy, its director, a tribute was given to him in gratitude for his services to the residents and to the community. It is a fitting summation of the efforts of all the Brothers in Kansas City, and indeed, everywhere.

Brother Jerome leaves behind him a truly splendid work at Good Shepherd Manor. He has brought the Manor from its beginnings and has formed it into a beautiful "oasis" of peace, joy and happiness for the handicapped and the mentally retarded persons who have made Good Shepherd Manor their home. Brother Jerome was truly a "Father" to his "boys." He has brought a spirit to this haven that we hope we can carry on and of which he may always be proud. We hope he will always feel part of the Manor and will come to visit those who love him so dearly.[88]

At the bottom of the page that carried this tribute was printed a short poem entitled simply ''Gratitude is the memory of the heart.''

10 .... **Brothers**

THE TRUTH OF THE LIFE OF A COMMUNITY IS NOT TO BE HAD IN STA-
tistics only. There is the unique relationship between the founder and
those who have chosen to follow him. Among the men Brother
Mathias has chosen, and who have themselves chosen to become Little Brothers of the Good Shepherd, there is not one who is like him.
Yet, from time to time, many have sought to be like him. Thus what
the Brotherhood calls "charisma" has been passed on. The word is
difficult to pin down, but in the end it embodies those qualities that
are most binding and bring out the highest aspirations in men. It is
the uniqueness of a group, its founder, and its mission. It is the spirit
of their corporate life. As such, it is more enduring than the life of any
one individual. Viewed in one sense, charisma is the fruit of the
founder's actions and achievements as carried on in the work of his
community. Viewed in another sense, it is his practical immortality.
Brother Michael Carlyle described it in these words: "The source of
every religious family is found in the charisma of its early beginnings. . . . Charisma lives in the works of the congregation."[1]

In 1951, Brother Mathias first undertook to feed the homeless in
the little house at 306 Iron Street, S.W., in Albuquerque by himself. He
had Monsignor José García to fall back on, Sister Frances Marie of
St. Joseph's Hospital to provide furniture and used coffee grounds,
and several local bakers to provide day-old bread. Principally, he had
Archbishop Edwin Byrne behind him. But in terms of answering the
doorbell at two in the morning to minister to the needs of some
"knight of the road," he was alone. So, the second item of business
was to remedy this situation. He wrote to all kinds of people asking
for financial help. He wrote to former Brothers of St. John of God
asking them to come to Albuquerque. He wrote to a host of Catholic
publications asking them to run little ads for him to recruit men seeking "Holiness and Happiness" in serving the poor.

Among the first who came to join him was George Bane, a Brother who had been in California with the Brothers of St. John of God but
had left his duties there. In Albuquerque, he lasted about three
months before he left again. He wrote a blistering letter to Archbishop Byrne, declaring that the work at the refuge was "laymen's work
and not suitable for a religious community." The letter raked Brother
Mathias over the coals. "Brother Mathias will never give you a true

report. . . . He is not very interested in this work. He is going to bring in postulants to live on the people of the diocese. . . . He is thinking of getting a place for a hospital with this as a front to get money for a building. He is not particular who he takes, sissies seem to be preffered [*sic*]. . . . Mathias is full of pride and just wants to be a big shot again."[2] Having relieved himself of these observations, Brother George Bane closed with, "Mathias will be pleased when I leave. . . ."[3] It is illustrative of Archbishop Byrne's already close relationship with Brother Mathias that he gave him the letter on the next trip to Albuquerque, where it was read with some amusement.

Brother Mathias's little ads resulted in a steady stream of young, and not so young, men beating a path to his door seeking "Holiness and Happiness." Few stayed. The door they had beaten a path to opened onto too stark a scene. There was as yet no formal religious order, no training program, no community life to speak of, nothing but a run-down old house in a sleazy neighborhood, manned by an Irishman who was a fanatic on the subject of sacrifice for the poor. One man who read such an ad in the diocesan paper of Scranton, Pennsylvania, was the future Brother Kevin Carr. On a Friday afternoon, after finishing his rounds as a salesman of hotel and restaurant equipment, he stopped at the Passionist Monastery for devotions and picked up the latest issue of *Catholic Life*. He had noticed a priest reading something at the bookrack.

> I went out and got into my car and threw the paper into the back seat where there were several other papers. Then I started off. But I remembered that the priest had been reading something. There must be something there. So I stopped and reached back and got it. A heading attracted me. "Vocations wanted. Men between the ages of 18-61 for a new community in New Mexico." I cut out the little ad and pasted it to a postcard and sent it to Albuquerque.[4]

After an exchange of letters, Kevin arranged to combine his two weeks of vacation with another two weeks of leave and headed by train for the Southwest. It was May, 1952. He was then exactly sixty-one years old. The scene that awaited him in Albuquerque was not what he had envisioned. "What a place it was then! Only two [Brothers] had habits. It was primitive indeed. . . . I went in there on 2nd Street. Two fellows rushed to open the door. Brother Mathias came in. . . . He had on a shirt and a pair of suspenders. I thought, 'Is this the head of a religious community?' He didn't look like the head of a religious community."[5] Brother Mathias was not impressed with Kevin either. He considered him too old and did what he could to discourage him from staying. "He told me that in the 15 months he had been there, everyone who had come left. He said that, 'At your age, I can't see any possibility of your staying.' "[6] That was that. But, since Kevin had nothing else he wanted to do with his vacation, he stayed. "The supper was passable but I felt perfectly at home at the table for my first meal."[7] In addition to Brother Mathias, there were Brothers Peter, Gerard, and Robert. Brother Patrick was in the East. He and Brother Enda arrived several days later. Certainly, the community was small. It is a credit to Brother Kevin that he saw potential in the group.

A tall, ramrod-straight man of few words, but with an amazing capacity for hard work, Kevin proved to be the St. Paul of the struggling community. He became a rock on which much of the organization was built. Mathias may have made the decisions, but Kevin carried them out. Moreover, Kevin found it deeply satisfying. In 1957, five years after his arrival in Albuquerque, he wrote to Brother Mathias, "These have been five years of solid happiness. There is no other place I would rather be nor anything that I would prefer to be doing. I look forward to the next five years with eager anticipation."[8]

Brother Mathias wrote a tribute to another early Brother whom he had asked to join him, Brother James Keily: "Brother James visited our Refuge in the early days of our Foundation. He seemed so frail, and not in his youth; but I know Almighty God is never outdone in generosity and Brother James Keily was generous. He had lively faith and great simple charity."[9] Brother James joined the community in October, 1952. He wrote of himself, "I am a religious Brother — Yes, a Little Brother of the Good Shepherd. I never wrote for the New York Times; never had an 'Identity Crisis' — just a happy Brother, thankful for the privilege of working full time for God."[10]

Brother Camillus Harbinson arrived on February 2, 1954. Like Kevin and James, he was a mature man. A veteran of inner struggles of his own concerning religious life, Camillus came to Albuquerque from New York searching for a community to which he could devote his life and energies. He too had read about the Little Brothers of the Good Shepherd in a Catholic newspaper. Arriving in Albuquerque, he found the situation at the refuge depressing. There were few Brothers there and conditions were still primitive.

> I absolutely refused to unpack my suitcase. I did not want to stay.
> It's hard to believe really. I said to myself, "This outfit is going
> nowhere rapidly." The food was awful. Most of the food we got
> was second-hand which was given to us by some of the local res-
> taurants. The coffee grounds came from St. Joseph's Hospital

and they were used coffee grounds. It was not a pleasant experience. They would dump the used coffee into large containers or cans outside the kitchen and the people who worked there would use the grounds as receptacles for the ashes of their cigarettes and the cigarette butts. So we had old tobacco mixed with used coffee.[11]

Brother Mathias sent Camillus to nursing school at St. Joseph's Hospital against his will. At first, he did not like nursing school; but, gradually, he grew to enjoy it. Suddenly, nine months later, Brother Mathias pulled him out of the school and told him he was going to New Orleans to establish the refuge in that city. He protested against having to leave his studies, but to no avail. Obedient to the letter of his vows, he went to New Orleans. It is conceivable that this change of scene was a factor in Camillus's decision to link his life with the fledgling community. An Irishman by birth, the desert and sand of Albuquerque had been a trial for him. "I was happy because going into lush Louisiana where it was green was like going home again."[12] Four years later he wrote to Brother Mathias, "I can now see that in all my previous years in another community, that God must have been preparing me for this great apostolate."[13]

Brother Francis Abraham, another major early figure in the community, joined at the age of thirty-six, after reading about the Brothers in *Time* magazine.[14] The year was 1954. He had been a technical sergeant in the U.S. Air Force and, later, a bookkeeper in Chicago. His obvious capacity for administration soon earned him the job of director of the refuge, then director of vocations, and later secretary-general. Brother Mathias found him both a valuable asset and a difficult man to live with, perhaps because both he and Francis shared similar character traits. "We had lots of difficulties, but that's normal. We had the same mentality. He was really straight and would stand for no nonsense." Once, a priest arrived from Via Coeli to serve as chaplain to the Brothers, at Brother Mathias's request. Shortly thereafter, Brother Mathias had to leave town, and, in his absence, the priest began running the show. Brother Francis retired to the refuge because "he couldn't take it." Upon his return, Brother Mathias relieved himself of the priest by a simple stratagem. It seemed that the priest had not paid his respects to the archbishop, and when asked about this duty he had the temerity to respond, "I've nothing to do with the archbishop." That did it. He found himself back in Jemez Springs. Brother Francis was soothed, and life returned to normal.[15]

Brother Francis died the day after Thanksgiving Day, 1968, after having gone shopping in bitter weather and returned feeling unwell. He went upstairs saying, "If I'm not down by 5 o'clock, don't come after me." Unfortunately, no one came after him when he did not appear. The next morning he was found, reaching for the telephone, dead of a heart attack. Brother Mathias in his tribute to Brother Francis, wrote, "He was first of all a Christian. Every minute of his life was dedicated to the works of Charity for the Society of the Little Brothers of the Good Shepherd. Every penny that came to him was for the works of charity."[16]

Brother Michael Carlyle differs from the preceding Brothers in that he joined the community as a much younger man. Together with Brothers Kevin, Camillus, Francis Abraham, Joseph Dooley, and John Hurley, Brother Michael has been the backbone of the houses in which he has worked, and is now one of the senior members of the order. A native of Syracuse, New York, Michael joined the Little Brothers in 1958 at the age of twenty-one. His mother was a psychiatric nurse who had spent much of her life working with the mentally retarded. Michael spent three weeks in Albuquerque, which he disliked, and was then sent to New Orleans, where he learned the fine art of feeding the poor from Brother John Hurley, another stalwart who had joined in 1955. In New Orleans, Michael was able to function also as the organist of St. Patrick's Church, thanks to an innate musical talent brought out by early training. An original and talented man, Michael has brought humor to his life as a Brother, plunged into the administration of one of the order's largest facilities for mentally retarded men — Mount Aloysius in New Lexington, Ohio — directed choirs, and put on organ concerts. In his leisure time he composes imaginary pieces for the organ with outrageous Latin titles, and wears striped suit coats with ties that do not match.[17]

Brother Lawrence Dillmuth arrived in 1961. Born in Hartford, Connecticut, he studied law and accounting at Fordham University and went into the textile business, ultimately with Dan River Corporation. His domestic goods division sold in excess of $92 million a year. After his wife's death, he went to a Jesuit retreat where he read an article about Brother Mathias entitled "Come Look Us Over." He did precisely that, commenting later, "The more I talked to him [Brother Mathias], the more I realized I was talking to a saint."[18] He joined the community and became director of the Good Samaritan Inn for alcoholics in Columbus, Ohio, after Brother Mathias had asked him what he knew about alcoholism. "I said living at the New York Athletic Club I had seen a lot of it."[19] Brother Lawrence later ran Camillus House in Miami, Florida, with the same kind of energy and skill that he had used in his former business life.

176

In 1968, Brother Jerome McCarthy arrived in Albuquerque from Chicago by a rather circuitous route. He had been a member of the Alexian Brothers (a nursing order) as a young man, and then had joined the U.S. Navy as a corpsman during World War II. Ultimately, he obtained a degree in chemistry from the University of Chicago.

> I had everything I wanted, cars, paintings, a second home, but I wasn't happy. I investigated vocation ads and wrote inquiries on Tiffany stationery. When I went looking for stamps to send them, I found in an old wallet Brother Mathias' ad about having opened a novitiate in a chicken coop. I wrote to him and within a week I had an answer. I made my decision, arranged my affairs, and bought a ticket to Albuquerque. In the restroom of the airport I threw away a brightly colored tie, and came.[20]

His first day in Albuquerque was memorable. After remarking to the newcomer with his customary frankness, "You're no spring chicken," Brother Mathias served dinner and the Brothers went to chapel. Then Jerome was taken upstairs to his room, where he went into momentary shock. "There were two colors of paint on the walls, dust bunnies on the floor and one leg missing on the bed. There was a lady's vanity table, a chest with no handles on the drawers, a door that didn't close, screens that didn't clasp, and a torn slanted shade. Brother Mathias said, 'Isn't this lovely! You've got cross ventilation!' "[21] Jerome swallowed hard and asked for a towel, soap, and a drinking glass. He stayed. He soon discovered that both he and Brother Francis liked Fannie Mae candy. But more than this, Jerome and Francis resembled each other strikingly. Because Francis was more of an authority figure than Jerome, the latter suffered because of the likeness. For a novice to look like the novice-master was not easy for the older professed Brothers.[22]

Through the years that the Little Brothers of the Good Shepherd has existed and seen candidates come and some of them persevere, the community has known death. The first Brother to die was Brother Eugene Steffen, on April 2, 1954. He had been working with the children of the Cupertino Catholic Club in Albuquerque when one of the children came with the news to other Brothers crying, "Brother is dead." Since the child had a blood brother in Korea, they assumed he meant his own brother, until the boy explained it was Brother Eugene. The day before the funeral, the children, in class groups, spent a half-hour at a time praying for Brother Eugene. Brother Mathias said, "If the prayers of little children can win one an immortal crown, Brother Eugene certainly has his."[23]

Next among the Brothers to die was Brother Francis Abraham,

on November 30, 1968.[24] Brother Joseph Dooley died on March 9, 1974, in a tragic automobile accident when his vehicle collided with two others and then caught on fire.[25] The youngest Brother to die was Brother Joseph O'Brien, about whose life and death his mother has written an unpublished manuscript, "The Year of the Flame."[26] After a short career at several different jobs, Joseph O'Brien developed cancer. He wanted desperately to join Brother Mathias's religious order, but there were questions about his suitability as a candidate. While his application was being considered, he was hospitalized. Lillian O'Brien wrote, "From this point on, the events in what remained of my son's life were utterly unbelievable. . . . He knew that he would not be prohibited from contributing to the community by his suffering. He explained his suffering as a gift to the Brotherhood for the sake of their community, for their work, for vocations."[27] Joseph was invested with the habit of the Little Brothers on September 14, 1976, and died in it three weeks later, on October 7. He was twenty-five years old. In his last days, he called Brother Mathias often and told him, "I have nobody." Brother Mathias responded, "You're not alone, you're talking to me."[28] Brother Majella Marchant, who was with him at the end, said, "He was awesome and radiant."[29] His mother's words were, "I could not grieve. I was shaken but I could not grieve, for one does not grieve in the face of victory."[30]

By their tenth anniversary year, the Brothers had given 100,000 nights of shelter to homeless men, as many meals, and thousands of items of clothing to those who sought their help.[31] It was clear that the value of these efforts was enough to inspire those who had chosen this life to renewed effort, hard work, and personal sacrifice. But the day-to-day difficulties of living the selfless life were always ready to pounce upon the overtired, the unprepared, or the doubtfully committed Brother. It is in meeting these situations head-on, as was his nature, and salvaging many a potentially ruinous situation, that Brother Mathias excelled. Part of the stress of religious life came from the sheer lack of gratitude that often confronted the Brothers. Ralph Looney, in his article "Derelicts at the Door," which appeared in *Catholic Digest* in 1962, saw this as a form of stress: "The lot of the Brothers is a thankless one. They deal with the lowest elements of society: bums, drifters, alcoholics. A steady stream of them ring the loud bell at the refuge daily. They get food, lodging or clothing — often all three — without question. When they leave, they rarely say, 'Thanks.' Even the transient families who stop for a handout of food or gasoline seldom express any appreciation."[32]

Brothers were taught to see Christ in all who came to the door and to do unto them as if the derelict at the door were indeed the

Lord. But this pious approach, inspiring as it could be from time to time, faltered beside the uninvited thought that often undermined it — Christ himself would have said, "Thank you."

Letters written to Brother Mathias, often in the heat of some argument that had yet to be resolved, give a glimpse of the struggles that day-to-day life as a soldier of charity entailed. These also express tensions inside the order itself as members took issue with one another over the goals and purposes for which they had dedicated their lives. In December of 1965, Brother John Hurley wrote a letter to Brother Mathias in which he questioned the entire operation of houses for the handicapped as opposed to what he viewed as the original thrust of the Brotherhood — serving the skid row poor.

> We hear vows on the New Year to work ourselves to death for the souls of God's most abandoned souls. . . . It is sad that after so many years you still have such a poor understanding of the services needed by the men of Skid Row and sadder still that so many Brothers are wasted on saving the saved. We will never get rich or own fancy houses in serving the Skid Row men as we will with the income groups such as the retarded, old age, youths, etc., but God will love us more for the terrible sacrifice it takes to care for the destitute men and more so to live and eat with them as He did. . . . I hope and pray that the Brothers get back to the Stable and out of the overcrowded inns where they are trying to save those who are already saved.[33]

The letter was signed, "Obediently yours in Christ the Good Shepherd," and professed vows of love and loyalty to Christ. "Make it harder if You wish, [O Lord,] we will only love You more."[34]

Such a cry from the heart illustrates the tremendous pressures under which the Brothers sometimes worked, as well as the genuine questions about the proper application of their talents. Brother Mathias lost no time in answering this particular letter but chose to ignore the attack on the other apostolates of the order — caring for the handicapped, the aged, and youth. Moreover, he was clearly upset. "It is Providential that this special delivery [letter] did not get into the hands of any other of our Brothers because it shows such a great lack of judgment for the simple fact that according to this letter, neither Brother Kevin at 76, or Brother Victor, or Brother Francis or Brother Joseph or Brother Columban or Brother Martin and what they do for the poor men on the road should not be considered just as much as what you do for the poor. . . ."[35] Then the tone softened. He left this subject for a discussion of the need for vocations to help lighten everyone's load, and then made mention of his own needs. "All this takes a great deal of time and when I remain up typing until one or two or three in the morning, thank God I am still able to get up for prayers with the Community and even make breakfast for them as well they know; then not hesitating going out to clean the side walks and curbs and if the streets are not cleaned I do not hesitate to call the City Fathers. . . ."[36]

Brother John stuck it out in Philadelphia, and a year later he received another letter from Brother Mathias. He reminded him that "Brother Kevin is now going on 76 and has done his share and more than that for the Society. He will take a place of rest in the most suitable house of his choice." But for himself, Brother Mathias continued, "I can still continue until a place be found in the cemetery." This letter closes with a reference to the devil, against whose wiles the Brothers must be ever vigilant, for he — Mathias warns — "must be busy doing all he can to destroy, for this is his tactic: to divide and conquer."[37] It was a curious mixture of community news, personal observations, and administrative matters that was typical of Brother Mathias. Simply to issue orders and not to have included references to various activities of the Brothers, and to his own sentiments at the time, would never have occurred to him. Business was often buried in the body of the text, together with spiritual exhortations and comments on the efforts, or lack thereof, of certain public officials. Such letters made interesting reading, but could be sources of exasperation when it came to communicating matters of vital substance.

As often happens when the load became too great, or the unresolved questions of a former life too insistent, or other unforeseen obstacles to religious life surfaced, men left their vocations. The Little Brothers of the Good Shepherd order was no exception. Often its members would write to Brother Mathias either during or after the fact of leaving. The men expressed regret that the reality had not proven equal to the dream. One such letter was written by a Brother who left the community and found himself fighting halfway around the world in Vietnam. Asking for forgiveness for things that had been done and said in the past and for his hasty departure, he wrote Brother Mathias: "I confess that I did wrong leaving the way I did, and now I am certain that had I waited a little longer and talked with you, I am sure that I would still be there." [38] He went on: "Last night we were hit and believe me, I prayed like I never prayed before, not knowing if I would live to see the next day or not, but with the grace [of God] I am here. And while I was in the fox hole I thought the first thing I had to do was write to you and tell you that I am sorry."[39] Brother Mathias got another letter from a Brother who left the community after three years to join the U.S. Army. Promising to "treasure all memories," the writer admitted to being unstable and professed hope that he would grow up in the army. "Amidst tears and supplications I begged our Good Shepherd to help me see religious life through, but to no avail. . . . Keep storming those Gates of Heaven for me as I shall not forget you, my father and brother."[40]

It was an odyssey not unusual for the 1960s. What is unusual, however, is the implied assumption that the rigors of the military would not demand more devotion than did the rigors of the religious life. Some measure of the degree of commitment required can be gleaned from this interesting situation where men left the community for the battlefield, not vice versa.

There was no end to the advice Brother Mathias was called upon to give, or that he gave unsolicited when he thought it needed giving. One such instance involved a Brother who was too active in outside affairs. In a letter to this individual, Mathias expressed the following sentiments: "So there it is, as I mentioned, temporarily and so you will avoid any commotion or upsetting anything while you are there; above all you will avoid any interference with outsiders or any involvements with outsiders or other works which do not deal directly with our Apostolate. I think you know me well enough as to see what I mean."[41]

With the press of the work ever upon them, Brothers would push themselves beyond their limits and from time to time their health would fail. Brother John developed a stomach ulcer in 1967, which although scarred and not active, caused continuous spasms "due to mental, physical fatigue and too long a time under tension without relief."[42] Informing Brother Mathias of the situation, he referred to his diagnosis and his efforts to get well: "I asked the doctor if he could recommend a good psychiatrist that I might talk to, to get to the root of it all so I would not repeat. He said there was no root, that I extended myself too long and too far in the performance of my duties, without adequate sleep, with poor eating habits, rushed eating and no recreation or a chance to get away from it all due to the circumstances under which we live."[43] He assured Brother Mathias that he would be ready to work again if he could have "two weeks to learn to sleep again."[44]

Brother Mathias advised him to take it easy "until such time as you have completely regained your health and especially that you have complete control over your nerves." Then he referred to the Brotherhood as one of the finest organizations in the Church and noted how besieged he was by requests for Brothers to undertake works of charity. Knowing this, he continued, "Oh, God, please send us many many more vocations and that they persevere 'till the end.''[45] One wonders if this letter was a comfort, or if it prompted new spasms as Brother John contemplated the immensity of the tasks that confronted him.

In addition to letters, Brother Mathias made frequent creative use of the telephone, often calling on the spur of the moment. Sometimes he would forget the time difference between Albuquerque and the houses in the East and roust Brothers out of bed. On other occasions, the telephone would prove to be an obdurate instrument and frustrate his best efforts to get through. Once, he wrote Brother Michael in exasperation: ''Greetings! I tried to call you many times this evening but each time the line was busy, so I told them to verify this as this was a very important Institution for the Mentally Handicapped and they discovered that the phone was out of order. Perhaps someone forgot to put the receiver back in place.''[46]

One matter that occasioned no end of correspondence, controversy, and occasional bitterness was the transfer of Brothers from one facility to another. It was one of those irksome tasks that an administrator is forced to do in order to meet staffing requirements and keep houses and programs going. But the fact that human beings were involved and that they would invest their emotions and energies into one place, only to be sent to another, was a constant source of conflict. Brother Mathias would try to temporize and counsel, but woe be unto the Brother who objected or who attempted to get in the way! On one occasion, Mathias wrote an angry letter to Brother Damian on the subject. ''I am somewhat surprised at this attitude all the time. There were reliable Brothers at Notre Dame and when Brother Mark is away, I send a Brother to take his place. If I do this it is for a serious reason and I should know and I am responsible for our reputation and I intend keeping it intact.''[47] He added, ''You would be indeed very surprised at some of the remarks I get when I call on the phone for advice.''[48] Then, characteristically, he concluded, ''So let us pray and forget all that,'' reminding Brother Damian that he was only concerned about what was best for the Good Shepherd Brothers.

From time to time, Brother Mathias would find himself admonishing the heads of the houses who, in their chronic search for more hands to lighten the load, would ask for the younger, untried Brothers before these were sufficiently prepared for the rigors of the work. In a letter to Brother Joseph, this message was clearly delivered: ''Now with regard to any young boys, like you mentioned on the phone, I still would hesitate to encourage you at this time, because I know the dangers no matter whether they are full of the best intentions. Now anything could happen and again you will be sorry. So let us be patient in all this.''[49]

182

There is a candid letter written to "My dear little Brother" dated July 14, 1968 (the identity of the Brother is not revealed), that illustrates what "anything could happen" meant. The Brother in question had written a letter to his parents, the contents of which were "vulgar and could merit dismissal." Brother Mathias referred to the fact that "I am of the opinion that too many of our young people are immature and that it is better to have them open their eyes and realize the seriousness of what they have done."[50] He then expressed his surprise that this particular individual had survived for a time in another religious house, and informed him that he was writing to that religious superior to inquire "where they put the six months of education."[51] He ended with an offer to talk the matter over if the errant Brother in question wished to do so. The remedy was offered in the light of Brother Mathias's resolve that this was exactly what the offender must do. "Please take your time and read this over very carefully and let me know when you will be here to see me."[52]

Several months later, Brother Mathias wrote to Brother Joseph about another Brother who had committed an obvious and public offense, namely, getting drunk and ending up in the local jail. This Brother's excuse, upon writing to Brother Mathias, had been simply, "I got drunk with friends."[53] Mathias's response to Joseph includes reference to the "fine group of young Brothers in Albuquerque" and that at the pontifical Mass everyone was saying "how dignified they are." Thus was poor Brother Joseph consoled by the fact that there were suitable Brothers to be had and that "you will get them."[54]

On June 11, 1968, Brother Paul got a very blunt letter from his superior on the subject of his objections to the transfers of certain Brothers.

> I wish again and once and for all that outsiders not be interfering when I come to change any Brother, also not to be after me for more Brothers. . . . I am well aware of the needs without having to be harassed by others. When I decide to change a Brother I have the reasons and very often when I make a remark about changing a Brother, the Local Superior gets upon his high horse and makes all kinds of remarks and declarations, while he is not in the least aware of the real cause of the change.[55]

Then, in a more conciliatory mood, he continued by reminding Brother Paul that "I have been so deceived in the past that I have to keep more alert."[56]

Occasionally, the correspondence was petulant, especially when he felt that the Brother he was trying to contact was avoiding him. A rather cryptic note to Brother Damian on July 11, 1968, illustrates this characteristic. "With regard to Philadelphia I wonder if you recall some weeks ago I called and you 'were out,' then when I 'called back you were 'ill in bed and could not be disturbed' but I fully understood the situation and will not dwell any longer on this."[57] One of Brother Mathias's most endearing characteristics is also in evidence here. Although he could flare up at a Brother for one reason or another — some mistake in judgment, some ill-advised act, or interference in matters outside his purview — Mathias could also quickly let the storm pass. One never sees references in letters to past wrongs or previous slights. The matter at hand was the one that was important. Once that matter was resolved, then it was time to move on.

Mathias was also quick to honor his fellow Brothers when they reached certain milestones in their careers. All the occasions when they made vows — temporary, renewed, or final — were times of celebration. He made every attempt to have the local diocesan ordinary — whether he be bishop or archbishop — present on such occasions, and to invite other members of the clergy and laity to celebrate along with the community. Moreover, public notice was given to honors bestowed on individual Brothers by the cities in which they labored, and Brother Mathias made sure everyone knew about such honors and appreciated the efforts that the Brothers involved had made to earn them. When Brother Columban was honored by the Metropolitan Council of Toronto for his work at the Richmond Street Family Hostel, *The Shepherd's Call* ran an article on the award.[58] Local newspapers were supplied with photographs of Brothers being invested or making vows. Lay boards, ladies' auxiliaries, and other groups allied with the Brothers in various communities were always given recognition: in the papers, at awards' luncheons and dinners, and in other ways. Brother Mathias truly recognized the propensity of the human being to thrive on praise. He made sure that when it was earned the world would know about it.

Mathias also went to bat for Brothers under the shadow of the military Selective Service Act. The case of Brother Savio Grover is an interesting example of this cautious confrontation between the head of a religious order and the authorities in charge of military procurement. After Brother Savio was classified 1-A by his draft board (which meant he was available for induction), Brother Mathias wrote to an attorney in Miami, Florida, to ask for intervention on his behalf. The attorney, Thomas Horkan, responded by advising Brother Mathias that if the local draft board had acted unanimously in the case, then there would be no further appeal possible. If, however, it could be shown that there were dissenting votes on the board at the time action was taken, Brother Savio would have the right to appeal directly to the president of the United States.[59] Brother Savio's fate hung in the balance. The decision had not been unanimous, and eleven days later, the Florida law firm entered an appeal to President Lyndon B. Johnson on behalf of William C. Grover, known in religious life as Brother Savio Grover.[60] The appeal, however, was unsuccessful and Brother Savio was ultimately drafted.[61]

The late 1960s brought changes to the Order of the Little Brothers of the Good Shepherd, as it did to the nation at large. President Johnson, in a move that surprised the country, jolted the American people with the announcement, early in 1968, that he would not be a candidate for reelection. The summer of that year saw the bitterest Democratic convention fight in the history of the nation played out in Chicago, under the clubs of Mayor Richard Daley's police and the ubiquitous eyes of the press. Four paraplegic veterans of the Vietnam War managed to get into the convention on passes from Senator Alan Cranston's office and made their way down to the front where they locked arms in their wheelchairs and chanted "Stop the bombing, stop the war!" at the top of their lungs.[62] When one of them, Ron Kovic, was being dragged away by security police, a delegate wearing a "Four More Years" button called Kovic a "dirty commie" and spat in his face.[63] That October, several hundred thousand people journeyed by bus to Washington, D.C., for the moratorium against the war. In 1969, over half a million endured the bitterly cold weather for the mobilization to protest President Richard M. Nixon's policies. The Civil Rights Movement — which had reached its pinnacle of triumph in August, 1965, with Martin Luther King, Jr.'s, speech at the Washington Monument — degenerated, after King's assassination in April, 1968, into riots and police confrontations. It seemed as though turbulence and despair gripped much of the country while its best young people turned a deaf ear to the government's exhortations. People everywhere began to wonder at the credibility of even the most hallowed traditions. It is not surprising that this ferment was felt within the Brotherhood.

In May, 1969, Brother Camillus Harbinson was named vicar general of the Little Brothers of the Good Shepherd, and in June, three more Brothers were invested with the white habit of the order.[64] In August, delegates from the Good Shepherd Brothers attended the fourth annual Brothers' institute in Massachusetts, at which two hundred Brothers from fifty congregations discussed such matters as job satisfaction, individual interests and talents, adaptability, direct-people contacts, the desire for less administration, and the desire for less desk work.[65] At the conference there was, for the first time, a black Brothers' caucus, and fifteen blacks were in attendance.

185

By November, 1969, the winds of change that had been breezes blowing through the windows of the Brotherhood making no more than passing eddies, suddenly became forceful and insistent. The challenge to the authority of the founder began in the East but was not confined to the Eastern houses. Its leader was Brother Joseph Dooley, director of the Eastern region. After having received a series of memos from Brother Mathias that he saw as unnecessary interference with the efficient and harmonious running of the houses under his jurisdiction, Brother Joseph wrote a remarkable answer to Brother Mathias on November 18, 1969, in which he said: "Please try to understand, Brother, that with all our respect for you as a long-time friend and your position as our superior and founder, I see no point to have constituted 'regions' if regional directors are not mature or responsible enough to look after brothers in their areas."[66] It was the culmination of a series of events that perhaps in an earlier age would not have amounted to more than grumbling and a collective gripe session. But in the context of the 1960s, they took on a shape and force that would, before long, transform the organization to which the Brothers had dedicated their lives. The following day, November 19, the Brothers in Philadelphia held a meeting for discussion and recommendations at which several key points were at issue:

> 1. The dislike of the word "little" in Little Brothers of the Good Shepherd. "Let us show to all that we are humble in our lives without broadcasting the often misconstrued, archaic word Little.
> 2. Recommendation that the General Chapter should be held as soon as possible with the election of Council members.
> 3. Recommendation that a lay lawyer for the community would be more objective than a Catholic lawyer.
> 4. Questioning the requirement that members of the Council all be in final vows.
> 5. Recommendation that the Regional Director be elected by the members from his region.
> 6. Recommendation that the day off should be seen as an "obligation to all the Brothers of the Society." Further, that when possible, Brothers should have a weekend off per month and that vacations should be a minimum of two weeks.[67]

Thus, the significance of the small pronoun "we" in Brother Joseph's letter to Brother Mathias becomes clear. For the first time, a Brother was representing the interests of other Brothers against the regulations and procedures that had been set forth by the Brother general. But the spirit of rebellion had the potential of going beyond reasonable demands and members were becoming puffed up with the possibility that they could restructure any and all aspects of the religious life. Brother Joseph sent a "Letter to all Brothers," to the Brothers in Philadelphia in order to gain time for reflection and to reduce the possibility that even stronger demands would be made in the heady atmosphere that was emerging. It was a minor masterpiece. Beginning with the assertion that "full authority" had been given to him as regional director from Brother Mathias, he rose to an eloquent defense of the man who had been his own inspiration for entry into religious life. "It was the law of love he was trying to emphasize and not just the letter of the law — and in this, his spirit we give and take, share and compromise, welcome and tolerate, in a time and place for everything. . . . So to question authority is not necessarily to undermine it but to establish authority in its rightful place with all due respect and honor."[68]

Brother Mathias did not answer the letter of November 18. Perhaps he reasoned that time would either solidify the feelings being expressed in the Eastern region, or dissipate them. He had been hurt. For once, the telephone did not ring and the mails did not carry their accustomed spontaneous prayer for the "final perseverance of us all." Brother Mathias remained silent. It is this silence, more than anything else that he might have said, that prevailed.

Life returned to its normal, demanding routines. Brother Joseph continued his active solicitation of views from his constituency of twenty-three Brothers, caring for their opinions, guiding and directing their lives. In March, he sent them a questionnaire in which they were asked to define the words authority, commitment, corporate poverty, identification, involvement, renewal, and witness.[69] Their answers to these, and to the other questions posed by the questionnaire, provide a map of the landscape of change that had been altering the society over the past nineteen years of its existence. They exhibit a sense of individual conscience and judgment, and show a breadth of experience beyond that of the novices of the 1950s. But then, those novices of the 1950s had not been asked such questions. Brother Mathias reasoned that it was enough to expect a prospective Brother to be willing to give up worldly pursuits and to dedicate himself to the service of the poor. The manner in which that service was rendered, and the degree to which the Brother would judge the communal life, were not questions that the Good Shepherd Brothers were asking of their membership. Thus it is as if the spirit of the 1960s had become the primary reference point for all endeavors, even for those whose bent, aims, and goals were clearly religious and removed from the heady realm of politics and social struggle.

From April 20 through April 25, 1970, all regional directors met in Albuquerque for the first seminar of its type in the history of the order. They concluded, after five days of sessions, that the community should seek "desirable changes in present policy and procedural operations of the Society."[70] Archbishop James P. Davis was a participant in the conference sessions, and, on April 24, Father Lucien Hendren of the archdiocese made a presentation on a proposed new constitution for the society.[71] It is interesting to note that the meeting was called by Brother Mathias, despite the obvious strain it put upon the operations in the various houses to have this many ranking Brothers absent for over a week. It is also interesting to speculate as to his motives for calling such a meeting and scheduling it for Albuquerque. The expression by the regional directors of their need for "desirable changes" could be willingly received without having to come to the battleground of specifics. Moreover, it would be possible to define "desirable" according to a number of agendas. Certainly, Brother Mathias was in full control of his directors, and both he and they acknowledged it. The meeting was cordial and open, and as one could have expected, full of affection on the part of the parties involved for one another. But the lines of authority had not changed. The Little Brothers of the Good Shepherd order was not yet a democracy. Tradition, respect, and — above all — obedience, were still strong, and it would take another seven years to shake them. By then, at age seventy-seven, Brother Mathias would be more willing to let go, although not all the Brothers would demand this of him, or welcome it when it finally took place.

11 .... Organization

THE LITTLE BROTHERS OF THE GOOD SHEPHERD BEGAN AS A PIOUS union of laymen. The group had no prescribed habit, constitution, or vows. Then, under the pressure of Brother Mathias's hopes for its future, the community became a secular institute, with a prescribed habit and private vows. In 1965, the Little Brothers became a Society for the Common Life, and, in 1977, it was recognized as a religious order with pontifical status and public vows.

All Brothers who entered the community underwent a ceremony of investiture during which they received the habit of the order. The ceremony was solemn and intended to convey all the dedication and faith with which the postulant offered himself to the service of the poor. During the investiture ceremony, the postulant prostrated himself on the floor, face down, arms extended, in a position of both worship and submission. The habit he received consisted of a white garment with long sleeves and a scapular that reached to the hem of the garment for the professed Brothers, but was of shorter length for novices. The rosary was worn on the right to make it distinctive. Sandals were also worn at first, although this practice did not last.[1] The white habits had been ordered from the Dominican Sisters in southern California, but they did not arrive in time for the first investiture ceremony, Sunday, May 27, 1951. So, the first habits were improvised by one of the Brothers.[2]

For his text at this first investiture ceremony, Archbishop Edwin Byrne chose Matthew 18:12, "If a man has a hundred sheep and one of them strays, will he not leave the ninety-nine and go in search of the one that has strayed?" Then, as he looked down at the members of the fledgling community that he had helped found, he gave them his blessing, and invoked the guidance of the Good Shepherd to increase their numbers.[3]

Through the years, many men with diverse views underwent this ceremony. But perhaps none was as unique as the experience of the order's humorous columnist, Brother "Uselessensis," who described his investiture in these words: "I was more or less in a daze and heard little, if anything, and being flat on the floor, I couldn't see much other than the polished hardwood. About the only thing that really concerned me was trying to breathe."[4] Continuing in the same vein, he went on to ask, "A nun takes the veil, but does a Brother take the cowl? In this outfit, we call a cowl a capuche. Why, I don't know. So long as the hood isn't on the front of the car and the capuche isn't running behind the train, who cares? Brothers may or may not take the cowl, but that last statement takes the cake."[5]

The Rule of St. Augustine was the framework of order for the religious life of the men from the beginning. The rule was intended to be a guide "for concretely living a life given to God."[6] The rule required that everyone entering "freely consent" to give up his possessions for the common use. "Let food and clothing be distributed to each of you by the Superior, not in equal measure to all, because you are not all of equal strength, but so as to provide for each one according to his need."[7] Eating, except at meals, was disallowed. "When you go to table, listen without noise and contention to that which is read to you according to custom, until you rise from your meal; nor let your mouth only receive food, but let your ears also be fed with the Word of God."[8] Chastity and mutual criticism were defended. Obedience to the superior was couched in such terms so that the superior would not feel guilty in reproving his subjects, "lest the authority of your government be weakened through too great regard to humility."[9] The Rule of St. Augustine goes on to say: "And although both love and fear be necessary, yet must the Superior rather desire to be loved than feared by you, ever remembering that he must give an account to God for you all. Be therefore the more obedient out of compassion not for yourselves only but also for him, who is in so much more danger in proportion as he is higher in authority over you."[10]

This was the rule under which the Order of St. John of God had been governed, and the one that Brother Mathias both knew and practiced. Thus it is not surprising to find that the first set of instructions for the common life that he drew up mirrored the language and spirit of the great fifth-century saint. Three vows were taken: poverty, chastity, and obedience. A fourth, that of hospitality, was not formerly required, for it seemed too cumbersome and difficult to observe.[11] But the practice of hospitality was embodied in the motto, "Charity Unlimited," which bound the Brothers to observe its spirit to the best of their ability.

In the first constitutions of the Little Brothers of the Good Shepherd, the purpose of the organization was defined as follows:

The care and assistance, both spiritual and corporal, of all poor, afflicted and unfortunate members of Christ, of every condition, more especially, the most abandoned of whatever race or creed that they may be. This includes fallen youth, convicts, derelicts,

190

all unfortunates. All this is to be done in the spirit of the Good Shepherd, who goes after the stray sheep and makes every effort to bring him back, more especially if he be in distress.[12]

For good measure, "all the other works of Charity and Mercy according as his Excellency, the Most Reverend Archbishop, may deem it necessary," was added. Recitation of the Little Office of the Blessed Virgin Mary, assistance at daily Mass, and morning and evening prayers were prescribed. Each day, an examination of conscience was made. Recitation of the Rosary and thirty minutes of spiritual reading were part of the Brothers' day, and periodic retreats were to be taken, if possible, on the first Friday of every month, and annually for eight days. "All should strive after perfection, especially by the practice of the virtues corresponding to the vows."[13] In case of illness, the aspirant was to inform the prefect "in order to know if he may make use of some remedy or present himself to the physician, or despise the pain and think no more about it."[14]

There were rules for cleaning and maintaining the novitiate; there also were rules governing the cutting of hair, shaving, entering the room of another, writing letters, taking baths, having one's clothes dry-cleaned, speaking to visitors, and leaving the premises. All of these regulations were designed to assist the new Brother in developing the "practice of submission." Novices were not to "lose time reading magazines and newspapers" and to avoid useless conversation because "the results of useless conversation are always disastrous."

There were instructions on the bearing of the head and face: "Hold it straight without either lifting or lowering it too much. . . . Avoid bursts of laughter which are a mark of levity, or that air of sadness which would lead others to believe one carries the yoke of religion with regret. . . Hold the body erect without stiffness, keeping one's hands usually under the scapular. . . . Strive to avoid yawning . . . as well as careless nonchalant posture. . . . No elbows on the table. . . . No dipping of bread into the drink. . . . No rinsing of the mouth too noisily."[15] This list of particulars for the regulation of personal appearance ends with the charming observation that "nothing looks worse on a religious than a dirty pair of shoes."

A variety of prayers were used by the Brothers. In addition to the Angelus, the Prayer to the Sacred Heart, and devotions to the Blessed Virgin, a "Night Litany for a Big City" was recited. In this prayer, Brothers prayed for ". . . those who are carrying on wicked trades and profit by sin, those tempted by suicide, those who are out for sin, those who are out to rescue others, those who work at night, those insane, those afraid to die. . . . Grant us pardon of our sins, our negligences and our ignorances."[16]

On March 3, 1961, Archbishop Byrne elevated the Little Brothers of the Good Shepherd to the status of a secular institute.[17] A constitution to conform to the new status had been written and submitted to the archbishop for his approval. The changes it embodied were minor. A new stipulation required that "one of the members will *always* be available to assist those who may be in need and ask for help."[18]

Article 10 declared that the constitutions "in themselves do not bind under pain of sin." The reason for this lay in the nature of the secular institute, which did not require the same commitment as did pontifical status. However, it warned that any member who would be so bold "as to transgress them [the constitutions] through contempt, or in matters which are contrary to the vows, the laws of God and His Church, or the formal precepts of the superiors cannot be excused from sin."[19]

Age restrictions were given as being between twenty-one and thirty-five, unless a dispensation was granted by the director general.[20] A training period of two years was prescribed for aspirants in "the process of mental prayers, in mortification, humility and self-denial . . . and Christlike methods of dealing with the sick and poor who seek their help." The list of stages in the development of the interior life was shortened to five items, dealing with the study of the Scriptures, the study of the constitutions of the secular institute, the practice of self-discipline, and the cultivation of a "recollected state of mind."[21] At the conclusion of the training period, the aspirant was required to pass a written examination on the constitutions and the customs of the institute. Vows were to be taken for one year, then for two periods of three years, and finally, for life. Aspirants would, in addition, sign a statement that they were joining "from a purely religious motive and charitable intent," and that if for any reason they left the order, "they can demand no temporal payment for services rendered."[22]

The admonitions for conduct, both personal and public, were retained, although in condensed form. Article 47 warned against the "sins of the tongue," among which are the going from one center to another and speaking of the "failings" of members in one community to those of another. Article 49 stipulated that "members will avoid all lazy and slouching positions; their walk should be simple, unaffected and as noiseless as possible." During meals and at recreation, members were to do their best to "contribute to an atmosphere of unity and companionship."[23]

Article 50 defined the "vow and virtue of poverty" in the following language:

> By their vow of poverty, members of the Institute retain the ownership of their property and the capacity to acquire further property, and they may retain the administration of it, under the supervision and control of their superiors. They may cede the administration of their property to whomsoever they wish, determine how it is to be used, and dispose of its income in favor of any charitable or pious work or in favor of anyone they wish, except themselves, unless they wish to add it to their patrimony.[24]

Four pages of explanation and stipulations on this subject followed. By contrast, the "vow and virtue" of chastity took only two pages to expound. Obedience took up six pages of text, and one stipulation stated that if the director general was issuing a "formal precept" under holy obedience, it must be made either in writing, or in the presence of two witnesses. The action was to be taken rarely and then only for "a grave reason and after mature consideration."[25] Likewise, the section on departure and dismissal was long, full of detail, and precise.

Finally, the constitutions of 1961 provided for officers, headed by the director general, who was to be elected for a term of six years by secret ballot of at least two thirds of the members present. Four councillors to assist him were also elected. Those cases in which councillors had a deliberative vote were enumerated.[26] In practice, these sections were never activated by Brother Mathias.

Four years later, the prefect of the Sacred Congregation of Religious approved the Little Brothers of the Good Shepherd as a Society for the Common Life.[27] Dated October 23, 1965, the promulgation entailed yet another constitution to reflect the new status of the community. The document was submitted to Archbishop James P. Davis of Santa Fe, "with the understanding that within two or three years from September 14, 1966, a General Chapter be held to implement the Constitutions of Vatican Council II regarding the Religious Life."[28] It took twelve years before this "understanding" was finally put into practice.

The new constitutions of the society borrowed whole sections from the previous constitutions of the secular institute. Certain titles disappeared and were replaced by others: "prefect" became "novice-master," while "aspirants" became "novices"; "director general" became "Brother General," and "local directors" were now "local superiors." Houses of the society were still subject to the local ordinaries of the districts in which they were located, and for most purposes, "ordinary" referred to the archbishop. There were now six, rather than four, councillors to assist the Brother General.

By 1960, it had become increasingly obvious that the community had grown too large, and that the houses they operated were too geographically dispersed, to make informal controls and communication feasible. With the invention of the various kinds of duplicating equipment, and the purchase by the Brothers of a photocopier and mimeograph machine, newsletters were increasingly used to disseminate information. Once he began utilizing an "open letter" to all the members of the Brotherhood, Brother Mathias warmed to the medium. Often he sent several out in the space of a month. As a source of both day-to-day trivia, and of matters of significance, they are invaluable. Moreover, they are written in his unique, engaging, and generally rambling style that is at times exasperating.

The letter to "My dear Brothers" dated December 27, 1960, for example, indicates Brother Mathias's irritation with the bureaucratic delays that had slowed final approval by the Sacred Congregation of the status of "Society" for the Brotherhood. Brother Mathias suggested that prayers offered up for the intention of speeding up the process "could not but be efficacious."[29]

In October, 1961, the letter to "Beloved Brothers in Christ" was full of news of openings of houses, proposed projects, and a request from the Philippines that had to be declined; but just to gear up for the next such request, "we are having a Brother taking Spanish and in due time he will be in a position to teach it to other young Brothers."[30] Brother Mathias praised the retreats that had been given for the Brothers by a certain Father Dumont, and "there is no room for mediocrity; on the contrary, our young Brothers are stimulated so well that love and zeal for perfection shine on all countenances."[31]

In April, 1962, the letter was full of news of the chapels in the various houses. In Hamilton, where Brother Kevin had Mass celebrated for the first time at the hostel chapel, Brother Mathias remarked that he was joyous that there was a chapel close to the hostel "where the poor men can come to visit their Lord and Master whenever they feel the need to call on Him."[32]

By July, he was rejoicing over all the anniversaries that had occurred and "will occur, please God," during the year.[33] He wrote, "Brother Camillus celebrated his 8th anniversary on February 2nd, and of course we know how he is working actively for the extension of the work in Columbus. September 21st will be the 8th anniversary of the day I arrived at St. Martin's home to take it over. It only took a few hours to decide that."[34] The last sentence took some liberties with the facts, but it is interesting to note that once things were "settled," the struggles and indecisions which accompanied the process faded into the past. "I am sure that you all realize that our group of Little Brothers of the Good Shepherd could conquer all hearts."[35]

In September of 1962, the letter to all Brothers launched into a recital of how nice it would be if each Brother — reporting on "his health, his status, and above all, his spiritual life"[36] — would write to Brother Mathias from time to time, and let him know how things were. Then, Brother Mathias turned to the subject of the new property, which had been acquired in the diocese of Columbus at Wakefield, and expressed amazement at its size. But, he pointed out, all things are explainable in terms of the solicitude of our Blessed Mother. He observed: "The vastness of this property and how it was acquired will be forever a mystery to me. But, then again when we call on Our Blessed Mother to come to our aid, what can we expect with our spirit of faith but that our Dear and Blessed Mother takes care of all."[37] The letter ended with "The more we pray, the better we become. . . ."[38]

In February, 1963, Archbishop Byrne expressed some doubts that an adequate preparation of candidates in the spiritual life was being pursued.[39] Brother Mathias quoted the archbishop in his letter to all Brothers and then exhorted them:

> Nothing should prevent any of us from making little visits to Jesus in the Most Blessed Sacrament. Just drop in the chapel and say hello to Jesus — become familiar with Jesus and His Blessed Mother. Do not wait until the bell rings for chapel and count the time. Be close to Jesus and He is close to you, so that when any difficulty arises (and indeed difficulties arise every day with some of us as we are all human), we can call on Him for help and it will come in a hurry.[40]

A number of personal matters were addressed in the June letter. Brothers were warned to avoid certain specific practices — for example, that "we should refrain from removing part of the rosary . . . chain, or adding to it, just to satisfy our own fancy," and "as regards to total abstinence [from alcohol], there should be no doubt that this is for life."[41] Moreover, the Brothers were to avoid getting involved in "all kinds of outside activities" because, "once started, . . . [such activities] may cause unnecessary commotion to try to discontinue." There was also a discourse on poverty and the admonition that "avarice is so ugly a vice." Brothers were chastised for complaining to outsiders and for not using their leisure time for reading. Moreover, some Brothers had apparently been allowing others to do more than their fair share of the work. "It makes me sad when I see a Brother trying to get his work finished in a tight spot, whether in the kitchen, washing dishes, or in the laundry, and close by another Brother just sitting down smoking a cigarette.[42] The spirit of this piece is summed up in the section on personal hygiene: "There is a great danger to use perfume, cologne and scented shaving lotions. . . . With these we are liable to be looked upon as not real genuine Good Shepherds who are supposed to be hardy men." The letter ended on the disquieting note that all the archbishop asked for was loyalty, "and he went so far as to say that when loyalty is missing, it is serious."[43]

There was sadness in this letter, the first of its kind in tone. There was also an undercurrent of reproach that sought almost to bring about confession and repentance. There was disappointment that such things even needed to be said. One senses the rebellion of the 1960s creeping in from the outside world. Certainly, if one recalls the mood of the country at the time, it is not surprising that some ripples of discontent would be felt inside the community. What Brother Mathias was trying to contain were those forces that would have made his Brotherhood a more impersonal, detached, and casual union of men, interested in the apostolate of the poor, but not knit together by the kind of love and submission he had known all his life. In this regard, Brother Mathias took on some measure of the mantle of Martin Luther, in that it was acceptable that he rebel against conditions which he found intolerable, but that no one in the future could do so against him.

Yet, one cannot help but sympathize. Here was a man who had stood in the snow in Montreal so that he could experience the hardships the men knew at the city shelter; who had eaten beans for days on end in order that the poor men could also eat; who had drunk coffee made from used grounds; who had carried stale bread in an improvised apron. He could not understand how one man could work and another could be "just sitting down smoking a cigarette." Moreover, as he knew from his own past, the Brothers of St. John of God didn't smoke. Brother Francis de Sales, who had been his teacher, recalled having thrown the last cigarette over the monastery wall before receiving his habit.[44] Now, there was a new generation emerging that Brother Mathias did not understand. This was a generation that would make an issue over long hair in the army, minority religious diets in the prisons, and the right to "relevance" in the classroom. It was a generation with both high ideals and petty demands, but chiefly one that shared a certain common ground, a distaste for and dislike of authority. For good or for ill, some of these young men were his Brothers.

It is easy to see much of what Brother Mathias wrote in his open letters to "My dear and Reverend Brothers" during the latter years of the 1960s as being excessively concerned with matters of detail. For example, on July 21, 1964, a circular letter went to all Brothers ordering them not to make any repairs or renovations on the buildings under their supervision without "having all plans approved by competent authority and the different departments of the location and then to submit all papers to our Motherhouse." The letter offered examples: ". . . this or that wall is out of place," or ". . . you could gain an inch or a foot here or there," or ". . . a tree should be removed"; these were admittedly small matters but ones that "can cause so much worry and trouble."[45] By October 26, 1965, a building committee had been established to oversee all remodeling of any and all parts of buildings whether they belonged to the society or not.[46] Moreover, "no publication will be put into print until previously submitted to the Motherhouse where Brother James, Censor Librorum, will examine it."[47] Perhaps most important was the declaration: "When I change a Brother from one house to another, or even give him a leave of absence, I would ask our local Superiors not to put up objections because very often there are motives that cannot be revealed to anyone and it is only between the Major Superior and Almighty God and the Little Brother."[48]

Another letter complained about excess luggage that certain Brothers had accumulated in their travels from one house to the next. "I have seen Brothers coming with a handful of clothing, and on being transferred, they need one of the moving companies to take their luggage to the depot."[49]

It is characteristic of Brother Mathias that he attacked the major difficulties with the same energy he used with minor ones. The spring of the following year found him trying to plug some of the leaks that had appeared in the dike of the spiritual life of the community. The chronic manpower shortage suffered by the Brotherhood necessitated the transfer of Brothers to work stations in the various houses before the prescribed two-year novitiate experience had been completed. There were nineteen novices in 1966 who were getting their training in community life while also on the job feeding homeless men, bathing teenagers with cerebral palsy, changing sheets for the elderly, collecting food, and doing a host of other tasks. It was inevitable that a studied development of spiritual life was impossible under the pressure of such activities. Brother Mathias complained:

> I do notice that many who come back from other houses have no idea of giving their full voice to the Office of Community prayers — but try to let it pass to the other Brother nearest him. . . . Also

they are astonished at hearing of the Martyrology, even though we did it simply, taking on the simplest names, so that there would be no embarrassment for the Brother reading. Also so few know that we have the Stations of the Cross in common every Friday, and on Mondays, Tuesdays and Fridays during Lent and Advent.[50]

By now, Brother Mathias was beginning to feel his own mortality. His letter to the Brothers admonished them, "Let us hurry and not lose our time. It is too precious because the night comes when we cannot do anything worthwhile."[51] By 1966, he was sixty-six. Aside from glaucoma and several operations on his eyes, however, his health was remarkably good and his constitution still able to keep pace with the grueling work he demanded of his body. Yet, one finds a more philosophical mood in his letters. In March, 1967, he came close to poetry in his description of the Little Brother on his rounds, giving comfort to the poor and afflicted, finding happiness in his "beautiful and noble vocation."[52]

In September, the Brothers got a four-page letter that ranged over a host of subjects. Brother Mathias had just returned from a cross-country trek, during which he had visited most of the houses of the community. The journey had given him the opportunity to see close at hand how his Little Brothers were going about their "beautiful and noble vocation." What he found both pleased and annoyed him. Obviously gratified with the progress he had observed, he looked forward to the future when even more would be possible and even greater things would be accomplished. ". . . We must be ready to accept whatever hardships come to us in this work" and ". . . each individual should beg of Our Blessed Mother final perseverance" are examples. But this letter was also the occasion for upbraiding those Brothers whom he felt to be insufficiently devoted to the work.

> You all know of the great affection I have for Aged and Infirm Priests and how I insist and, I will ever insist, that they receive the best possible care and attention. We promised this on the day of our Profession and unless we take this to heart we are not serious in our vocation. Let no one dare to advise you to the contrary, whether he be a theologian or a philosopher. We are Little Brothers of the Good Shepherd and that is our calling and we must accept it completely or not at all. We must be ever ready to sacrifice our time, our welfare for the care of the needy and unfortunate. Let this be the last time that I write this kind of a sentence.[53]

He also took this opportunity to lecture those Brothers who had been intemperate. "The Brother who indulges in liquor knows perfectly well that he is not following his Constitutions because in this there is no human frailty but malice and he will be called to render an account to Almighty God for the scandal he has given."[54] The instructions at the end of this long letter directed local superiors to "read it once a month until further notice." Previously, superiors had been told only to read letters once, and then to inscribe them in the records of the house. Now it seems, however, that Brother Mathias felt that repetition could achieve what force of example had failed to accomplish.

On September 19, the Brothers learned that they would all be taking CCD (Confraternity of Christian Doctrine) courses and that they would soon receive their first lessons. It was a new task laid upon their shoulders, which they were asked to "accept in the right spirit." Such study would prepare them to be ready when called upon to assist in teaching Christian doctrine and catechism. Brother Mathias ended this letter with the prediction that the Little Brothers "will be one of the finest groups in the Catholic Church, a consolation to the Ecclesiastical Authority and a comfort to all."[55]

In May, 1968, Brother Mathias wrote one of his most beautiful letters on the subject of the humanity of the Brothers. He reminded them that some were now growing old and would soon have to "lay down their tools someday and serve our mission in prayer." He continued: "The Motherhouse owes this to every Brother — that he will be assured of security; that he who has given up worldly pleasures, honor and gain to serve humbly in poverty within the framework of our Mission, will know that he at least will receive proper care."[56] It is a moving plea for perseverance in the face of disappointment and hardship. "The weight of the world's complexities does not make our task easier; in fact the burden becomes almost unbearably heavy." It ends with the humble request, "Pray for me, dear Brothers, that I may remain worthy of your trust."[57]

This was followed, in January of 1969, by another remarkable letter. In this one, vision and faith seem to combine with an even greater intensity than in the earlier letters. Brother Mathias reported on the death of Brother Francis Abraham as a great tragedy and a shock. Furthermore, he and most of the other Brothers in the novitiate were stricken with the flu and were laid low in the "dark shadows that had suddenly fallen across the bright vistas of hope." Frankly admitting that he had struggled with despair during this period, he describes the luminous reconciliation that brought an end to his sadness. "Let us look backward for a moment through the pages of Brother Francis' Book of Life, use this as a precept in our own life and take an example

199

from the way he met our many problems, especially in the infancy of our Society when each problem seemed the challenge of the Matterhorn to a climber without shoes."[58]

The year 1969 would see more struggles than those with poverty, sickness, and mortality. There would begin a movement among the Brothers that would culminate in the transfer of authority from the hands of the one who had been its titular head and founder into the hands of another. The argument over whether the religious order needed a "restoration," or a "renewal," was about to begin. In some ways, this struggle would be more of a Matterhorn "to a climber without shoes" than had any previous struggle been for Brother Mathias.

12 .... The 1960s

THE DECADE OF THE 1960S WOULD PROVE TO BE PIVOTAL IN THE HIS-
tory of the Little Brothers of the Good Shepherd. It was marked by a
series of achievements. Expansion continued in both the numbers of
institutions operated by the Brothers and in the size of their membership. But the original thrust of Brother Mathias's vision was being
challenged. No longer were candidates content to dedicate themselves without question to whatever service he chose for them.
Moreover, there was an increased spirit of independence in the older
Brothers, coupled with an inevitable shift toward institutionalization.
The latter was unavoidable as administrative demands multiplied.
Government regulations had to be adhered to, forms for various government support programs had to be filled out and submitted. The
new tasks placed upon the order demanded new capabilities. That the
order would emerge from the 1960s with a different orientation toward the world, and toward its own mission, could have been predicted. Perhaps more than any other single factor, the death of Archbishop Edwin Byrne in July, 1963, accelerated the process.

The establishment of a refuge for transient men in Toronto, Ontario, Canada, required much of Brother Mathias's time and energy
during 1960. He corresponded with Charles J. Heffernan, a member of
Toronto's St. Vincent de Paul Society, which was financing the facility. As usual, Archbishop Byrne was cautious about new foundations.
He wrote to Brother Mathias in January, "Your interesting letter . . .
indicates there is no need of rushing into this new foundation in Toronto. In fact, it seems to me better not to make any new foundations until we get the Nihil Obstat [that is, official approval] from the Holy
See."[1] The Canadians, however, were not holding back. In February,
Brother Mathias got a second letter from Canada. This one came
from the St. Vincent de Paul Society in Hamilton, Ontario. They too
were anxious to explore the possibilities of establishing a men's hostel "for the poor, the homeless and unfortunate members of Christ's
Mystical Body."[2] Brother Mathias responded with guarded encouragement but added, "At this time I am in no position to make any
commitment, and I would also ask you not to mention me in any
way. . . ."[3] He advised the members of the Hamilton society to have
their bishop contact Archbishop Byrne; then, if the response was encouraging, plans might proceed.

Shortly thereafter, the bishop of Hamilton wrote to Archbishop Byrne and enclosed a copy of Brother Mathias's letter to the Hamilton group. Byrne shot a letter off to Brother Mathias, complaining, "Only today did I read your correspondence with the Society of St. Vincent de Paul in Hamilton, Ontario." He warned Brother Mathias not to accept obligations that he could not fulfill.[4] Brother Mathias duly read the letter and then set out on a trip back East to visit the Brothers at the Brother Martin Home in Columbus, Ohio. But he arranged to come home by way of Hamilton, Ontario.

Once back in Albuquerque, Brother Mathias reported to Archbishop Byrne that the St. Vincent de Paul Society in Hamilton wasn't well organized. "They are very anxious to do something at this time, but they do not know the way to go about it." He added, for Byrne's benefit, "Hamilton is only 42 miles from Toronto and I have been told that by 1970, Toronto will be 100% Catholic. . . ."[5] Moreover, Mathias pointed out, there were four Brothers in Columbus, and one of them could surely be spared to go to Hamilton. At length, as negotiations developed further with the Hamilton group, Byrne's misgivings were laid to rest and he gave his permission to proceed. In February, 1961, he wrote to Mathias, "I rejoice with you at the opportunity presented in Canada. . . . Whatever arrangement you make about going will be agreeable to me."[6] In the meantime, Brother Mathias had made his famous one-man trek to Miami, and Camillus House was in full swing feeding and housing the poor of that city. Having reached his sixtieth birthday, Mathias was showing no signs of slowing down.

As January, 1961, opened, the order made preparations for its tenth anniversary celebration. The bishop of Columbus, Clarence Issenman, was planning to attend in person. Other prelates, including Cardinal Richard Cushing of Boston, Archbishop Joseph Rummel of New Orleans, Bishop Coleman Carroll of Miami, and Bishop Charles Buddy of San Diego sent personal letters of congratulation to Brother Mathias. Daniel Donohue, gentleman-in-waiting to the pope, and his wife, Bernardine, a papal countess, wrote the introductory letter for the program. It was a day of celebration, prayer, and feasting. Brother Mathias paid tribute to Archbishop Byrne and called him "my ecclesiastical Protector."[7] Byrne reciprocated in kind, saying, "I am honored in being able to congratulate the Little Brothers of the Good Shepherd, and to promise them my continued paternal guidance and affection."[8]

The remainder of the year was occupied by yet another new project. This one involved acquiring the land to the northwest of the novitiate for the purpose of Brother Mathias's long-standing dream of erecting a home for the chronically ill. He wrote an update on the negotiations to Archbishop Byrne in October. "I am still awaiting news from Daniel to whom I wrote a few days ago about that fine project for the chronically ill. I feel so sure that he and Bernardine will do something as it will be a great monument of Charity."[9] The archbishop responded, "Cordially do I bless the study, knowing that you will keep me advised before taking any definite action. . . ."[10]

In January, 1962, a check arrived from Daniel Donohue in the amount of $10,000 to purchase the Springer property behind the novitiate on Thirteenth Street.[11] Brother Mathias also again took up the issue of acquiring the apartment house next door. For months he had carried on a running battle with the tenants who occupied the place. He reported to Archbishop Byrne that "we have great annoyances with the neighbors who occupy this apartment house. I have had to call on the police officers several times and the results do not last too long."[12] He also wrote Daniel Donohue for help, and the latter told Archbishop Byrne that he would be willing to assist with the purchase of the apartment building if it was the archbishop's recommendation to proceed.[13] It took close to four more years, but Brother Mathias prevailed and got his building. As he described the process that led to the happy outcome, "The property at the corner of Mountain Road and 14th Street had very undesirable tenants for a good time and I feared that it would be detrimental. [Eventually] . . . they moved out and I made enquiries and also wrote Daniel Donohue in Los Angeles, for you know of the deep interest he has in our welfare."[14] Donohue did offer to send $5,000 for a down payment, if the owners would accept an offer of $12,000 with the balance payable at $75 or $100 per month.[15] In this fashion, the building was acquired. Brother Mathias later admitted that his having copied down license plate numbers during a noisy party they were having may have contributed to encouraging the tenants to move out.[16]

Meanwhile, the ladies' auxiliary continued its support of the Second Street refuge. *The Shepherd's Call*, in lauding the group for their work, reported: "With the financial aid of the Ladies' Auxiliary, our old, rickety front porch at the Good Shepherd Refuge was replaced this past year by a brand new one that now allows the Brothers to get a breath of fresh air on the second floor. Further improvements to the refuge included the renovation of the chapel and installation of new appointments (but wow, we need to import some heat for this cold spell we are having — we shiver in our prayers)."[17]

During 1962, the Good Shepherd Refuge served 63,110 meals to "unfortunate souls," distributed 6,439 pieces of clothing, and gave 6,119 men shelter for the night.[18] In addition, the Brothers continued their regular visits to the county jail, and assisted needy families and travelers "stranded far from home." *The Shepherd's Call* commented, "Sounds like a lot, doesn't it?"[19]

The year 1963 marked the opening of the hostel for poor men in Toronto, Ontario, Canada. The coadjutor archbishop of Toronto, Philip F. Pocock, paid tribute to the Little Brothers at the dedication of the facility and praised their "quiet, unobtrusive work . . . to feed the hungry, clothe the naked and shelter the homeless."[20] Brother Mathias returned the compliment, noting that "the close cooperation of all the people in Toronto and the kindness of His Excellency, Archbishop Pocock of Toronto, will go down in history."[21] The remodeling of the building that housed the refuge had cost over $100,000, for which the city of Toronto had contributed $40,000. On the day of dedication, people of all creeds as well as clergy from all faiths attended. Another triumph had been achieved, and Brother Mathias made sure that Archbishop Byrne was filled in on all the details.[22]

On July 25, 1963, the blow fell. Archbishop Edwin V. Byrne, superior and co-founder of the Little Brothers of the Good Shepherd, died at St. Vincent's Hospital in Santa Fe.[23] He had undergone gall bladder surgery, and complications had set in from which he did not recover. *The Shepherd's Call* paid tribute to the man who, along with Brother Mathias, had been the mainstay and chief support of the religious order. A few days before his death, Byrne had relayed to Brother Mathias that Pope John XXIII had conferred upon him (Mathias) the papal award Pro Ecclesia et Pontifice.[24] It was a bittersweet period for Brother Mathias. He had been honored by the head of his Church, but he had lost a steadfast friend. Although the two men had often disagreed, they had held each other in the highest esteem. Byrne's death would signal the beginning of a time of change for Mathias and for the community he led. The implications would be slow to emerge, but when they finally took shape, the damage would be irreparable.

Archbishop Byrne's successor, James P. Davis, was installed on February 25, 1964. Born in Houghton, Michigan, and reared in Flagstaff, Arizona, the new prelate had also followed Byrne's footsteps as bishop of San Juan, Puerto Rico, before coming to New Mexico. But there the similarities ended. Soon, the new style in Santa Fe became all too clear.

Brother Mathias wrote to his new superior asking for an appointment to see him about remodeling the building that had been moved to Villa Maria in Alameda.[25] The archbishop's secretary answered the letter, saying: "His Excellency, Archbishop Davis, kindly directs me to inform you that your appointment will be on April 7 at 11:00 A.M. Bring a written memo showing pertinent details of project remodeling, proposed budget, financing, etc., when you come."[26] Brother

Mathias followed the instructions. When it became clear that a second appointment would be necessary, he wrote Davis to "humbly ask you for another date to visit."[27] It was a new tone for him, one that he had not used with Archbishop Byrne. Archbishop Davis had placed his relationship with Brother Mathias on a businesslike basis. In this spirit, he authorized Mathias to take out a loan "not to exceed $48,000 for a term of ten years with interest not to exceed 6% . . . to be negotiated with Albuquerque Federal Savings and Loan and secured by a first mortgage on your properties."[28] Brother Mathias complied, but the personal touch was gone.

The difficulties with Archbishop Davis may have begun with the dedication of this new wing to the Alameda facility, which he had authorized. The archbishop was scheduled to preside at the ceremony, but was considerably delayed in his arrival. Brother Mathias felt that the congregation was getting restless and nudged a Father Boniface to begin with the invocation. When Mass was almost finished, the archbishop arrived on the scene, and Brother Mathias told him, "Father Boniface is taking your place." Unfortunately, the archbishop was not one to appreciate the innocence of this remark. Brother Mathias recalls that Archbishop Davis "was not pleased."[29]

Brother Mathias attempted to bridge the gap with his new prelate by inviting the latter to social functions that were held from time to time at the refuge or the motherhouse. One such event was a senior citizens' garden party. Brother Mathias wrote to the archbishop saying, "Many were anxious to meet you and to kiss our Archbishop's ring, and some were enquiring how to act when you arrived."[30] The senior citizens were not the only ones who were uncertain how to approach the archbishop. It is not surprising that the correspondence between Mathias and Davis dwindled to once or twice a month. In the past, when Archbishop Byrne was alive, letters had gone to Santa Fe from Thirteenth Street once or twice a week.

As yet another anniversary approached, the *Albuquerque Journal* ran an article entitled "Brother Louis Devotes Life to Helping Friendless Poor."[31] It recounted the history of a young man who had recently entered the Little Brothers of the Good Shepherd from Chicago. There was nothing particularly remarkable about him. Like so many other young men casting around for something meaningful to do with their lives, the desire to serve the poor had brought him to Albuquerque. Brother Louis McRoy explained: "Because I had worked in many cities, I saw poverty at first hand. It is difficult to walk down a street of Chicago without having someone ask you for a handout. . . . No matter what you do, it is nothing unless you have charity. There are many ways to practice charity, but for me I felt

205

the best way was to give my whole self to it. The little I could do would help alleviate some of this misery."[32] It was clear that there was no decrease in the power of the Little Brothers to inspire new members to join them and to share their demanding life. As Brother Mathias reported to Archbishop Davis in June, "The number of requests for admission to our Institute coming from our young candidates is very encouraging."[33]

Yet, despite the steady growth in the membership of the Little Brothers, Brother Mathias could not keep up with the demand for their services. During 1966, he turned down three requests: one to operate a halfway house for delinquent boys in Cincinnati, another to take over a segregated home for black boys in Alabama, and a third to administer an orphanage in Cuzco, Peru. The last was refused partly because of the shortage of Brothers who knew the Spanish language. Brother Mathias was reluctant, however, to let any of their projects go.

On January 19, 1966, as part of the celebration of the fifteenth anniversary of the founding of the community, the Brothers burned the mortgage for the motherhouse and novitiate on Thirteenth Street. Photographs were taken of the happy event that showed Brother Mathias and Archbishop Davis in a jovial mood. In April, Brother Mathias wrote to Donohue that he was about to get possession of the remaining houses on the block. He gave him the financial details and then commented, "When I look back on all this and to say that only a short 15 years ago we had or at least I had nothing — no, not a cent to my name. But sure I have nothing today either of my own and I do not worry either. We have a fine Society and we can be thankful mostly to yourself — when I and you went into that building and made the decision. This was a happy day."[34]

Brother Mathias spent much of the new year working on a new home for retarded boys in the South Valley of Albuquerque, which he proposed to call "Notre Dame of the Southwest on the Rio Grande." He carried on an extensive correspondence with federal and state licensing officials, Archbishop Davis, and prospective parents of boys to be accepted by the facility. He arranged for a men's advisory board to assist the Brothers in the project. As part of the publicity efforts, he wrote to the editor of the *Valley News*, a local paper:

I wonder if you have not yet heard of our new venture in the South Valley where we intend operating a Home for the Mentally Retarded Boys. . . . Due to the great care lavished on the little ones in our Good Shepherd Manor in Wakefield and Columbus, Ohio, the news spread across the Country and into Canada, so that requests are coming to the Brothers for the admission of young boys over 13 years of age for custodial care. The only therapeutics that the Brothers will extend, with the exception of education in behavior is loving tender care.[35]

Also quick to support this new venture was Daniel Donohue, who wrote his encouragement to Brother Mathias, adding, "I know the quality of service which the Brothers will render and the love with which they will surround these children. This will do much to surmount the red tape and 'professional' double talk which so encompasses Welfare work today."[36] The *Albuquerque Journal* reported that "Brother Mathias plans to open a house for 28 retarded boys, 13 and older." A large adobe structure south of Albuquerque was being remodeled for the purpose.[37] And, as Brother Francis reported in *The Shepherd's Call*, "We can only say to a Brother who works directly with these children of God, 'Yours is an exalted labor.'"[38]

The germ of this enterprise had been Archbishop Davis's request to Brother Mathias for two Brothers to operate a home for about twenty Cuban boys that was floundering. Brother Mathias took a tour of the home and was appalled by the conditions. The fittings were gone in the shower room, and there were tiles missing everywhere. Moreover, it was his view that rather than caring for Cuban boys, the Brothers should take over the place and operate it for the retarded. He informed Archbishop Davis of this decision, and Davis had instructed him to "submit in writing for my study a detailed account of how you propose to operate a home for retarded children.'"[39] This, of course, was easier said than done. Brother Mathias, as we have seen, was not an accountant and was not used to proceeding according to itemized lists of anything. He made, however, a valiant attempt to comply with his superior's request. This reply is worth quoting at some length. It began with the following sentiments, "It was nice receiving your gracious letter on the Feast of Saint Mathias, a Feastday here and the Second Anniversary of your Installation as Archbishop of Santa Fe. In fact, last year you officiated at the Mass and Ceremony of Profession here at the Novitiate."[40]

Having reminded the archbishop of these charming events, Brother Mathias proceeded to address the request for a "detailed account." He noted that there were long waiting lists all over the country for facilities for the retarded and said, "This alone should warrant us to do something." He estimated that four Brothers would be needed to operate the home. These Brothers would be trained at the novitiate where several "elderly priests" would help train them "so that when they are engaged in the Refuge work such as at 601 Second

Street or in New Orleans or Philadelphia or Miami, they would have that great respect for the poor men in need." The Brothers would also take a nursing course. "The only expense would be food, heat and Public Utilities and of course the maintenance of the building and grounds." He thought that if $100 per month could be obtained from each boy, "we most certainly could meet all obligations." The letter ended with an expression of humility and his willingness to "accept whatever decision Your Excellency may have for me."[41]

The next bombshell for Davis was the submission by Brother Mathias of a $12,000 plumbing bill to Catholic Charities, owners of the building the Brothers had leased. There were several explosive meetings on the plumbing bill. Brother Mathias recalls, "I told them what people had done for me in New Orleans. They said they didn't want to know about New Orleans. I said I wanted them to know about it! I wouldn't give in."[42] The issue was ultimately resolved by including the disputed bill in the total renovation package amount of $50,000.

The new home for retarded boys held its open house on June 12, 1966. Brother Mathias invited Archbishop Davis to attend the affair, adding, "I am sure that if Your Excellency should have a few minutes that day to come and visit us, you would be happy and comforted. . . ."[43] He apologized for the condition of the grounds but assured Davis that the problem would be taken care of in good time.

In July, a major milestone in his life was marked when Brother Mathias celebrated his golden jubilee of fifty years in religious life. Archbishop Davis presided at Mass, which was held in a large downtown church. Brothers came from all over the country to attend: Brother Camillus from Wakefield, Brother Joseph from Toronto, Brother John from Philadelphia, and Brothers Lawrence and Michael from Columbus. Also in attendance were the vicar general, the chancellor, and local clergy and religious. Brother Mathias heard his favorite hymn sung — "On this day, O Beautiful Mother" — and lunch was served at the Alvarado Hotel. A reception followed at St. Vincent Academy Auditorium, and the festivities concluded with benediction at the novitiate and a cookout in the community garden. *The Shepherd's Call* reported, "During the past 50 years, Brother Mathias has washed dishes and scrubbed floors from Montreal to Miami. He has borrowed beds and begged for chairs, food and light bulbs from Watts to Wakefield. . . . While Brother Mathias had requested a Mass at the Novitiate house followed by a little party with his Brothers, his Brothers thought otherwise and made it a day he will always remember."[44] Daniel and Bernardine Donohue sent a check for $2,700 to buy a 1966 station wagon as their gift for the occasion. The letter accompanying the check said, "It goes without saying, no amount of money or worldly possessions could amply reward a Religious man or woman for the years of devoted service given for the love of God."[45]

Notre Dame on the Rio Grande was soon filled to capacity with "little ones," and a long waiting list was rapidly developing. The Brothers also took on a new apostolate teaching CCD classes. Four Brothers were assigned as religious instructors in the local parish of St. Anne, also in Albuquerque's South Valley. The pastor of the church, Monsignor Francis O'Byrne, lauded their services in his education program, noting what he called "the crying need for convert work." As he said to Brother Mathias, "For example, we lose people to the Jehovah Witnesses due to a lack of religious instruction. With only two priests and a mere handful of trained laity, it is almost impossible to cope with the problem. . . ."[46] Archbishop Davis was likewise very pleased by the religious-education program and made a special point to say so.[47] The effort also brought in additional revenue as Monsignor O'Byrne contributed $200 a month to the motherhouse for the services of the Brothers.

The January, 1967, celebration of the founding of the Brotherhood was marked by the investiture of the sixty-fifth Brother to enter the community — Brother Stephen Conner of Florida.[48] Brother Mathias wrote to Cardinal Richard Cushing of Boston shortly thereafter with a long letter of news and reflections. One subject that concerned him was the prospect of sending Brothers to Peru, a possibility which had been hovering on the horizon for some time. He wrote Cardinal Cushing, in his usual rambling manner:

> I am beginning to get afraid of all this and looking back at the way I was treated many years ago, as you well know. I might meet with too many difficulties and troubles with my Brothers so far away, while things are doing so nicely now. . . . Right here at 901 13th Street, we have a unique School of Law — Yes, the Law of Love, where our Faculty consists of 9 aged priests; Father Julius Hartmann, 84 years old and almost 60 years a priest. He is Dean; then Father Blackburn, 77, Prefect of Discipline; of course Father Gallagher, also 77, who fails to meet any changes in the Liturgy and he is Agitator.[49]

The mention of the "School of the Law of Love" was a diplomatic way of referring to the sometimes trying task of caring for aged priests. At one point there were nine in residence at the motherhouse. Although the care of elderly priests was a major priority for Brother Mathias, there were times when it verged on the burdensome, and even the ridiculous. But he never let their needs or "peculiarities" defeat him. Nor did he allow his Brothers to slight them in any way.

Brother Mathias also had to contend with the vagaries of the federal government's inspectors for the programs that the community utilized. A case in point was the surplus commodities program, which was supplying the refuge with milk, margarine, and cheese. Fed up with the requirements of the agency to whom he had to report, and incensed at the latter's questioning of the amounts of milk and margarine the refuge required, Brother Mathias wrote to New Mexico Senator Joseph M. Montoya. He told the senator that the officials in charge of the surplus foods program should realize "that we have only one purpose — helping . . . the needy" and that one reason the refuge required more milk than usual was because "during these hot days of over the 90s the poor men drink more milk."[50]

The next project that Brother Mathias embarked on was a home for elderly ladies. After several locations had been investigated without favorable results, Brother Mathias found a piece of property in Bernalillo, a farming community north of Albuquerque, which had been a convent for the Sisters of Loretto. The letter of inquiry he sent to Miss Helen Raveling of the State Department of Institutional Licensure indicated that the home would be "not a Rest Home or a Convalescent Home, but just for the Aged."[51] At the same time, he wrote to the mother superior of the Sisters of Loretto. "I do notice that there is no care taken of the property and I feel that if the property is left vacant too long it could be greatly damaged by vandals. At this time I wonder if you would not consider leasing the property at a nominal sum. If I had this information I could communicate with His Excellency, Most Reverend Archbishop James P. Davis who is, I know, very interested in a Home for Elderly Ladies."[52] The reply to this interesting letter instructed Brother Mathias to get in touch with Judge James Maloney, the legal agent for the Sisters of Loretto in Albuquerque, and he did so without delay. By this time, the nature of the project had shifted away from the care of elderly ladies. The letter to the judge said, "Now comes to my mind a more feasible solution, a second Home for the Mentally Handicapped, but for those over 16 years of age. We continue to keep the little ones under 16 at Notre Dame. Also, we could continue the same name — Loretto Manor. This is only one phase of the work. The other will be for young men to join our Society and coming from Ireland, in preparation for service in Latin America."[53] The same day as this letter went out to Judge Maloney, Brother Mathias wrote Archbishop Davis to advise him that the home for elderly ladies was being put on hold in order that the home for retarded men could take its place. He reminded the archbishop that "I did write to you about the study of securing young Irish Vocations for the works of Charity of the Little Brothers of the Good

Shepherd, but especially for Latin America. . . ." These Irish Brothers would "care for the multiple Handicapped and perhaps also help in the CCD Program in Bernalillo."[54] Pursuing multiple goals in the same letter was typical of Mathias. He never saw any problem in fitting them all together. Moreover, it was good insurance. If one set of possibilities was not convincing, another might carry the day.

In January, 1968, Brother Mathias wrote to Senator Joseph Montoya with details of two projects, one for elderly ladies, and one for the "Elderly Mentally Handicapped from 16 years up." The letter ended with the sentence, "Whatever encouragement you may give me will be greatly appreciated."[55] There is no record of whether Senator Montoya answered this letter. Nor is it clear what sort of "encouragement" Brother Mathias had in mind. However, the senator did write on June 4 to wish the Brothers every success in their endeavors.

Also in January came Brother Mathias's offer of $90,000 to purchase the former convent in Bernalillo, with a $20,000 down payment and $500 per month at four percent interest.[56] The response from the Sisters of Loretto was delivered to the chancery office by mistake. It was the first Archbishop Davis had heard of the negotiations, and as Brother Mathias recalls, "He was mad."[57] But, as the Sisters had accepted the offer, Brother Mathias was able to make peace with the archbishop and the papers were signed.

The property was inspected by the local fire department, and, with Brother Isadore appointed caretaker, the gas was turned on during the first week of April.[58] Brother Mathias's instructions to Brother Isadore were very specific. After informing him that the lights, heat, gas, and water would be on and that the parish church was next door, he said, "All that is needed is that you take care of our own business and not the business of the parish. . . . Once we mind our own business, all goes well."[59]

In June, the State Health and Social Services Department submitted an itemized list of renovations that were required for the Bernalillo facility, now named St. Joseph's Manor, before a license could be issued. The list, which contained eleven items, included the following stipulations: "Lavatories are needed in the kitchen and the laundry"; "a segregation room is required, complete with toilet, bathing and handwashing"; and "solid core doors are required on all corridors in children's areas."[60]

St. Joseph's Manor was dedicated on February 2, 1969, by Archbishop Davis. The home began with six residents and had a capacity of thirty. There was a staff of five Brothers, headed by Brother Edward, superior. He noted that "there are many homes for young chil-

211

dren but few for boys 16 and older.''[61] Very quickly, the home gathered the support of the community. Most notable was the joint donation, in 1973, by the Springer Corporation, Albuquerque Gravel Products, and the Jayne's Corporation, of volleyball and basketball courts that were paid for and constructed by the businesses and their employees.[62]

The elderly ladies were shortly to have their day, after having been sidetracked in favor of the Bernalillo project. Brother Mathias had his eye on The Sleepy Hollow Motel at Eleventh and Central in downtown Albuquerque. In order to "get some details about that Motel," he sent Brother Hubert to look it over. Brother Hubert was not to reveal that he was a Good Shepherd Brother, but rather to let it be known that he was "just a visitor passing through," according to Brother Mathias's instructions. In order to bolster the visitor image, he showed the owner his Washington library card and no other information.[63] Brother Mathias reported this subterfuge to Richard Krannawitter (attorney for the archdiocese), with the interesting comment that "I must keep out of all this now." He added, "In all these great needs of humanity I am doing all I can but again I must also take special care of our own or at least my special work which is the recruiting and cultivation of our own Brothers. . . .''[64] The allusion to "keeping out of all this now" may be understood in light of a letter Brother Mathias received several months later from Archbishop Davis on the subject of extending himself too thin. The letter was also a plea for what Davis understood to be "sound business practices." The archbishop warned, "Do not spread your activities and resources too thin. . . . Many promising businesses have suffered from 'over-extended virus' and in most instances this is fatal. . . . Deviation on the part of those in charge or requests to condone 'after the fact' will not be favorably considered.''[65] The substance of this communication was quite similar to that contained in Davis's letter to Brother Mathias during the negotiations for the purchase of the Loretto Convent. That letter had said, "Before obligating your Corporation in any way for loans and before contracting for the purchase of property, the written permission of the Ordinary shall be obtained. This will obviate any misunderstanding and will insure the proper protection of the best interest of all.''[66]

In terms of more concrete control, Archbishop Davis was already beginning to direct certain changes in the administration and operation of the Little Brothers. He now insisted that Brother Mathias utilize Richard Krannawitter as legal counsel. Then in June, 1968, in accordance with the wishes of the archbishop, Brother Mathias reported that he had appointed six Brothers to the general council of the order.[67] Brother Mathias was feeling the stern hand of his prelate. In a letter to Brother Kevin, he told his old friend that the archbishop had said to third parties, "I gave Brother Mathias a line of conduct to follow and I want everything down in writing." He told Kevin that he had been trying to do this anyway, but that things would happen at the various houses and he would be presented with a *fait accompli*. In those instances, he asked Brother Kevin, "What can I do but pay the price?"[68]

An example of what "paying the price" meant occurred with respect to an interhouse loan within the community. Notre Dame on the Rio Grande had asked to borrow money from Camillus House in Miami to pay for Brother Mark's hydroponic tomato project. Attorney Richard Krannawitter addressed a cool letter on the subject to Brother Mathias, reminding him of the archbishop's displeasure toward such loans unless he was directly consulted in each instance. Further, "His Excellency also asked that this, as well as other policies, which he has referred to you governing your order, should be brought to the attention of all your local superiors. The superiors of your various houses should bring their problems and proposals to you and you then should submit your requests or proposals to His Excellency in writing and then await a return reply."[69]

The same week that he received the above communication from Richard Krannawitter, Brother Mathias wrote to Archbishop Davis with the same disarming candor he had used with Byrne. The letter was about an elderly priest whom he referred to as Father H.:

> It is hard sometimes to get any information at all from Father H., since if he is asked one question he becomes suspicious and goes off on a tangent with all kinds of references about the War and the Jews, etc., etc. However, we have been able to get some information but it is far from being complete. . . . We are doing all we can to keep Father happy, although at times he becomes a little irritated. But all this is good for the training of our Good Shepherd Brothers. . . .[70]

The archbishop's reply, however, made no mention of Father H. Instead, it addressed the vexing question of whether Notre Dame on the Rio Grande should be permitted to borrow $7,500 from Camillus House in Miami. Ultimately, Davis approved the request on the condition that all legal instruments with respect to the transaction were to be drawn up by Richard Krannawitter.[71] The tomato-raising project went forward.

Brother Mark had pursued this scheme as a business venture for the handicapped residents of the home. He had been greatly encouraged by a group called the Ladies of the Albuquerque Alcohol and Beverage Institute. The latter had mounted a wine-tasting party as a fund raiser, and also had arranged a major concert by singer Nancy Ames in an Albuquerque auditorium. Together, these events had brought in over $20,000.[72] Obviously impressed, Brother Mathias now included the budding tomato business as one of the accomplishments of the order in his letters to public figures, benefactors, and friends.

One of the sorrows of 1968 for Brother Mathias was the death of Bernardine Donohue, a steadfast and loyal friend of the Little Brothers. Daniel Donohue sent a donation in her memory to Mathias to be used for the purchase of a car for St. Joseph's Manor in Bernalillo. But complications soon arose. As Brother Mathias wrote to Daniel:

> You thought and even told Brother Francis that I would like that a car be purchased for St. Joseph's Manor, as that is where it is really needed now. The distance is some 20 miles from Albuquerque. I even said we could call the car "Bernardine" and it would keep the memory of our dear departed in our mind and prayers. But Brother Francis did not agree in purchasing any car as he said this was given on the down payment of the property. Perhaps if you have an opportunity of coming to our celebration you might see the whole situation.[73]

The 1960s were drawing to a close. Brother Mathias wrote an open letter to his fellow Brothers in the summer of 1968. He expressed the hope that all of them had advanced spiritually because "you know as well as I do, that if we do not advance we just go back, because there is no standing still."[74] Although the religious order had opened new houses and extended services to the indigent, retarded, and elderly, nine requests for new foundations had been turned down. Mathias was particularly grieved that four of those requests had come for refuges or hostels for the poor. The care of poor, needy, homeless men was still, in his mind, "our main Apostolate."[75]

As has been earlier noted, in mid-summer of 1968, Brother Mathias appointed six Brothers to the general council as requested by Archbishop Davis. His letter to Davis carried the curious sentence, "I fully understand that our Life is completely different from that of any other Order, Congregation or Institute, and how the Brothers still have me around. . . ."[76] The tensions that had begun to show in outline would be fleshed out in the decade to come. Brother Mathias was seeing the last of the triumphant years. The 1970s would be a time of struggle, discord, and bitterness. Yet, they would also see the beginnings of the nationwide acclaim that would bear fruit in the 1980s.

13 .... Into the Seventies

BROTHER MATHIAS IS OFTEN CALLED THE "MOTHER TERESA OF America." There are also remarkable similarities between him and both Peter Maurin and Dorothy Day, founders of the Catholic Worker Movement in the United States. Peter Maurin, born in France, had, like Brother Mathias, emigrated to the United States by way of Canada. Also like Brother Mathias, he was a man of vision, but his vision was more in line with the peasant-based socialist movements of Europe. He saw in a return to the land a remedy for the urban ills of poverty and want. "We all ought to go back to the land and live together as a social and religious community without barriers. We ought to give ourselves to each other and work without money. We ought to join hands with each other in a common pursuit of a decent and dignified life. This can begin in small but concrete ways."[1] Peter Maurin not only worked with the poor, he had lived as one of them. He had been arrested as a vagrant and was the habitué of flophouses. As Robert Coles has described him: "Indifferent to worldly things, he concentrated his vision on the evils of this world."[2] He accepted the Gospel injunction that he should give his own coat to anyone who asked him for it. Thus he gave away his own clothing or whatever else he had to those in need. He spent most of his time talking to anyone who would listen, outlining in meticulous fashion his ideas for a better world. His followers today attempt to put them into practice on the Peter Maurin Farm in Marlboro, New York.

Dorothy Day came to the Catholic Worker Movement by a different route. An educated and talented journalist with radical leanings, she became a convert to Catholicism after personal suffering. The combination of these two aspects of her personality created a powerful and persuasive talent. Her editorship of the *Catholic Worker* newspaper gave wide coverage to her own and Peter Maurin's social programs. The paper advocated equality, the sharing of the world's resources, compassion for the poor, and pacifism. As an outgrowth of the goals that the paper espoused, Catholic Worker houses ministering to the needs of the urban poor began to appear. Day called this "active love," and wrote, "When one loves, there is at that time a correlation between the spiritual and the material. Even the flesh itself is energized, the human spirit is made strong. All sacrifice, all suffering is easy for the sake of love. . . . This is the foundation stone of the Catholic Worker Movement. It is on this that we build."[3]

Thus, the aims of the Catholic Worker Movement and of the Brothers of the Good Shepherd appear in this respect to be identical. The major divergence between the two organizations lay in what might be called their philosophical grounding. The Good Shepherd Brothers based their service on Christ's call to his followers to "feed the poor, clothe the naked, and comfort the homeless." There was no profound philosophical underpinning to this call. What mattered was to do it, over and over, without tiring, without discouragement, without bickering with one's fellows, and with unquestioned faith in Christ the Good Shepherd and his Blessed Mother. On the other hand, the *Catholic Worker* has been the forum for social philosophies and political programs. In line with Peter Maurin's "Easy Essays" — which are far from easy — the paper has always taken the position that simply doing good on the level of the individual is not sufficient. One's efforts must also be directed at eradicating the institutional evils of society. Without a restructuring of the social conditions that create poverty, there will be no end to its continuance. With this in view, the *Catholic Worker* has printed a wide variety of articles ranging from the proper raising of crops to washing dishes in a refuge, to visiting refugee camps in Central America, to boycotting certain products in support of labor unions. It has advocated civil disobedience to further racial equality, and has long taken a stand against war.

None of these concerns are primarily those of the Little Brothers. Brother Mathias does not hold forth on complex philosophical issues. As one of his close friends explained it, "Getting him to talk about philosophy would be like trying to get him to talk about the force of gravity."[4] It is the individual who is called by God to minister unto other individual souls. In Mathias's view, there is no greater or more compelling duty of mankind. With their emphasis on immediate service in concrete terms — food, clothing, and shelter — the Brothers have found a welcome reception wherever they have established shelters. One reason for this is implied in Gerald D. Suttles's *The Social Order of the Slum*. His analysis illustrates why society is grateful to organizations that will take care of the undesirables in its midst.

> The standards of American society are severe and a very large proportion of our population is regarded with suspicion and caution. Typically, these are poor people from a low-status minority group and unable to manage very well their "public relations." The presence of such a group of people is disruptive because it undermines the trust residents must share to go about their daily

216

rounds. In American society, a common solution to this difficulty has been to relegate all suspicious people to "slums" and "skid rows." As a result, respectable and essential citizens can carry on their corporate life undisturbed by their own apprehensions.[5]

One study of skid row neighborhoods done in Chicago revealed that the residents of the "row" were eighty-six percent to ninety-eight percent Caucasian, and that "skid rows tend to be Caucasian islands in a sea of Negroes, Puerto Ricans and Mexicans. . . ."[6] The study also discovered that fifty-five percent of the residents had lived on skid row longer than a year, and that one fourth of the population had been there more than five years.[7] The kinds of jobs that the men obtained were "spot jobs" such as unloading freight cars and trucks, washing dishes, and peddling popcorn and candy bars at major public events. The skid row itself was not a tightly knit community but "seems to be composed largely of discontented individuals who live in semi-isolation, who have few if any close friends and who survive by being suspicious of everybody."[8]

These analyses of the poverty areas of the big cities raise some questions about the relevance of the solutions offered by the Good Shepherd Brothers and the Catholic Worker Movement. The Brotherhood has been successful at meeting the needs of individuals because it functions in an environment where alienated individuals gravitate. If there is in fact little or no community structure to a skid row, then it makes little sense trying to establish one using people who are in effect refugees from such structures. On the other hand, if a lack of community, or of trust (as Suttles suggests), is a cause of skid row, then it would make sense to keep such disintegration from occurring in the first place.

For years, Brother Mathias has told stories about the skid row "knights of the road" whom he has helped. There was the case of a man who took off to Las Vegas, Nevada, where his mind snapped. Weeping and in a depressed state of mind, he was arrested by a sheriff. Since his papers indicated an Albuquerque address, welfare workers put him on a bus back to New Mexico where he ended up with Brother Mathias. "We sat down and I found out his name was Martin and that he spoke French and had been to Montreal," Brother Mathias recalls. Having established his memory sufficiently to find out who his relatives were, Brother Mathias called the man's brother-in-law, who came to get him.[9]

Then there was the sixty-two-year-old woman, a secretary "from somewhere," who was picked up on the street by Brother Anthony. Brother Mathias put her up at the Town House Motel, an establishment where he had several rooms on perpetual reserve for such emergencies. The woman stayed the weekend but really needed a longer-term solution to her homelessness. A third person, a woman who insisted that the FBI was tapping her telephone, was unable to get food stamps without a permanent residence. Brother Mathias gave her the address of his motherhouse on Thirteenth Street and she was able to get her stamps.[10]

Often Brother Mathias assisted travelers to get from Albuquerque to a home or a relative in another state. He called these journeys "flights into Egypt." When he had difficulty getting through to the airlines or bus lines, he would inform the telephone operator that he was the archbishop's secretary. This announcement always got him a clear phone line. The same approach also worked if the telephones in a particular place were tied up. Operators would then break into the line in question and ask the parties to hang up. Then they would put Brother Mathias through.

The decade of the 1970s opened with these concerns as well as others of a more intimate nature. Brother Mathias wrote to all the Brothers of the Good Shepherd in January, 1970: "We have just completed another decade of this century, one which will certainly go down in history on both the good and bad side of the ledger. Man conquered space and brought back a portion of the moon; however, we have not been able to halt the spread of crime, ill will, war and pestilence. The Four Horsemen of the Apocalypse ride the Earth unchecked." He also pointed out that scores of children in Biafra were dying of starvation and malnutrition. (In 1967, Biafra declared its independence from Nigeria in west Africa; civil war broke out, and Biafra surrendered in 1970 after three years of fighting.) "In our own country of abundance," he continued, "hunger persists and race tension mounts."[11] Brothers were not, however, to give in to complacency, or to let "the forecasters of doom discourage you or turn you from your path."[12]

In his letter to Archbishop Davis the next day, Brother Mathias voiced his determination to seek vocations in Ireland by renting a small dwelling in Waterford, "not far from the Little Sisters of the Poor." He announced that Brother Mark would go to Waterford to get the program underway, adding, "Brother Mark is not at all Irish, but rather of German ancestry and this too might help."[13]

Not only did the program get underway, it spread in the following year to England. By this time, Brother Justin was in Waterford and he attracted the interest of the auxiliary bishop of Birmingham to the works of the Good Shepherd Brothers. In his report on these successes to Archbishop Davis, Brother Mathias said:

Brother Justin, an Australian Brother, who . . . [has been] with us for the last six years and attached to our Canadian Region, is recruiting in Ireland, while residing in a rented house in Waterford. He has many prospective candidates, but due to the Emigration Laws, I was unable to get them into the United States. . . . However, I am able to get them into Canada. We have one Novice there already and another soon to arrive. . . . So, Your Excellency, all this I think shows the great vitality of our group. . . .[14]

There was reason to be optimistic. There were now eighty-five Little Brothers of the Good Shepherd. In January, 1971, the *Catholic News Register* did an article on some of the newest members of the religious order. Included were Brothers John Patrick Wall, Mathew Papenmeyer, Eugene Reis, Juan Diego Salazar, and Magella Marchand. Among these new members one had been a national coordinator for a real estate firm; another had been a Methodist minister for twelve years; and the other three had joined the Brotherhood as high-school graduates. The *Register* noted, "These are the newest of the Brothers of the Good Shepherd; but Brother Mathias, who sees the need almost inexhaustible, wants more and more men." It quoted him as saying, "God will give us the work to do and the money to do it with but men must make the choice themselves."[15]

To mark the twentieth anniversary of the founding of the community on January 19, 1971, the *Albuquerque Journal* ran a feature article on Brother Mathias. Reporting on a surprise honor arranged for him by his friends, the paper said, "His friends kept the celebration secret because the merry Irishman with the twinkling blue eyes and thatch of white hair is a man of simple taste."[16] For his part, Brother Mathias used the occasion to announce another new project, a home for retarded youths and adults in Momence, Illinois. Guests and Brothers were served pieces of a cake topped by a small figure of a Brother in a white habit. Activities were not curtailed to mark the anniversary. A week later, Brother Justin cabled from Ireland, "Bishop Cleary wants small refuge. Birmingham would like you to visit."[17]

Brother Mathias reported on the new projects to Archbishop Davis. Apparently there had been some resistance on the part of the local residents in Momence to the establishment of the facility for the retarded, but these objections had been "straightened out." The new home would have room for one hundred twenty, and, according to Brother Mathias, "it is one of the most modern facilities in the Country for our type of Apostolate." The second item was the cheery announcement that Mathias was going to Ireland and from there to England "to see what Bishop Cleary of Birmingham has to offer."[18]

One month later Archbishop Davis opened another letter. This one advised him that there was now a working refuge in Birmingham, England. "Brother Justin and Brother Raphael are now there. Auxiliary Bishop Cleary and the Clergy are so happy to have us and I am sure that it will be a success."[19] The archbishop was not surprised. He had become accustomed to having projects proposed one day and finalized the next. He wrote back that he was pleased with these developments.[20]

Within three weeks, the archbishop received a third letter from Brother Mathias about still another "proposal" — a refuge for transient men to be located in Washington, D.C. This time, the prelate's response was less accepting. He wrote directly to Monsignor Ralph Kuehner of the Washington archdiocese as follows: "I must tell you that Brother Mathias enjoys all the privileges and perquisites of a 'founder.' He keeps me young trying to keep up with him. Do not please misinterpret these remarks. I am all for expansion if and when personnel are available."[21] And to Brother Mathias, he sent a short note that said, "I must of course remind you since you are 'a founding father' that new commitments of personnel must not be made at the expense of existing ones."[22]

Spurred to produce new members of the order to staff these projects, Brother Mathias wrote to his Brothers, "But now the time has come for each and every one of us Superiors to show a real supernatural interest in Vocations; in the young Candidates and Novices who come to us with great enthusiasm and a strong desire to be Good Shepherd Brothers." All were exhorted to pray for an increase in vocations and that these might continue to "flow" into the Brotherhood.[23]

As it turned out, the Washington project soured on several accounts. Brother Mathias made a whirlwind trip to the nation's capital to inspect the facility at first hand. Here is his report on the visit: "A group of well-intentioned people, known as S.O.M.E. (So others may eat) were trying to get a refuge under way there. Indeed it was very depressing for us Brothers of the Good Shepherd to be offered in Washington, D.C., an old shack, which needed lots of remodeling and repairing. . . . They all debated about getting free material, cheap labor and money and I listened very carefully, when one of the Members said to me: 'Reverend, what are you going to give, as I am giving a hundred dollars?' I replied, very bravely: 'I have given fifty-six years of my life to this work, caring for Christ's poor needy unfortunate, and I would willingly do it all over again, even to the last drop of my blood and your one hundred dollars is not worth talking about. . . .' "[24] He went on to tell the hushed group that although he had worked out of shacks in the past, in Montreal, Los Angeles, and Albuquerque, "I would never be able to find a Brother in our Group today to accept these conditions."[25] Needless to say, the Washington venture did not materialize.

Internal matters in the community had not been going smoothly. These problems have been alluded to in Chapter 10. The normal difficulties of life as a Brother had been compounded by frustrations of an organizational nature that would soon erupt openly. In this regard, Brother Camillus's letter to Brother Joseph is pivotal, and worth quoting at some length.

> As you know, I too have been deeply concerned about the future of our Society. I was quite disappointed that nothing too constructive came out of the Spring Seminar, 1970. However, we do have general guidelines and it is up to the Regional Superiors to adhere to them as much as possible in preparation for an eventual chapter. . . . One other point I would like to bring to the surface, and that is that I would not discredit the power, the influence and the authority, of the Founder-Superior General. . . . Like you, I do not feel secure with the way some matters are being handled by Brother Mathias. . . . It would be in order to contact the chancellor of Santa Fe asking him when we can expect to have the draft of the Constitution ready for the Brothers, so that we can continue with our seminars in preparation for the General Chapter. Upon receipt of his reply, communicated to all the Brothers, everyone would be satisfied.[26]

The reference to the general chapter refers to the community-wide convocation that would result — when it finally took place in December of 1977 — in the election of a new Brother General to head the order. In 1971, however, plans to hold the general chapter were still in the formulating stages. Archbishop Davis had taken a major role in these preparations. It was his desire that the community be counseled by an outside authority on religious life. The person chosen to do this was a Franciscan Father, David Temple, based in California at the San Damiano Retreat Center. Brother Mathias wrote Father Temple requesting that he "come on a visitation and interview all our Brothers of all our Houses."[27] Archbishop Davis sent a separate letter to Father Temple that contained this interesting information:

> The years and the burden of being the founding father have taken their toll of dear Brother Mathias. But he has plenty of fire left and a solid group of men. . . . I think that you will enjoy the copy of a letter which Brother Camillus wrote to Brother Joseph last

April. . . . At the Spring meeting of the Bishops in Detroit I met with Brother Joseph and Archbishop Donnellan. Upon my return from Detroit Brother Mathias met with Father Hendren and me and the result was Brother Mathias' appeal to you for assistance.[28]

Archbishop Davis also reported these matters to his Washington, D.C., contact whom he was endeavoring to discourage from inviting the Little Brothers to establish another refuge. This letter said: "We are in the process of preparing for the first general chapter of the society, and placing the revered founder in a context with which he and the members can live and communicate profitably, both with respect to themselves as religious and the apostolates undertaken by them to date."[29]

Meanwhile, two Brothers of the Good Shepherd decided to leave the community but petitioned Archbishop Davis to allow them to remain as religious in his diocese as "exclaustrated Brothers of the Good Shepherd" ("exclaustrated" meaning "formerly being confined to a monastery or cloister"). They were soon joined by a third. The three formed what they termed a Pious Union.[30] This, in effect, constituted the first schism in the order.

Conditions in the Eastern region headed by Brother Joseph were the most turbulent. There was an exchange of letters between Brother Joseph and Brother Mathias in June. These illuminated with painful clarity the gap that had widened between them. Brother Joseph reported that Brother William Hudspeth had left Canada and moved to Kansas City on his own, and that this action "no doubt leaves yourself to doubt the motivation of this action and his continuance in the life of the Good Shepherd." He continued: "The sad estrangement that has developed between the Motherhouse and the Cdn. [Canadian] region, whether justly or unjustly, was not on the part of the Regional Director to cause disturbance or isolation, nor to doubt the charisma values of yourself as Founder. Problems are realized by all of us. . . . For the many privileges granted with confidence from yourself in the past to have guided the Eastern Region, I am humbly grateful. At this time, however, it should be given to another who may be able to better evaluate the moods and contradictions that many now experience in adapting to and living the religious life. This request is sincerely made, for I realize that I have misplaced your trust and confidence that was once mine."[31]

Brother Mathias answered with a cool reply that said, "Under our policy, Brother Camillus had no authority to accept Brother William Hudspeth into his region without consent from me. I was completely bypassed in this." With respect to Brother Joseph's request to be relieved of his duties as regional director, Brother Mathias was equally distant. "Your request to be relieved as Eastern Regional Director has been noted. The Archbishop has been in Puerto Rico. I feel in light of your charges against me to him that the matter should be brought to his attention so that there will be no question of undue influence on my part. . . . It may be that you will desire to delay this until the official Visitator has investigated your complaints. A copy of this letter is going to Archbishop Davis for his information."[32] Missing were the customary requests "for prayers, for reliance on the Good Shepherd and His Blessed Mother, and for the final perseverance of us all." The estrangement was obvious.

Then, in July, there was trouble at Good Shepherd Manor in Alameda. The board of directors of the manor submitted a letter to Archbishop Davis regarding the use of monies left to the manor by a deceased resident. The letter complained that "in this process we have encountered opposition from the Mother House of the Brotherhood. One most serious result of this opposition is the abrupt removal of Brother Isadore, Director of the Manor."[33] The letter voiced the distress of the board over this precipitous action, and the members offered to resign if it appeared that their services were no longer needed. Archbishop Davis took action. His letter to Brother Mathias, dated July 6, 1971, directed that Brother Isadore be reinstated as director of the manor and that "it is my wish that the lay board of Good Shepherd Manor continue the administration of the fiscal affairs of the Manor to insure an orderly transition in the event the same is indicated."[34]

It was due to pressure brought to bear by the archbishop that Brother Jerome McCarthy became procurator general, in July, for the houses operated by the Brothers in New Mexico. In this capacity, he co-signed all financial transactions and was put in charge of the staffing of all houses. This included the "placing of competent administrators in each."[35] Archbishop Davis stated in his letter to Brother Mathias, Brother Jerome, and the board of Good Shepherd Manor: "It is not necessary for me to go into the minutiae of the Brothers' life such as vacations, days off, etc., nor do I propose to do so. I do, however, charge Brother Jerome with full responsibility of his position and want him to reflect upon the weight thereof and the confidence that has been placed in him by his Superior General and me as Religious Superior of the Society."[36] In his letter to Brother Mathias alone, the archbishop reiterated that Brother Jerome was to be in fact the fiscal and administrative director of the New Mexico houses. "I want his full authorization that any other religious director has and, in addition, that his authority be not infringed upon by you in any way whatsoever." If he wished, Brother Mathias was invited to call his office and "make an appointment to see me for any necessary discussion."[37] Thus had matters been dealt with by the Santa Fe prelate. But if he thought that the difficulties had been "settled," to use one of Brother Mathias's favorite words, he was mistaken. Among other things, the board of Good Shepherd Manor was not happy to have had the financial responsibility taken from its directors and vested in Brother Jerome. For another, Brother Mathias continued to function as superior general, despite the archbishop's desire to shift most of the substantive functions of that office onto the shoulders of Brother Jerome. For his part, Brother Jerome accepted his new duties willingly in the spirit of obedience, but he later felt that he had been used in a power play between Archbishop Davis and Brother Mathias.[38]

In a letter to Sam Hartnett, member of the board of Good Shepherd Manor, Archbishop Davis attempted to placate that group. But he also launched into a discussion of the intimate affairs of the Good Shepherd Brotherhood. The significant portions of that letter revealed that "given the present circumstances within a Community in transition from a highly personalized one man rule to structured authority by election delegation it is somewhat problematical and premature to forecast performance."[39]

Meanwhile, Brother Mathias held the first meeting ever of the general council of the Brotherhood. It took place in Momence, Illinois, in August. The council "unanimously decided that immediate action be taken to prepare for the General Chapter of our Society by holding sessions in March 1972."[40] A second communication relating to the Momence meeting went out to all Brothers over the signature of Brother Vincent de Paul Woodhouse on August 18, and constituted something of a bombshell. This letter reported the council's unanimous decision that Brother Mathias still "exercises full authority as Superior General over the entire Society without exception until such time as a successor is *elected* by the membership of the Society in plenary session in General Chapter."[41] Further, Brother Lawrence Dillmuth was appointed to investigate matters in the Southwest houses and report to the general council at their next meeting. Finally, Brothers Camillus and Vincent de Paul were delegated to proceed to Rome to meet with the secretary of the Sacred Congregation of Religious on the subject of the forthcoming general chapter.[42] In the meantime, Brother Mathias transferred Brother Jerome to Philadelphia.[43] This removed Jerome effectively from the scene, and from his duties as procurator general.

Archbishop Davis endeavored to keep Father Temple abreast of these developments and wrote to advise him of Brother Jerome's transfer, and of the correspondence that Brother Mathias had been carrying on with Bishop (now Cardinal) Joseph L. Bernardin of the National Catholic Council of Bishops' Committee on Arbitration and Mediation. The letter contained this rather curious sentence: "Since you have been fired along with me and Mr. Krannawitter, I assume you might want to know what has taken place."[44] And in a letter to a relative outsider, Davis relieved himself of the following sentiments:

> I regret to say that the present condition of the Little Brothers of the Good Shepherd is somewhat precarious. The venerable founder, Brother Mathias, is in his eighties and is quite confused and senile. Within the last two years a considerable number of candidates and Brothers have left the congregation because of a lack of a consistent program of formation and the eccentric conduct of the Superior, Brother Mathias. Attempts to assist Brother Mathias by myself and members of the staff of the Chancery, clerical and lay, notably the Chancellor and General counsel, have failed utterly to evoke any acceptance by the Superior General, and any member who endeavored to cooperate with us has been harshly disciplined or dismissed.[45]

Archdiocesan attorney Richard Krannawitter penned a three-page memorandum for Archbishop Davis in September. In it, the words "senile" and "irrational" were repeated along with Brother Mathias's view of Brothers Camillus and Joseph as "threats" in trying to unseat him as superior general. Also detailed were the phone bills that Brother Mathias had run up by "calling constantly and screaming and yelling" at the above two Brothers to the tune of $100 and $200 per month. Said Krannawitter, "These calls were not for the most part necessary nor did they accomplish anything."[46] Moreover, with the departure of Brother Jerome, Brother Lawrence had announced that he was the new regional director for New Mexico. Finally, "When Brother Mathias returned from Momence he was completely submissive to those he formerly considered traitors to him and turned strongly against those of us who had always helped him, namely yourself, Father Temple and me. . . . They are trying to axe the old fellow and at the same time convince him that his only hope of staying in power was to throw in with them."[47]

It is most interesting to note that Brother Mathias's letters do not reflect any of this turmoil. He wrote to Father Temple in October, apologizing for not having informed him earlier that the general council had decided to "work toward a General Chapter; thus the delay in the visitation of our Houses until a later date." He expressed hope that Father Temple would not be inconvenienced, and asked for his blessing.[48]

A period of waiting ensued. Brother Mathias did not contact Archbishop Davis, nor did the latter contact him. In December, Davis wrote to Father Temple in California that he had had no communication with Mathias "since the receipt of a letter some months ago." He confided that "I have decided to leave the Brothers alone unless and until they seek some assistance or require some attention. As you say, the time is not now."[49]

In his next general letter to all Brothers, Brother Mathias told them, "As you are well aware, our Society needed a restoration — not a renewal. . . . With the help of Our Blessed Mother, Our Lady of Mount Carmel, the restoration took place on July 16th, 1971, and now I am happy to announce that all things in our Society are shaping up and once again we can be certain that nothing like this will ever happen again."[50] He rejoiced over the ninety inquiries that had been received in the first half of 1972 from prospective candidates, adding, "Thank God we are getting some very fine young men — clean and cultured, who will, through the example of our Senior Brothers, build upon the finest religious societies in the Church." The tone of the letter revealed the fact that Mathias was still firmly in charge. It ended with the sentiment, "So, dear Brothers, what a responsibility we have! I am sure you will all ever remember this when you are dealing with the poor needy and the afflicted."[51]

The main item of business in August — and the occasion for the first letter in months from Brother Mathias to Archbishop Davis — was Brother Mathias's desire to sell the hydroponic tomato-plant project at Notre Dame on the Rio Grande. "The Hydroponic Tomato Plant has been a headache for me and a source of great anxiety," he said. Further, the work for the retarded being done at Notre Dame would be merged with that being done in Bernalillo at St. Joseph's Manor. The letter ended with the sentence, "Thanking Your Excellency for your paternal solicitude and humbly begging your blessing on all my endeavors," as though nothing had ever happened between the two men.[52] The archbishop, in a short reply, gave his permission to sell the tomato-plant project and to merge the two facilities.

In October, Brother Mathias wrote to Archbishop Davis, this time with respect to the home for elderly ladies. A certain benefactor, Mrs. Brian O'Neill, had been the instigator in helping the Brothers to obtain the Sleepy Hollow Motel on Central Avenue and Eleventh Street, and in getting the price reduced from $100,000 to $75,000. He asked for no money to proceed, only for the archbishop's blessing on the project to be called "Our Lady's Home."[53] According to Brother Thomas Driber, the place was a real dump with "cardboard on the windows and loose tiles that came off the floor when you walked on them."[54] But, true to his vision of what it could be like, Brother Mathias got the right man and the right resources together, and wonders emerged. The "right man" in this case was the rehabilitated Brother Jerome.

In December, Brother Mathias sent Archbishop Davis a Christmas message. He invited him to be present at the opening of the home for elderly ladies, now called Our Lady's Manor, on January 19, the twenty-second anniversary celebration of the Good Shepherd Brotherhood. There was even a personal touch: "The story of this Work is very interesting. One day I will tell it to you."[55] The archbishop attended the dedication. The breach was healing.

By the beginning of 1973, the Good Shepherd Brothers had reason to be proud. There were now twenty houses, including refuges, homes for the aged, and homes for the retarded. To the list of earlier institutions (those in New Mexico, Ohio, Illinois, Florida, Pennsylvania, and Kansas) were added houses in Canada as well as houses in Birmingham and Wolverhampton, England. Admirers pointed out that this record averaged almost one new house per year of the existence of the society. The celebration of the twenty-second anniversary was capped by Brother Mathias's receipt of a twenty-five-thousand-dollar check from Daniel Donohue and the Dan Murphy Foundation to be used for the renovation of Our Lady's Manor, the new facility for elderly women. Brother Mathias was overwhelmed. He wrote, "All my anxiety is dissipated."[56]

His concern for women continued full force, and the next project initiated on their behalf was achieved with the acquisition of the property at 212 Iron Street, S.W., adjacent to the refuge. This building provided shelter for the "poor women presently lined up at the Refuge and mingling with the poor men."[57] In addition, the women would now have their own dining room. The winter, 1973, edition of *The Shepherd's Call* announced that the purchase of this facility "completes our Program in Albuquerque."[58] As is true of many predictions, this one later turned out to be premature. Three new facilities have been opened in Albuquerque since 1973, and a fourth, a home for aged priests, is on the drawing boards. As his Christmas gift that year from a friend in Waterford, Ireland, Brother Mathias was sent a "beautiful white knitted jacket." True to form, he decided not to keep it for himself but to raffle it off to raise money for meat for the annual corned beef and cabbage dinner on March 17.[59]

The year 1974 marked the retirement of Archbishop Davis. He

had served as the head of the New Mexico Church for ten years and, according to Catholic historian Fray Angelico Chávez, had stood up to the "winds of religious as well as social turmoil that have marked our current era."[60] Further, he had the foresight to arrange the appointment of his successor, Robert F. Sanchez, as the new archbishop of Santa Fe. This appointment was a landmark one in that the new prelate was the first Hispanic to be raised to the level of archbishop in New Mexico's history. A young man in his forties in tune with the political and social tensions of his times, his elevation fired the imagination of people in all walks of life, Catholic and non-Catholic alike. His initial relations with Brother Mathias were cordial, a continuation of their association based on his years as pastor of San Felipe Church in Old Town.

In December, Brother Mathias wrote his new superior on the subject of his "Procession around the block," telling him: "We have been holding our Procession around the block on the 28th of each month, while our Brothers chant hymns and accompany the Little Handicapped Boys while carrying our Traditional Banner with the Slogan: 'Light a Light for Life.' We are sure that Almighty God and His Blessed Mother will bless our efforts in view of combating Abortion and Euthanasia."[61] Also in 1974, the national Catholic newspaper *Our Sunday Visitor* published a lead article on Brother Mathias entitled "The Dream of an Irish Beggar," in which he was characterized as a small man who looks like Jimmy Durante. The article stressed Mathias's personal campaign against the "anti-life forces who would destroy those whom the world finds a burden." It concluded with a characteristic remark of Brother Mathias: "I never stop begging."[62]

Not reported in the press, but making a mark on the lives of the Albuquerque Brothers, was the death of a fifteen-year-old retarded boy called Little Richard. Brother Mathias had been deeply attached to this "little violet." The two of them would often recite the alphabet letter by letter. When the child died on Christmas Eve after seven hours of intensive care, Brother Mathias was grief-stricken. According to Brother James Keily: "It took all that evening and the next day for Brother Mathias to be comforted but then we were able to arrange for the Holy Sacrifice of the Mass to be offered in our Novitiate Chapel for Little Richard who lay there lifeless before the Altar, clothed in a white habit. . . . Since Christmas Eve, Brother Mathias does not cease to remind us Brothers of our great obligation to care for Christ's dearest Little Ones, the Severely Handicapped, and to constantly check on their needs and keep them clean, comfortable and happy without counting the cost. . . ."[63]

228

Life at the houses and the refuges went on with the same kinds of problems and opportunities that they had always weathered. In its Spring, 1974, issue, *The Shepherd's Call* described a typical weekend in Albuquerque:

(1) The phone rang on Friday announcing, "This is the Public Defender's Office. We have a young lady here who has been a week in jail. She is only 18 years of age. Could you accommodate her until the day of the trial?"

(2) At 6:00 P.M. on Friday there was a knock on the door. . . . A father and two children came seeking assistance. They were on their way to Grants, New Mexico, when their car broke down.

(3) At 7:00 P.M. we received a call from another stranded family. The husband expects to find employment on Monday morning and so they need accommodations in the meantime.

(4) At 7:30 P.M. one of the Funeral Parlors called up asking for a Brother to recite the Rosary.

(5) At Midnight a young man called up from the Bus Station seeking accommodations and a meal. . . .[64]

Meanwhile, the weightier matters of the order's internal organization and authority remained unsolved. Brother Mathias's first communication with his new archbishop on the subject of the long-delayed general chapter occurred on July 6, 1975. In it he said, "I sincerely thank you for your kind letter of June 25th and of course I fully agree about going slow on this question of the General Chapter, as there are so many points to study and which are liable to change from day to day."[65] The remainder of the letter concerned itself with a little girl who had made her First Holy Communion in the refuge chapel. In Brother Mathias's view, these two items were of equal importance. By August, he wrote to assure Archbishop Sanchez that he was continually working on the constitutions and the general chapter. The work was being done in "close cooperation" with Father John A. Hardon.

In the meantime, Bishop Floyd L. Begin, of Oakland, California, had written to Archbishop Sanchez requesting an evaluation of the Little Brothers of the Good Shepherd, whom he was considering inviting into his diocese. The draft of the archbishop's reply, which carried the comment "This may need editing, etc." said:

I do not hesitate to recommend the Brothers. . . . Perhaps the internal affairs of this community would cause some trepidation. Brother Mathias is certainly a saintly person but, possibly, difficult to live with — a true "founders" type! The old gentleman exercises a firm leadership in many areas, and differences arise on occasion. . . . The Brothers have worked in harmony with various agencies and have a good reputation. A "corned beef and cabbage" dinner annually offered to Albuquerque has been sold out for a number of years, which indicates considerable popular support.[66]

To Brother Mathias, he wrote, "I never cease to be amazed at the marvelous blessings which you receive from Our Lord as you continue to expand your services and love to the poor and needy." He expressed enthusiasm over the final purchase of the union building at Third and Iron Streets, and offered to stop by and visit on Thanksgiving Day "to greet you and the brothers and others who may be present there that afternoon." Brother Mathias was not to delay any meal plans, because "I would prefer simply to arrive informally."[67] This letter was typical of the simple, direct, and disarming style of leadership Robert Sanchez was bringing to the New Mexico Church. Needless to say, when he arrived at the refuge on Thanksgiving, he was warmly welcomed.

By the end of 1975, the Brothers could look back over still another year of accomplishment. Another center to feed transient men had been opened in Oakland, California, under the auspices of the St. Vincent de Paul Society. A new home for the mentally handicapped was operating in Kilkenny, Ireland. A senior citizens center serving the Barelas area of Albuquerque had been opened at Third and Iron Streets. Finally, an addition of twenty-four new beds had been made to the facility for the elderly in Alameda. But the "question" of the general chapter was still pending. The organization of the community was still under discussion, some of it bitter and divisive. The future of the community was never in doubt, and Brother Mathias continued to forge ahead with his projects, but discontent behind the scenes had reached serious dimensions. He would control his order for only two more years. The showdown would occur at the general chapter in 1977, the holding of which was, according to Brother Mathias, "the biggest mistake we ever made."[68]

14 .... Sorrow and Acclaim

THE LAST CHAPTER OF THE BIOGRAPHY OF A LIVING PERSON OUGHT to address the kinds of profound questions that occur as life draws to a close. There should be, perhaps, a contemplation of the meaning of existence and its approaching end. Brother Mathias, of course, has never spent much time contemplating ends, or conclusions. He has continued to plan beginnings. Even so, the story of the last ten years, from 1976 to 1986, is a story of sorrow as well as of worldwide acclaim for the man who has become "the Mother Teresa of America."

In 1976, the ladies' auxiliary, which Brother Mathias had initiated the first year he arrived in Albuquerque, celebrated its twenty-fifth anniversary of service. Archbishop Robert Sanchez sent his congratulations on the occasion: "Your continuing efforts and support of the work of the Little Brothers of the Good Shepherd is a work that has been blessed by Almighty God and praised and respected by the Community of Albuquerque. I join with the thousands of poor that have received love and assistance from your hands during these past years in saying thank you for your kindness and for your Christian charity."[1] The auxiliary honored the memory of its first president, Carre Gallagher, who had presided at the meeting held November 26, 1951, when ten women attended. Mrs. Gallagher had met Brother Mathias and had organized her friends in the country-club neighborhood of Albuquerque to assist the Little Brothers. Her leadership and inspiration were inspiring. "There was no task that the newly founded Ladies' Auxiliary wouldn't try for that extra dime for the Little Brothers. . . . There were tag days, teas, linen showers, garden parties, and fair booths."[2]

By 1976, the auxiliary had grown to a membership of one hundred sixty women and had seen seven remarkable presidents. Celina Raff was the first woman in New Mexico to own and operate her own finance company. Margaret Spence raised four children and, according to one of them, especially liked poker. Dr. Catherine Clarke, a dentist, served as president from 1956-1967 and earned the Archbishop Lamy award. Daisy Davis initiated the Council of Jewish Women and "if she could help someone, she would go to the end of the earth to do it."[3] Frances Hardwick served on numerous boards and organizations. She enjoyed world travel but always assured Brother Mathias that no matter where she went, she loved Ireland. Mary Burke, a grade-school teacher, started her career in the coal-mine camps in Gallup. Kathryn Kelly, president in 1976, had held the post for twelve years. A businesswoman with a keen sense of civic responsibility and a quick wit, she brought charm and vigor to the ladies' auxiliary. In addition, she also became a trusted friend of Brother Mathias. As one anonymous member of the group confided, "I'm very fond of Brother Mathias. It's a blessing to even have anything to do with him and the Little Brothers. And I'm not even Catholic!"[4]

The auxiliary had held the first corned beef and cabbage dinner on March 17 in honor of Brother Mathias's "birthday." (As mentioned earlier, Mathias was actually born on March 15 but "adopted" St. Patrick's Day as his birthday.) As the 1976 memorial program recalls: "It [the first corned beef and cabbage dinner] was almost a disaster. Because of poor ticket sales, auxiliary members feared that no one would come and the ladies began to make plans to carry the extra food to the Refuge. However, the lines began to form and continued so steadily that before long, people were patiently standing throughout the building and down the block. Local restaurants saved the day [when the corned beef began to run out] with their offerings of chickens, hamburgers and any meat they could spare. Their meat may not have been corned, but it was tasty with cabbage and no one left hungry."[5] Mrs. Celina Raff recalls that her heart sank when she first entered the empty hall and realized how sparse the ticket sales had been. When Brother Mathias arrived, he tried to cheer her up. Her response was, "You had better get out your Rosary."[6] He did. Shortly thereafter, the lines began to form. Calling this a miracle might be far-fetched, but it certainly appeared that way to the overworked volunteer staff.

In 1962, one volunteer boasted that in the last eleven years he had carved ten thousand heads of cabbage.[7] The next year, over two thousand people partook of the "traditional Jiggs' dinner," and the crowd almost overflowed the space available. The *Albuquerque Journal* reported that "all the Irish and the would-be Irish in Albuquerque had a rip-snorting time at the corned beef and cabbage dinner."[8] For the next five years, the money raised for the refuge from the dinner remained fairly constant, ranging between $1,884 and $1,658.[9]

The St. Patrick's Day dinner outgrew the facilities at the Knights of Columbus Hall and was moved to the fairgrounds for several years. One of the chairmen who put on the dinner at that location recalls that "you had to run a garden hose from the stables to make the coffee."[10] Finally, the dinner site was moved to the new convention center, which was equipped to serve six thousand people. In 1982, Brother Thomas Byrne came over from Ireland for the celebrated event. He

232

got out his harmonica and, assisted by Judge Thomas Mescall on the concertina and soloists from the Civil Light Opera, played all the Irish music any of them knew. The *Albuquerque Journal* reported, "You'll be as welcome as the flowers in spring at the Convention Center next Wednesday when doors swing wide and the air is filled with lovely Irish melodies and the aroma of corned beef and cabbage."[11] By 1983, it took 1,800 pounds of cabbage, 2,500 pounds of potatoes, and 2,600 pounds of beef to feed the happy throng.[12]

Although, in 1976, the Brotherhood seemed as strong and vigorous as ever, major changes were about to take place. The most fundamental change in the order's history occurred in 1978. And it came in a snowstorm. The Little Brothers of the Good Shepherd had been through four stages of organization within the Church. In addition, the requirements laid upon it as a religious community by Vatican II were far-reaching. These affected internal organization, dress, relationship of members to authority figures, finances, and the relationship of the community to society. These questions were met — one might say weathered — by religious communities in various ways. But Brother Mathias largely ignored them. He preferred to operate as he always had, trusting that the values he had espoused all his life were still the most reliable. He viewed the Brotherhood as a "special group and no one should interfere."[13] Not everyone agreed with him. The most vexing question of all was how to prepare for and hold the first general chapter meeting. Due to the complexities of the process, and Brother Mathias's passive resistance to it, these preparations had lasted for ten years. The event took place at last in Albuquerque in December of 1977.

The pre-chapter meetings were held in Momence, Illinois, in November. An early winter had clamped down on the state and it was snowing heavily. Due to delays caused by the weather, the trip from Albuquerque to Momence took thirty-six hours. In places the snow was seven feet deep. When Brother Mathias arrived at the airport in Chicago, there was no one to meet him. He recalls, "There wasn't a soul. I thought there must be a revolution. Well, there was a revolution."[14] Brothers Jerome, Victor, and Fenton, and a Father Harden were also coming. They arrived and sat down to plan how to get out of Chicago and down to Momence, a distance of about sixty miles. They went first to a friend's house and then to a hotel, continuing to dispute over the best course of action. News came that the road was clear. So they set out in a car and made it as far as Joliet. By that time, it was eleven o'clock at night. Brother Mathias recalls that "Father Harden was a very holy man. He was a Jesuit. He wasn't going to go to any hotel." Debating what to do took up more time. Then Father Harden suggested St. Joseph's Hospital. Brother Mathias remembered he knew a Sister there. The hospital had room for the travelers, although only Brother Mathias, Brother Jerome, and Father Harden stayed at the hospital. There they were put up in the psychiatric ward. After breakfast the next morning, Brother Mathias returned to the psychiatric ward to get his things when he was stopped by a doctor. He explained, "Doctor, I'm not a patient here. I just spent the night. Let me in. And he did!"[15]

Meanwhile, the meeting was already underway in Momence. When Brother Mathias arrived at 4:00 P.M., much business had already been transacted. (During one of my interviews with Brother Mathias, I asked him what decisions had been made at the meetings. His response was, "I wonder. I wonder. They are still making them." His view was that all they needed to do was adhere to the Ten Commandments, the six commandments of the Church, the eight beatitudes, and the seven sacraments. I also asked him, "Did you make any speeches?" His answer was, "Ridiculous. The most ridiculous questions you ask!"[16] Then he proceeded to tell me again the story of the early days at the refuge in Albuquerque and how it all began. In this way, we skirted the pain these memories still held for him.)

The major decision taken at the general chapter in Albuquerque the following month was, of course, the election of Brother Camillus as the new Brother General. Brother Camillus recalled that after the election, Brother Mathias went back to the motherhouse on Thirteenth Street and moved his things out of his room. He told Camillus, "Now you can have that too."[17] Camillus assured him that he did not need the room and that Brother Mathias did not need to move out. In actuality, what the election meant was that only the formal administration of the order would be moved to Momence, where the new Brother General resided. Mathias would continue as Brother Founder. In that respect, no one could replace him. The election results were hardly a surprise. However, some felt privately that matters could have been handled with more finesse. Daniel Donohue felt that the Brothers should have chosen Brother Mathias at this first general chapter out of respect for his role as founder. "They could have found ways to work with him and around him. It would not have been that difficult."[18] Brother Mathias took little part in the actual proceedings. When asked to make a statement to the Brothers, he said simply, "It's all so very simple, just love God, love our Blessed Mother and love the poor. I love you all. Thanks a lot."[19]

Life went on as before, with this difference: Brother Mathias was no longer the titular head of the order he had founded. He was now the

Brother Founder, with indeterminate duties but with no limits, as he saw it, to his activities. The letters, the telephone calls, and the exhortations to his fellow Brothers continued as before. There was no change in his relationship to the community of Albuquerque, where the internal shift in power within the Brotherhood passed almost unnoticed by the public.

Brother Mathias continued to pursue his goal of a home for women on the road, and for families in need of shelter. Writing in the *National Hibernian Digest*, Noel Martin remarked:

> Albuquerque is a cross-roads of two transcontinental highways. With the recession and high unemployment rate in this country, he [Brother Mathias] gets many calls in the middle of the night from stranded families with no money, no food, no shelter. Usually the social agencies have long quit their nine-to-five jobs. And it is particularly rough on weekends. The police department, courts, mental health centers, halfway houses, and ordinary families with problems are constantly making demands on him. The Good Shepherd always responds.[20]

In July, *The Shepherd's Call* reminded its readership that the need for a shelter for women was a first priority. The weekends were times of particular difficulty because from Friday to Sunday the welfare department and other social agencies were closed. Brother Mathias tried to house women in the building next to the refuge, but this failed because of its closeness to the men's facility. Placing people in cheap hotels also left much to be desired. "Brother Mathias and Brother Jerome are working with keen interest," the newsletter reported, ". . . securing the proper facilities for the poor stranded families and single women."[21] On one occasion, a woman telephoned Brother Mathias in the author's presence about the plight of a transient lady. He did not even know his caller's name, but within minutes, he advised her first to become a Roman Catholic, and then to become a nun and open a house for poor transient women herself!

Brother Mathias also continued his jail visits. *The Shepherd's Call* noted: "Brother can be often seen visiting the jails and attending the hearings and ready to vouch for a poor unfortunate who is lodged in jail for an infraction of the rules on the streets or some small misbehavior."[22]

One of the closest contacts between Brother Mathias and the world of the law was Thomas Mescall. A judge of the Second Judicial District, Mescall first met the Brother Founder in 1976. The two visited with each other an average of twice a week for ten years. Brother Mathias sent over "knights of the road" who were in difficulty with

235

the law. Thomas Mescall responded, often spending hours with indigent, confused, and disoriented people whose problems were obviously not confined to the legal realm. When court appearances came up, Brother Mathias would appear as a witness, testify, and often suggest that the person come to stay with him. Once, a case involved a priest who was arrested for disorderly conduct. Brother Mathias called Judge Mescall and then went down to the jail. The judge recalls:

> The jailor was amazed that I would show an interest and said, "We don't think this guy is a priest. He has a dialect like a sailor." I didn't think he was either. Brother Mathias went into the cell and spoke to him. "I assure you, Tom, he's a priest," he said. I had an order issued to have him released. We verified through the Archbishop that he was from a diocese in the East. Brother Mathias insisted that we stay on the case and that he be defended.[23]

In his years of work with Brother Mathias, Thomas Mescall has often been amazed by the former's willingness to thrust himself into a case without hesitation. As a result of his reputation for veracity and genuine concern, Brother Mathias is respected by judges on all levels. He can get sentences reduced to probation. He will extend himself for a man who will be here one day and gone the next. According to Mescall, "It's like doing something for a child. We don't expect children to be grateful." Of his own role, Thomas Mescall said, "It is a need. It is my job to plug that hole in the wall. Somebody else picks out size 8 shoes from size 10 shoes at the refuge. Somebody else hands out food. I do this." During the time when Judge Mescall held evening court, he would stop to see Brother Mathias afterward. He recalls, "I found a respite there. There is something healing in his presence."[24]

Throughout 1983, Brother Mathias continued to work to get emergency housing for transient, needy families. The *Albuquerque Journal* ran an article on the problem in August. Using a fictitious name for a real family to highlight the dilemma they faced, the paper pointed out that single men and women fared better than those with children. The city had only one shelter besides the Salvation Army facility available for families.

> Since the Martínez family gave up its apartment, it has sold furniture and other belongings for money to live on. Martínez, 32, has been unemployed since he was laid off from his truck-driving job nine months ago, and his unemployment benefits ran out in March. . . . Since a small grill they were using to cook on burned

last week, the Martinezes are living on sandwiches and other cold foods. They have taken showers in the locker rooms of a community center. . . .[25]

For years, Brother Mathias had been aiding such stranded families. The cost expended for such temporary aid over a three-year period by him amounted to nearly $22,000, with the bulk of the amount expended from August 16, 1982, through August 16, 1983.[26] The monies were spent for such items as "shelter, food, transportation, medications, rents, utility bills. . . ."[27] This, however, was not enough to satisfy him. He wrote numerous letters to Archbishop Sanchez on the subject of a shelter. The archbishop established a committee to research the problem. Brother Mathias wrote to Mr. J.H. Hottenroth, consultant to the committee, that a motel like the El Vado Court on East Central "could be obtained and all these needs attended to on the same grounds."[28] Further, "I have experienced in the past few days very sad cases and to date nothing seems to be accomplished except that I maintain these poor people in Motels. Again as I said, feeding-clothing are no great burdens but the sheltering is the most serious because anything could happen to a poor unfortunate especially a Lady on the Road and then the whole City and even the State are in an uproar. . . ."[29] He also confided, "I am leaving for the General Chapter after refusing to travel for many days but with pressure on many sides I am going." He added that he hoped it would be his last trip anywhere, since his eighty-fourth birthday was fast approaching.[30]

In November, 1983, the general congregation of the Brothers of the Good Shepherd met and reelected Brother Camillus Harbinson as Brother General. The honor had not been expected by Brother Camillus; as he confided to Archbishop Sanchez shortly thereafter, "Again, I believe myself to be totally unworthy. . . . I was quite amazed and rather embarrassed that our Chapter of Elections took so little time; seemingly the community was of the opinion to have me recycled." Camillus asked for the archbishop's prayers "to carry out what has been mandated to me."[31] The second session of the chapter was held in June, 1984. Brother Mathias also attended this session and had this to say to Archbishop Sanchez as he prepared to leave for the meetings: "I am going to the second half of the Brothers' Chapter next Tuesday and, indeed, I have a lot to say; and I was informed by the proper authorities that it is my duty as I am the Founder and I have every right to see that the work I established is carefully followed up and in the manner in which I wanted. We cannot afford to have every Tom, Dick and Harry join and impose their methods and spend money so easily. Money does not grow on trees."[32] As for

237

Brother Camillus, Brother Mathias felt that Camillus, as Brother General, should have moved to Albuquerque. It was also Mathias's view that Camillus had "done nothing in seven years."[33] Apparently one of the difficulties the new Brother General faced was how to please the founder of his order. Together with his other duties, this one didn't make Camillus's job any easier. (Brother Camillus died in October of 1986, after nearly nine years as head of the Little Brothers.)

Meanwhile, ordinary people and their experiences continued to put the Little Brothers of the Good Shepherd in the newspapers. There was the matter of a sheep, bought for $45 by a certain James Marquez, who planned to slaughter and dress the animal and then donate it to the refuge. In an article entitled, "Good Shepherds Get Their Sheep," the *Albuquerque Journal* quoted Marquez as to his reasons for undertaking this unusual task:

> I've been down that sort of street before. . . . Ten, 15 years ago, I was an alcoholic. I lived on the streets with nothing. I had no wife, no children, no one was depending on me. I would go in there (the shelter) and they would give me food. I've seen hundreds of guys eating at the place. . . . Every night I come home and have something good for dinner. Sometimes, chicken fried steak, sometimes roast beef. I always think of the shelter and what those guys must be eating.[34]

Then there was the story of a seventeen-year-old Mexican boy who had come north for work; he was riding the train to Kansas City and caught his foot in the wheels. His foot was later amputated at an Albuquerque hospital. Brother Raphael Mieszala took on his case and, aided by the citizens of Albuquerque, raised $1,000 to buy him an artificial foot. He was fitted with the new prosthesis and given extra money to use for alterations when he arrived back in Mexico. In this fashion, he did not return home a cripple.[35]

Major renovations were undertaken at the Second Street refuge in 1984. Archbishop Sanchez met with the directors of all the Albuquerque houses in October. The principal item of discussion was the projected cost of the renovations. Brother Jerome displayed his talent at making money and resources appear out of thin air. Having taken over the refuge with approximately $19,000 available, he estimated that the cost of refurbishing the dormitory would be $65,000 "plus $10,000 for beds, mattresses, linens, etc., and furnishings for the TV lounge." He informed the group that he had a promise from a "personal source" for $30,000. Impressed, the archbishop then added $25,000.[36] It was also at this meeting that Archbishop Sanchez brought up the subject of the Lumen Christi Award. It was his desire, he told the Brothers, to nominate Brother Mathias for this prestigious honor, which, incidentally, carried with it a grant of $26,000. Brother Vincent de Paul agreed to assist in preparing the papers for the nomination process.[37] Thus was set in motion the machinery for one of the major honors that would be bestowed on Brother Mathias.

The year 1984 was a year of awards for the man who had done little more, in his opinion, than follow the dictates of Christ to feed the poor and comfort the homeless, and to involve everyone he could in the process. In January, his native city of Waterford, Ireland, bestowed on him the Freedom of the City Award. Noel Martin, friend and confidant, recalls that Brother Mathias was invited to attend the ceremony but that no one appeared willing or able to go with him. Since Martin had been in Ireland with Brother Mathias on a previous occasion in 1974 — when he had taken time out from a vacation to go over to Kilkenny and Brother Mathias had met his train — he talked himself into going again. He recalls, "That's where I ran into trouble."[38] As it turned out, a third person joined the entourage in New York: Brother Bonaventure who had been sent by Brother Camillus to look after the Brother Founder on the trip.

The three men then flew the Atlantic Ocean and arrived in Ireland in the chill of a January winter. The ceremony was held on January 19 in Waterford's City Hall. According to the *Belfast Morning Star*: "Brother Mathias Barrett, the tough little former cabinetmaker who has become one of the Catholic Church's foremost social workers, is approaching his 84th birthday. As founder of the Little Brothers of the Good Shepherd, he is to be recognized for his outstanding and selfless efforts on behalf of the poor and needy."[39] The part about being a "cabinetmaker" referred to his job as a teenager in the furniture warehouse. The phrase was later picked up and used in other papers, including the *Albuquerque Journal* where it raised a few eyebrows. The Irish paper also noted that since the Freedom Award had been established in 1876, the city had used the privilege "sparingly." The original charter of the city of Waterford, dating from 1205, had granted "diverse liberties, pribileges (sic), immunities and exemptions to the Citizens and their successors. . . ."[40] The last honorary awards had been given in 1980 — to Noel Griffin of the Waterford Glass Company, and to the Reverend John Ward Armstrong, Catholic primate of Ireland. A total of only twenty-two awards had been given in the previous one hundred four years.[41] Among the recipients had been such notables as Andrew Carnegie, Charles Stewart Parnell, John Redman, Eamon de Valera, and John O'Connor.[42]

Brother Mathias was escorted up the steps of City Hall by the lord mayor, Mr. Dick Jones. Inside the crowded hall, he was greeted by the councilmen of the city. One of these, Thomas Brown, gave the nominating speech for the award. After listing the accomplishments of Brother Mathias's life, he reflected:

> It is difficult to believe that all this has been achieved by a little fellow from Ballybricken, as Brother Mathias describes himself. . . . He is an extraordinary man whose great love for his fellow man affects all those who come in contact with him. This can be seen in the widespread support Brother Mathias of the Little Brothers of the Good Shepherd received from the ordinary people wherever a house of the Order is opened. Brother Mathias and his Order stand fast against the empty life forces who would destroy those whom the world finds a burden. How very necessary are such dedicated persons in today's world.[43]

Alderman Stephen Rogers noted that Brother Mathias had "followed the path laid out for him in a single-minded, unquestioning manner."[44] He also repeated Mathias's aphorism, "What good in life is theology if you can't cook?" This latter remark was widely quoted in the Irish newspapers and appeared on several radio programs and talk shows.[45]

When it came time for Brother Mathias to address the audience, he told them about the news article in the Albuquerque paper entitled "Ten Best Dressed Men in Town." He said that he had taken down the names of the men in the article, found their addresses, and then written to them to ask, "What did you do with your old clothes?"[46] From then on, the audience was his. For over forty minutes, the Waterford councilmen and guests got some of the best stories retold from the past. He told them stories of his childhood, about Ned Scully, and the Hoolihans, who had returned penniless from the land of opportunity — the United States. They heard about the "copy" of his baptismal certificate that he had used to cross the border from Canada to the United States in 1941, and about parsimonious Bishop Cantwell of Los Angeles. When told about the new refuge, "He gave me his blessing. That's all." They heard about the leaky plumbing from the apartment upstairs and the burglary of sheets, blankets, and the electric razor. In this spontaneous speech, the mixture of his efforts to set up houses for the poor, with the ridiculous and comical events that had accompanied those efforts, gave this Irish audience an evening of entertainment they would not forget.

The second day they were in Ireland, Noel Martin went to visit a ninety-year-old lady and was concerned about her navigating the frozen sidewalks. As it turned out, it was Martin who broke his leg. Not realizing that he was entangled in his seat-belt, he had gotten out of the car in which he was riding and fell. After a harrowing journey to the hospital over the snowy streets, he fell asleep only to awake to see Brother Mathias's gnomish countenance bending over him. Martin spent the next five months in Ireland. Brother Mathias went back home to Albuquerque.[47]

In March, Brother Mathias was awarded the John F. Kennedy Memorial by the Ancient Order of Hibernians. Peter Moughan, president of the local chapter, noted that Brother Mathias was one of twenty-six people who had been nominated from across the country. Brother Mathias, who had known President Kennedy personally, remarked, typically, "I am happy to receive it but I can't understand why I was picked for it."[48] Later, in an interview given to *Albuquerque Living Magazine*, he commented on his dedication to the poor by saying simply, "It's hard work but you make it lovely."[49]

Then, in February, 1985, the New Mexico Legislature passed a memorial in his honor. Introduced by Representative Alfonso Otero of Bernalillo County, the memorial stated:

> Whereas, while his followers claim that he is a Saint and those in the temporal world say he is persuasive enough to have been a politician, Brother Mathias Barrett of the Brothers of the Good Shepherd Refuge says he is just a simple man; and. . .
> Whereas, in December 1984 over eight hundred people were given a hot turkey Christmas dinner at the refuge and the Ladies' Auxiliary to the Refuge passed out presents to the homeless visitors whom Brother Mathias calls the "knights of the road," and. . .
> Whereas, in 1984 over six thousand five hundred people attended Brother Mathias' eighty-fourth birthday party at the Albuquerque Civic Center downtown;
> Now, therefore, be it resolved by the House of Representatives of the State of New Mexico that it most highly commends Brother Mathias Barrett of the Brothers of the Good Shepherd Refuge for his dedicated, devoted, untiring and loving work for and with the homeless, the sick, the elderly, in fact, with anyone in need. . . .[50]

The year 1985 would bring Brother Mathias the Lumen Christi Award from the Catholic Church Extension Society. In this connection, and for the first time, Brother Mathias's photograph appeared on the front page of *Our Sunday Visitor*, and was seen in Catholic homes all over the nation. The lead article was entitled "The Irish Brother Who Turns No One Away."[51]

The award itself was given at a ceremony in Chicago in May.

241

Brother Mathias traveled with Brother Jerome and Archbishop Sanchez, who had proposed Mathias's name for the honor. There were fifty-four nominees in 1985. The committee was composed of seven leading Catholic figures, including Father Theodore M. Hesburgh of Notre Dame, John Tracy Ellis of Catholic University, Archbishop John L. May of St. Louis, and Bishop James W. Malone, president of the National Conference of Catholic Bishops. Brother Jerome advised the committee not to put their honored guest in a fancy hotel, or he would walk out on them.[52] Archbishop Sanchez arranged for a new suit and shoes to be delivered for Brother Mathias to wear, but instructed that they be given to him just before the airplane left or he would give them away to some poor man.[53]

The Lumen Christi Award, established in 1978 by the Catholic Extension Society (which was founded in 1905), was designed to honor "quiet, unselfish people whose heroic labors have remained hidden and unseen."[54] Father Edward Slattery's opening remarks at the award dinner praised Brother Mathias not only for his "compassion for the weak and willingness to forgive without limits," but for "his sense of humor, strength in adversity, energy and continued sense of wonder."[55] He compared Brother Mathias to outstanding Irish Catholics of the past, including Edmund Rice and Nan O'Nagle. Cardinal Joseph Bernardin presented Brother Mathias with a one-thousand-dollar check and the small glass head of Christ on a wooden stand, the outward symbols of the award. In addition, a check for $25,000 was presented to Archbishop Sanchez, which the latter turned over to the Brothers for their work. Brother Mathias then made a few simple comments of his own. He said, "When I find a man like Father Slattery who gave such a lovely sermon, I think we should make him master of novices. . . . If Nan O'Nagle had been a man she'd have beaten Johnny O'Connor in any debate." He thanked the Extension Society for the new institution for transient women that their money would make possible. "I thank everybody because that's the way we live. The people have always been good to me." Then he grinned and added, "And thanks also for paying my expenses to come here."[56]

Archbishop Sanchez then rose to make his remarks. He began by telling the audience about the story of a raindrop in the desert. The sun looked down and asked the raindrop, "Who are you?" and received the reply, "I'm just a little raindrop." The sun then said, "But, oh, how you sparkle."

The Lord took a little raindrop from Ireland and transferred that raindrop to the deserts of New Mexico thirty-five years ago and the sparkle of that raindrop has continued to provide the light of

Christ for the poor, the abandoned, the street people, for elderly men and women who have no place to retire, for retarded men and women not only in New Mexico but throughout the country. These were the marginated people that this little raindrop looked out for and loved. Because he could reflect the light of Christ, the Lumen Christi in his own life, so much good has been done.[57]

The twenty-five-thousand-dollar check from the Catholic Extension Society made possible Barrett House. A committee had been working on this shelter for women and children with the kind of zeal that Brother Mathias could inspire. According to Don and Barbara Brennan, who headed the committee's efforts, "Brother Mathias supplied the inspiration and the obstacles just seemed to disappear."[58] Brother Mathias gave half of his residence on Thirteenth Street for the project, and the Presentation Sisters, who were to administer the shelter, moved in for renovations. Quickly, the face of the old house changed as new paint went on the walls and new carpet was laid on the floors. The few old men who had been situated on the upper floor were moved to other quarters, and Brother Anthony had to move his files as the whirlwind of activity advanced. Barrett House opened on August 18, 1985. Sister Rita Johnson, one of the two nuns who composed the staff of the shelter said, "Brother Mathias has been putting up some of the homeless ladies in motels. . . . This is one of his long-time dreams."[59] One of the remarkable occurrences that accompanied the opening of Barrett House was an unexpected gift. While praying in the chapel one afternoon, Brother Mathias was handed an envelope by a woman who entered and then quickly left. When he opened it later he found a check for $50,000.[60]

Aside from the money from the Lumen Christi Award, the lease on the building, and the use of his name, Brother Mathias and the Little Brothers had no formal connection with the house for women. However, he proudly presided at its opening along with Don Brennan, the president of Presentation, Inc., and Barbara Brennan, who hosted the event. Visitors were fed and taken on tours of the newly refurbished house. Even those who had seen it in its former role as bachelor quarters for an assortment of men, found it hard to recognize so complete was the transformation. Tidy rooms with carpet, beds, and curtains greeted the public. Fresh flowers in vases, magazines on tables, clothing in closets, and toys for children in a playroom were charming additions to the basic decor. Throughout the day, Brother Mathias greeted visitors, shook hands, and enjoyed the happy commotion. Once again he was in his element, opening yet another house for the poor.

Since then, some confusion has arisen as to the address of Barrett House, since the Brothers still maintain their residence next door and the two are combined in the same building. Brother Mathias has several handwritten signs up on his front window with arrows that point to Barrett House to inform any newcomers that "this is not Barrett House." Moreover, there have been occasional differences of opinion between the Brother Founder and the staff of the home for women of how certain matters should be handled. Other than these, Brother Mathias says, "I keep out of their hair."

The 1986 edition of the St. Patrick's Day dinner was the most successful to date. Thousands of people crowded into the convention center to eat corned beef and cabbage and hear the Ballut Abyad Shrine Bagpipe Band, the Duke City Fiddlers, and other timely entertainment. The affair boasted all the traditional trappings of Irish patriotism, from shamrocks and green tissue paper to green beer. But this year, for the first time, the program devoted considerable space to a serious discussion of Irish opposition to British rule. The lead article by Timothy Meehan, headlined "When Irish Eyes Are Not Smiling," chronicled the deaths of Irish children at the hands of British troops using sawed-off shotguns and plastic bullets. Readers were invited to support an end to the partition of Ireland, the departure of British soldiers, and an end to political and economic discrimination against Irish Catholics and Nationalists in Eastern Ulster. The goal proclaimed was "an Ireland: united, Gaelic and Free."[61]

In a sense, Brother Mathias had come full circle. Born in Ireland, and raised with its history of struggle, he now presided over an Irish dinner, which not only raised money for a refuge for the poor but which also reflected the age-old dreams of Irish freedom.

A further evidence of this renewed commitment to the cause of Ireland was Brother Mathias's insistence that Albuquerque have a branch of the Ancient Order of Hibernians. As a result of his agitation, and Noel Martin's efforts in behalf of this dream, the chapter was organized in 1982. Brother Mathias recalls the process by which this all came about: "Their [the Hibernians'] goals are to protect the church and the clergy, be a friend of charity, and have no enmity between them. I wrote to the President of the Hibernians, Joe Roche, and said, 'If you help me, I'll help you.' So I pursued getting a branch here in Albuquerque. They wanted to call it Division Mathias and I protested. 'You leave the name Mathias alone!' The big man in this was Noel Martin. He kept up all the negotiations."[62]

The first group of members was sworn in at the Hilton Hotel. Brother Mathias became one of the most loyal members of the new organization and lost no time in finding projects for them to do. As he remarked, "Meetings are all very fine but you have to have something real, tangible."[63] One of the more interesting projects was the pilgrimage to San Patricio (a little chapel in southern New Mexico), first held in October, 1984. The green-and-white flyers that advertised the event had a drawing of St. Patrick dressed as a Viking warrior, the coat of arms of the Hibernians, and the message "He Was Needed Then, You Are Needed Now." The pilgrimage fulfilled a promise Brother Mathias had made to St. Patrick. The group left on the bus in the morning for the three-hour drive. On the way, they sang hymns and recited the Rosary. The actual location of the little chapel of San Patricio, which had not been used for years, was down the main highway about a mile from the main chapel where Mass was held. Then everyone walked, carrying banners and singing. There was a chill wind. Brother Mathias, his sparse hair blowing in the wind, held on to Judge Mescall's arm. Someone offered him a woolen cap, but he brushed it away. Later, people were heard to remark that the Lord had not preserved him this long to have him catch cold on the pilgrimage in honor of St. Patrick.

When the assemblage arrived at the chapel of San Patricio, they found a structure that had been hastily swept and put into presentable condition, complete with flowers on the altar and the banners of the Hibernian Society. The work had been done by Brother Thomas, who in fact was the behind-the-scenes wonder-worker for the entire event. There was something hauntingly beautiful about the bright colors, the strong sunshine, the wind, the prayers, and the old church. Brother Mathias talked for a while about how he had come to New Mexico, then recounted the various stories about Father Gerald Fitzgerald and the used coffee grounds. Most people could not hear above the wind, but they listened intently anyway. It was not the substance of what he said that mattered, but the fact that he was there.

Brother Mathias was invited to return to Ireland in the spring of 1986 for another honor at the hands of the city fathers of Waterford. As part of urban renewal in that city, the street where he had been raised was to be renamed Barrett Place and a plaque placed at the site of the house where he was born. The mayor of Waterford sent his hat by special delivery to be used at the celebration in Albuquerque to send him on his journey. The festivities were held outside in early May on the grounds of the motherhouse. Mass was celebrated by several priests, and the audience of several hundred, including Brother Mathias, sat in folding chairs on the lawn. Partway through the ceremony he pulled his cowl over his head to keep off the hot sun. Sam Baca, chief of police, commended Brother Mathias and his fellow Brothers for having aided the police in keeping desperate men off the streets. He said, "We not only look at you as part of the community, but as part of the law enforcement community. Thank you for the fine work you have done."[64] Ken Schultz, mayor of Albuquerque, gave Brother Mathias the keys to the city. He praised him in these words: "He has consistently worked for all the people of our community, but particularly the poor. Government alone cannot do the job. I believe that one cannot say enough about the decent, kind and compassionate people like Brother Mathias. . . . I am lucky enough to know him, and to love him. He is a tremendous person."[65] Then the mayor gave him twelve yellow roses and Mrs. Schultz gave him twelve red roses and kissed him. The invitation from the city of Waterford was read aloud: ". . . The Waterford Corporation voted unanimously to invite you to urban renewal housing and to name it Barrett Place after your family in recognition of your work for the poor, homeless and destitute."[66]

But of all that was said on that day, Brother Mathias's remarks were the most memorable. Putting aside the cowl that had covered his head, he looked out at all the people gathered in his honor and said:

> All this is a big surprise to me. I depend on the people. I am very proud today. Everybody is kind to us. We don't need big fortunes. Don't try to burden the mayor with all kinds of problems. Let's try to help him. . . . I never had any difficulties with authorities. Once I was down getting a man out of jail. I had no license, no bank account, no papers. So I pulled out my scapular from under my habit and this guy said, "That's all right with me. I'm a Pentecostal."[67]

Monsignor Francis O'Byrne, chaplain of the Brothers and long-time friend, said in his homily, "We are here to crown you king. Of course, you'd be king of the hobos. . . . You will have a great time in Waterford and they will greet you with great joy because you are a Shepherd of the people."[68]

By July, Brother Mathias had not yet gone to Ireland and appeared to have no intention of going. Nevertheless, a majority of the public thought he had already gone. Some believed he had gone there to retire and would not come back. The long-awaited trip was finally set for August. Brother Mathias was simply reluctant to leave his work and go. Moreover, he enjoyed the mystery he created.

Earlier in the year, Noel Martin and Thomas Mescall had accompanied Brother Mathias to Via Coeli in Jemez Springs for the burial of a priest. Mathias had walked on ahead and was busy pointing out the spot where he intends to be buried some day. The spot is close, but not too close, to Father Gerald Fitzgerald's grave. When Noel Martin caught up with him, Brother Mathias turned and remarked that even after burial, he would still be "flitting around like a bird." His hands moved in the air to illustrate. Later, Thomas Mescall confided to Noel Martin, "I don't know what I'm going to do when that man dies." The latter's response was, "Don't worry; he told me he isn't going anywhere."[69]

In an interview he gave to the *Irish American News* in May, 1986, Brother Mathias reflected on his long life and said, "The Lord gave me energy, health, strength and courage to face people. When I was young, I was timid. It's all by the mercy of God. You know, a lot of people forget God's mercy."[70] Examples of the exercise of human mercy by Brother Mathias have blessed all who have known him. Eurath Lucas, a writer for the *Albuquerque Tribune*, recalls that Brother Mathias "could talk to the lowliest person and treat him with dignity as though his story, unreal as it might sound, was the absolute truth."[71] Virginia Reva recalls that when she would go to parishes to speak on the beatification cause of Brother André Bessette (who was beatified in 1982), Brother Mathias went with her. She introduced him with the words, "Naturally you all know Brother Mathias. He is a friend of everybody in the city."[72] Frances Hardwick, longtime member of the ladies' auxiliary and former president of the group, when asked to sum up the importance of Brother Mathias's life, said, "I'd have to write an encyclopedia. He's the closest thing to God I'll ever know."[73]

Of all the memories to end with, perhaps Noel Martin's is appropriate. He received a phone call from Brother Mathias one evening with instructions to come down "before nine o'clock because I have a little fella here for you." Convinced that the "little fella" was probably a retarded boy that needed lodging, or some old man for whom there was no room at the refuge, Martin drove with some apprehension to the motherhouse. There he was met by a jubilant Mathias carrying a statue of the Infant of Prague about two feet high. "Here's the little fella!" he announced. Martin took the statue and breathed a sigh of relief.[74]

Brother Mathias has created a legend with his life. This book has tried to chronicle the achievements as well as the aggravations and disappointments of that life. Comparisons with other figures notwithstanding, he stands alone, unique, and compelling. Every time a visitor leaves the motherhouse in Albuquerque, the diminutive old man in the white habit has stood in the doorway and called out, "Toot the horn so I know you are all right." Looking back at that beloved figure with the gnomish countenance, a visitor cannot help but feel that yes, it is true, Brother Mathias won't be going anywhere.

Appendixes

Names and Locations

The following are the names and locations of the various residences, refuges, and other institutions run by the Little Brothers of the Good Shepherd, including a description of their purpose:

- Motherhouse, P.O. Box 389, 901 Thirteenth St., N.W., Albuquerque, New Mexico 87102 *(residence of the Brother Founder)*
- Good Shepherd Manor, P.O. Box 10248, 10127 Guadalupe Trail, N.W., Albuquerque, New Mexico 87184 *(home for elderly men and women)*
- Our Lady's Manor, 1023 Central Ave., N.W., Albuquerque, New Mexico 87102 *(retirement center for women)*
- Good Shepherd Refuge, P.O. Box 749, 601 Second St., S.W., Albuquerque, New Mexico 87102 *(shelter for the transient poor)*
- St. Joseph's Manor, P.O. Box 610, 2027 Camino del Pueblo, Bernalillo, New Mexico 87004 *(home for mentally handicapped men)*
- Good Shepherd Manor, P.O. Box 4461, 3220 East 23rd St., Kansas City, Missouri 64127 *(home for mentally handicapped men)*
- Ozanam Inn, P.O. Box 30565, 843 Camp St., New Orleans, Louisiana 70190 *(shelter for the transient poor)*
- Camillus House, P.O. Box 1829, 726 N.E. First Ave., Miami, Florida 33132 *(shelter for the transient poor)*
- Mount Aloysius, P.O. Box 598, Rte. 32, New Lexington, Ohio 43764 *(home for mentally handicapped men)*
- St. John's Hospice, 1221 Race St., Philadelphia, Pennsylvania 19107 *(shelter for the transient poor)*
- Good Shepherd Manor, P.O. Box 260, Dixie Highway, Momence, Illinois 60954 *(home for mentally handicapped men)*
- Good Shepherd Centre, P.O. Box 1003, 135 Mary St., Hamilton, Ontario, Canada L8N 3R1 *(shelter for the transient poor and residence for homeless men)*
- Good Shepherd Refuge, 412 Queen St., East, Toronto, Ontario, Canada M5A 1T3 *(shelter for the transient poor)*
- House of Formation, P.O. Box 2357—Station B, Richmond Hill, Ontario, Canada L4E 1A5 *(novitiate)*
- Good Shepherd Centre, Troys Lane, Kilkenny, Ireland *(shelter for the transient poor and home for the mentally handicapped)*
- Good Shepherd Manor, Ardmore Estate, 10-12 Sycamore, Kilkenny, Ireland *(group home for mentally handicapped men)*
- Good Shepherd Centre, 27 Thornley St., Wolverhampton, England WVi iJP *(shelter for the transient poor and residence for homeless men)*

Sources

Primary and Archival

Archives, Archdiocese of Boston (AAB).
Archives, Archdiocese of Santa Fe (AASF).
Archives, Archdiocese of Los Angeles (AALA).
Archives, Hospitaller Order of St. John of God, Montreal (ASJGM).
Archives, Hospitaller Order of St. John of God, Ojai (ASJGO).
Archives, Little Brothers of the Good Shepherd (ALBGS).
The Tidings Archives, Los Angeles.

Newspapers

The Albuquerque Journal, 1951-1986.
The Albuquerque Tribune, 1951-1986.
The Boston Pilot, 1945-1949.
The Flame of Charity, 1940-1945.
The Shepherd's Call, 1941-1982.
Selected issues of: *The Miami Voice; The Philadelphia Inquirer; The Boston Globe; The Philadelphia Daily News; The Philadelphia Bulletin; The Columbus Dispatch; Belfast Morning Star; Kilkenny People.*

Interviews

Among those interviewed for this work were: James Barrett; Thomas Barrett; Barbara Brennan; Don Brennan; Daniel Donohue; Frances Hardwick; Kathryn Kelly; Richard Krannawitter; Eurath Lucas; Timothy Cardinal Manning; Noel Martin; Thomas Mescall; Peter Moughan; Monsignor Francis O'Byrne; Celina Raff; Virginia Reva; Archbishop Robert Sanchez; Dr. Hubert Teague.

Also, Brothers Anthony Aucoin, O.H.; Kevin Carr, B.G.S.; Patrick Corr, O.H.; Michael Carlyle, B.G.S.; Thomas Driber (former B.G.S.); Camillus Harbinson, B.G.S.; Jerome McCarthy, B.G.S.; Oliver McGivern, O.H.; Laurier Ouellette, O.H.; Andrew Scully, O.H.; Hugo Stippler, O.H.

Secondary Sources: Books

Akenson, Donald Harman. *The United States and Ireland* (Cambridge, Mass.: Harvard University Press, 1973).

Allen, T.D. *Not Ordered by Men* (Santa Fe: The Rydal Press, 1967).

Almon, Albert. *Rochefort Point: A Silent City in Louisbourg* (Glace Bay, Cape Breton, N.S.: MacDonald Printers, 1940).

Aragón, de, Ray John. *Padre Martínez and Bishop Lamy* (Las Vegas: Pan-American Publishing Co., 1978).

Barber, Ruth K. and Edith J. Agnew. *Sowers Went Forth* (Menaul Historical Library of the Southwest, 1981).

Bastien, Hermas. *L'Ordre Hospitalier de Saint-Juan-de-Dieu au Canada* (Montreal: Therien Frères Limitée, 1947).

Blyth, Jack A. *The Canadian Social Inheritance* (Toronto: Copp Clark Publishing Co., 1972).

Bogue, Donald J. *Skid Row in American Cities* (Chicago: University of Chicago Press: 1963).

Cather, Willa. *Death Comes for the Archbishop* (New York: Vintage Books, 1927 and 1971).

Caulfield, Max. *The Irish Mystique* (Englewood Cliffs, N.J.: Prentice-Hall, 1973).

Chávez, Fray Angelico. *But Time and Chance: The Story of Padre Martínez of Taos, 1793-1867* (Santa Fe: Sunstone Press, 1981).

Cleeve, Brian. *A View of the Irish* (London: Buchan and Enright, 1983).

Coles, Robert. *A Spectacle Unto the World: The Catholic Worker Movement* (New York: Viking Press, 1973).

Curtis, L.P., Jr. *Anglo-Saxons and Celts: A Study of Anti-Irish Prejudice in Victorian England* (Bridgeport, Conn.: Conference on British Studies at the University of Bridgeport, 1968).

Cutler, John Henry. *Cardinal Cushing of Boston* (New York: Hawthorn Books, Inc., 1970).

Defouri, James H. *Historical Sketch of the Catholic Church in New Mexico* (San Francisco: McCormick Bros., 1887).

Dever, Joseph. *Cushing of Boston: A Candid Portrait* (Boston: Bruce Humphries, 1965).

Doherty, Eddie. *Matt Talbot* (Milwaukee: Bruce Publishing Co., 1953).

Ellis, John Tracy. *American Catholicism* (Chicago: University of Chicago Press, 1969).

Fenton, John. *Salt of the Earth: An Informal Profile of Richard Cardinal Cushing* (New York: Coward, McCann, Inc., 1965).

Greeley, Andrew. *The Catholic Experience* (New York: Image Books, 1969).

Gregg, Josiah. *Commerce of the Prairies*, Max L. Moorhead, ed. (Norman, Okla.: University of Oklahoma Press, 1954).

Historical Manuscripts Commission, *Tenth Report*, Appendix Part V; "Manuscripts of the Marquis of Ormonde, the Earl of Fingall, the Corporations of Waterford, Galway & Co." (London: Eyre and Spottiswoode, 1845).

Horgan, Paul. *Lamy of Santa Fe, His Life and Times* (New York: Farrar, Straus and Giroux, 1975).

Howard, Brett. *Boston: A Social History* (New York: Hawthorn Books, 1976).

Howlett, W.J. *Life of the Right Reverend Joseph P. Machebeuf, D.D.* (Pueblo, Colo., 1908).

Kovic, Ron. *Born on the Fourth of July* (New York: McGraw-Hill, 1976).

Lamar, Howard Roberts. *The Far Southwest 1846-1912, A Territorial History* (New Haven, Conn.: Yale University Press, 1966).

Lawlor, Shiela. *Britain and Ireland, 1914-1923* (Totowa, N.J.: Barnes & Noble Books, 1983).

MacDonaugh, Oliver, W.F. Mandle, and Pauric Travers, eds. *Irish Culture and Nationalism, 1750-1950* (Canberra: Australian National University, 1983).

McCaffrey, Lawrence J. *Ireland from Colony to Nation State* (Englewood Cliffs, N.J.: Prentice-Hall, 1979).

McCarthy, Joe and the editors of *Life* magazine. *Ireland* (New York: Time Inc., 1964).

McMahon, Norbert, O.H. *The Story of the Hospitallers of St. John of God* (Westminster, Md.: The Newman Press, 1959).

_____, *St. John of God: Heavenly Patron of the Sick and Dying, Nurses and Hospitals* (New York: McMullen Books, Inc., 1951).

Miller, William D. *Dorothy Day: A Biography* (San Francisco: Harper & Row Publisher, 1982).

_____, *A Harsh and Dreadful Love: Dorothy Day and The Catholic Worker Movement* (New York: Liveright Publishing Corp., 1973).

Ministries for the Lord: A Resource Guide and Directory of Church Vocations for Men (Ramsey, N.J.: Paulist Press, 1981).

Montesano, Pat. *Sing a New Song: The Story of a Mentally Retarded Boy Seeking Acceptance* (Colorado Springs, Colo.: Century One Press, 1982).

O'Broin, Leon. *Dublin Castle and the 1916 Rising* (New York: New York University Press, 1971).

O'Connor, Ulick. *A Terrible Beauty Is Born: The Irish Troubles 1912-1922* (London: Hamish Hamilton, 1973).

Piehl, Mel. *Breaking Bread, the Catholic Worker and the Origin of Catholic Radicalism in America* (Philadelphia: Temple University Press, 1982).

Purcell, Mary. *A Time for Sowing: The History of St. John of God Brothers in Ireland 1879-1979* (Dublin: Allograph Design, 1980).

Roberts, Nancy L. *Dorothy Day and the Catholic Worker* (Albany, N.Y.: State University of New York Press, 1984).

Salpointe, J.B. *Soldiers of the Cross* (Banning, Calif.: St. Boniface Indian Industrial School, 1898).

Sanchez, George. *Forgotten People* (Albuquerque: University of New Mexico Press, 1940).

Seaburg, Carl. *Boston Observed* (Boston: Beacon Press, 1971).

Sisters of St. Dominic, Congregation of the Most Holy Rosary. *The Rule of St. Augustine* (Adrian, Mich.: 1973).

Suttles, Gerald D. *The Social Order of the Slum: Ethnicity and Territory in the Inner City* (Chicago: University of Chicago Press, 1968).

Twitchell, Ralph D. *Leading Facts of New Mexico History* (Cedar Rapids, Iowa: The Torch Press, 1912).

Vásquez, Dora Ortiz. *Enchanted Temples of Taos: My Story of Rosario* (Santa Fe: Rydal Press, 1975).

Ward, Alan J. *The Easter Rising: Revolution and Irish Nationalism* (Arlington Heights, Ill.: AHM Publishing Corp., 1980).

Ward, Leo R. *All Over God's Irish Heaven* (Chicago: Henry Regnery Co., 1964).

Weston, George F., Jr. *Boston Ways*, updated by Charlotte Cecil Raymond (Boston: Beacon Press, 1972).

Woods, Robert A., ed. *The City Wilderness: A Settlement Study by Residents and Associates of the South End House* (New York: Garrett Press, Inc., 1970).

Secondary Sources:
Articles, Pamphlets, Unpublished Manuscripts

Bauer, Pam. "The Irish Brother Who Turns No One Away," *Our Sunday Visitor*, Vol. 74, No. 7 (June 16, 1985).

Bowden, Henry Warner. "Richard James Cushing," *Dictionary of Religious Biography* (Westport, Conn.: Greenwood Press, 1977).

Callan, Benignus, O.H. "The Life of Outstanding Hospitaller Brothers of St. John of God," unpublished manuscript, 1972.

Carlyle, Michael, B.G.S. "Soldiers of Charity: The Life Story of the Little Brothers of the Good Shepherd," unpublished manuscript, n.d.

Currivan, Earl J. "Brother Mathias," in *St. Anthony's Messenger*, January 19, 1944.

Flood, Jeanne. "James Joyce, Patrick Pearse and the theme of execution," in P.J. Drudy, ed., *Irish Studies I* (London: Cambridge University Press, 1980).

Francis, E.K. "Padre Martínez: A New Mexican Myth," *New Mexico Historical Review*, Vol. 31 (October, 1956).

Gaustad, Edwin S. "Religion in America: History and Historiography," *American Historical Association Pamphlets*, No. 260 (Washington, D.C., 1973).

Heitz, Henry. "Historical Notes on St. Vincent de Paul's Parish, 1874-1924" (Silver City, N.M.: Citizen Printers, 1924).

Looney, Ralph. "Derelicts at the Door," *Catholic Digest*, September, 1962.

Mann, W.E. "The Social System of a Slum: The Lower Ward, Toronto," in S.D. Clark, ed., *Urbanism and the Changing Canadian Society* (Toronto: University of Toronto Press, 1961).

Martin, Noel. "Brother Mathias: A True Servant," *National Hibernian Digest*, September/October, 1983.

Munn, T.J. "Ireland," *New Catholic Encyclopedia* (Washington, D.C.: Catholic University of America, 1967).

O'Brien, Lillian. "Year of the Flame," unpublished manuscript, 1976.

O'Connell, Patricia. "Brother Mathias," *Albuquerque Living Magazine*, Vol. 2, No. 12 (December, 1984).

Scott, John Charles. "Between Fiction and History: An Exploration into Willa Cather's *Death Comes for the Archbishop*," unpublished Ph.D. dissertation, University of New Mexico, 1980.

"Seventh Synod of the Archdiocese of Santa Fe, celebrated on December 2, 1958 by His Excellency the Most Reverend Edwin Vincent Byrne D.D." (Albuquerque: Moulton Printers, 1958).

"Twenty Five Years of Service," Albuquerque Ladies Auxiliary, 1976.

Vigil, Ralph H. "Willa Cather and Historical Reality," *New Mexico Historical Review*, Vol. 50 (April, 1975).

Wermes, Joanmarie McLaughlin. "Mathias: 'I'm Tired Now and Want to get on Home to Heaven,' " *Irish American News*, Vol. 10, No. 3 (May, 1986).

Chapter Notes

Chapter One

1. Joe McCarthy and the editors of *Life* magazine, *Ireland* (New York: Time Inc., 1964), p. 10.
2. *Ibid.*
3. Ten times as many Irish live outside the island as on it. They have been driven to emigrate by famine, religious persecution, and hardship. "The Irish have won respect as missionaries and teachers, prize fighters, doctors and lawyers, military leaders and cannon fodder, navvies [unskilled laborers] and tavern keepers, actors and politicians, dramatists and philosophers, artists and thinkers, wits and buffoons." Brian Cleeve, *A View of the Irish* (London: Buchan and Enright, 1983), p. 170.
4. McCarthy, *op. cit.*, p. 46.
5. Lawrence J. McCaffrey, *Ireland from Colony to Nation State* (Englewood Cliffs, N.J.: Prentice-Hall, 1979), p. 13.
6. Max Caulfield, *The Irish Mystique* (Englewood Cliffs, N.J.: Prentice-Hall, 1973), p. 227.
7. "One sometimes has the feeling that Ireland is a single, great, open-air monastery. Since 1870, the population has fallen 23%, yet the number of priests has risen by 87%. There are 6,100 priests or one for every 550 Catholics in the country. In Dublin, one in every 600 is a priest, nun, or member of a religious order." McCarthy, *op. cit.*, pp. 76, 225.
8. "The priest was also involved in every other concern in his town, including business and legal disputes, arguments over land ownership and whether there will be a new dance hall or saloon." *Ibid.*, p. 76.
9. Oliver MacDonaugh, W.F. Mandle, and Pauric Travers, eds., *Irish Culture and Nationalism 1750-1950* (Canberra: Australian National University, 1983), p. 45.
10. *Ibid.*, p. 270.
11. *Ibid.*, p. 139.
12. MacDonaugh, *op. cit.*, p. 126. When John Millington Synge's "Playboy of the Western World" was staged in 1907, it caused a riot because Irish peasants were portrayed as doing something other than saying the Rosary — namely as being capable of violence. McCaffrey, *op. cit.*, p. 123.
13. Cleeve, *op. cit.*, p. 57. The fabulous character of Irish Catholicism dates back to St. Patrick. When Irish monks began flooding the Continent, they found a receptive audience for their tales. One of these was Patrick's struggle with the angel on Croagh Patrick, the result of which was the agreement that he be allowed to judge the Irish on the Last Day, and that Ireland, of all nations, be spared the torments of the Last Judgment. Caulfield, *op. cit.*, p. 113.
14. McCaffrey, *op. cit.*, p. 36.

15. *Ibid.*, p. 121.
16. L.P. Curtis, Jr., *Anglo-Saxons and Celts: A Study of Anti-Irish Prejudice in Victorian England* (Bridgeport, Conn.: Conference on British Studies at the University of Bridgeport, 1968), p. 63.
17. *Ibid.*, p. 81.
18. McCaffrey, *op. cit.*
19. *Ibid.*
20. Ulick O'Connor, *A Terrible Beauty Is Born: The Irish Troubles 1912-1922* (London: Hamish Hamilton, 1973), p. 14. Hurling and Gaelic football became popular pastimes under the aegis of the Gaelic Athletic Association, which was pledged to protect the Irish against "alien and effeminate English games." McCaffrey, *op. cit*, p. 121.
21. The league was founded by Douglas Hyde, son of a Protestant parson, who had discovered that Irish peasants spoke poetry in the fields. *Ibid.*, p. 160.
22. *Ibid.*, p. 122.
23. O'Connor, *op. cit.*, p. 24.
24. The Irish Republican Brotherhood was at first known for its efforts at staging patriotic funerals, but new leadership was shortly to give the movement a new lease on life during the Easter Rebellion. McCaffrey, *op. cit.*, p. 124.
25. *Ibid.*, p. 68.
26. Interview with Brother Mathias, September 17, 1984. The leather workers were paid in leather money which, due to the importance of the industry, was acceptable currency.
27. *Ibid.* The house no longer stands, but there is a plaque on the spot, erected by the city of Waterford in honor of Brother Mathias.
28. Interview with Brother Mathias, October 5, 1984.
29. *Ibid.*
30. *Ibid.*
31. McCarthy, *op. cit.*, p. 84.
32. McCaffrey, *op. cit.*, p. 129. Home rule was jokingly defined by Tom Kettle, a young Irish member of Parliament as "the art of minding your own business well," whereas Unionism was "the art of minding someone else's business badly." O'Connor, *op. cit.*, p. 23.
33. McCaffrey, *op. cit.*, p. 132.
34. Leon O'Broin, *Dublin Castle and the 1916 Rising* (New York: New York University Press, 1971), p. 20.
35. The records of St. Stephen's School, Waterford, Ireland. Copy in the possession of Brother Thomas, Kilkenny, Ireland.
36. Brother Mathias also wrote a composition on the *Titanic*, a "terrible big boat," which had a race course. He could never understand the race course, until years later when he came to America on a ship that had one. It was a little game played with squares of wood. "You would shake up the numbers. Can you imagine how stupid I was!" Interview with Brother Mathias, October 14, 1984.

37. Brother Thomas became an engineer in the United States and then converted to the Catholic faith. He then joined the De La Salle Brothers and returned to Ireland, where he "covered Ireland with teachers." Brother Mathias is the source of this information.

38. Interview with Brother Mathias, October 26, 1984.

39. Letter from Brother Camillus Harbinson, B.G.S., to the author, August 14, 1985.

40. Interview with Brother Mathias, August 14, 1984.

41. *Ibid.* The old lady was also "fond of drink and conducted business with a bottle under the counter."

42. *Ibid.*

43. McCaffrey, *op. cit.*, p. 125.

44. O'Connor, *op. cit.*, p. 18. "The north side of Dublin, that became the fashionable side in the 18th century, full of Georgian houses and elegant squares and side streets — town planning was first tried out on the Irish to see if it was dangerous — the north side declined right through the last hundred years to become a desert of neglect, slums, tenements, demolition sites and parking lots." Cleeve, *op. cit.*, p. 145.

45. McCaffrey, *op. cit.*, p. 125.

46. O'Broin, *op. cit.*, p. 20.

47. McCaffrey, *op. cit.*, p. 134.

48. Interview with Brother Mathias, October 5, 1984.

49. *Ibid.* Margaret Foley had a lovely singing voice, and Brother Mathias recalls he could tell something was wrong if she wasn't singing.

50. "Love Shines in Brother Mathias," pamphlet published by the Little Brothers of the Good Shepherd, Albuquerque, New Mexico, n.d., p. 4. Archives, Little Brothers of the Good Shepherd. (From hereon, this reference will appear as ALBGS.) He also checked out the schedule of the Cunard Steamship Line to get information on ships sailing to America. Interview with Brother Mathias, August 14, 1984.

51. *Ibid.*

52. Brother Mathias probably precipitated the explosion by having lit a candle to see inside. Flames then came out of the building. His mother nursed him with a combination of olive oil, egg yolk, and lime water, which she placed on a cloth and secured over the burns.

Chapter Two

1. Norbert McMahon, *St. John of God: Heavenly Patron of the Sick and Dying, Nurses and Hospitals* (New York: McMullen Books, Inc., 1951), p. 72. The floggings, an attempt to shake patients out of their delusions, have been compared to modern electric-shock therapy and, as such, were not as "inhumane" as might first appear. The physical condition of these hospitals was, however, awful.

2. *Ibid.* "John's strange form of penance was explained to the directors of the hospital by Father John of Ávila. They immediately discontinued

their treatment, which, perhaps they looked upon as being responsible for his cure.''

3. *Ibid.*, p. 82.
4. *Ibid.*, p. 143.
5. Another such story has John of God taking the corpse of a poor man and laying it on the steps of a wealthy noble's residence, refusing to remove the body until the noble came up with the money to give the man a decent burial. *Ibid.*, p. 151.
6. Norbert McMahon, *The Story of the Hospitallers of St. John of God* (Westminster, Md.: The Newman Press, 1959), p. 11.
7. *Ibid.*, p. 12.
8. *Ibid.*, p. 23. An inspiring story survives concerning two of the earliest adherents. A man, hardened by hatred for the supposed killer of his brother, arrived in Granada. John accosted him in the streets and made such a profound impression on him that the two proceeded to the jail and obtained the release of the accused man. Both men joined John as fervent servants of the poor, and so remained until their deaths.
9. *Ibid.*, p. 69.
10. McMahon, *St. John of God*, p. 134.
11. Brother Benignus Callan to author, June 12, 1986.
12. Mary Purcell, *A Time for Sowing: The History of St. John of God Brothers in Ireland 1879-1979* (Dublin: Allograph Design, 1980), p. 25. The name comes from Stig Lorcan, a Gaelic hero whose tomb was discovered nearby. The mental hospital was established after a short fling at taking in gentleman boarders. On one occasion, a horse was raffled off to raise funds. *Ibid.*, p. 29.
13. *Ibid.*
14. *Ibid.*, p. 40.
15. *Ibid.*, p. 44.
16. *Ibid.*, p. 48.
17. *Ibid.*
18. Quoted in Eddie Doherty, *Matt Talbot* (Milwaukee: Bruce Publishing Co., 1953), p. 76.
19. *Ibid.*
20. *Ibid.*
21. *Ibid.*, p. 78.
22. An American historian presents a less idealized picture of Matt Talbot: "Talbot was a Dublin alcoholic who, in middle life, suddenly turned from alcohol to religion. He would arise every morning at 2 A.M. and pray on his knees until 4:30 in his room, then at 5:00 go to church for Mass. He would next go to his job at 6:00 A.M. At noon hour, instead of taking lunch, he would spend most of his time in private prayer. At 5:30 in the afternoon, he again went to church. . . . He spent the evening in prayer and spiritual reading up to his bedtime, 10:30. Each Sunday he spent a minimum of eight consecutive hours on his knees in prayer, rising only to receive communion. . . . Men like Talbot whose histories

belong in the pages of textbooks on abnormal psychology are rare, but the neurotic use of religion in Ireland is far from uncommon." Donald Harman Akenson, *The United States and Ireland* (Cambridge, Mass.: Harvard University Press, 1973), p. 164.

23. Conscription was finally extended to Ireland in 1918. It aroused such a storm of protest that voluntary recruitment was substituted. In this struggle, the Irish Catholic bishops took a leading role and agreed that conscription should be resisted by every means "consonant with the law of God." MacDonaugh, *op. cit.*, p.. 172ff.

24. McCaffrey, *op. cit.*, p. 134.

25. Before the war, the predominant Irish party had been John Redmond's party. It had been prepared to recommend that Irish voters accept home rule. The effect of the war was to radicalize Irish demands. Shiela Lawlor, *Britain and Ireland 1914-1923* (Totowa, N.J.: Barnes & Noble Books, 1983), p. 1.

26. O'Broin, *op. cit.*, p. 25ff.

27. *Ibid.*, p. 69.

28. *Ibid.*, p. 90.

29. *Ibid.*, p. 94.

30. Alan J. Ward, *The Easter Rising: Revolution and Irish Nationalism* (Arlington Heights, Ill.: AHM Publishing Corp., 1980), p. 7.

31. O'Broin, *op. cit.*, p. 110.

32. The middle class regarded the Easter Rebellion with a certain horror. Gas supplies were cut off, banks and shops were closed. Public transport and postal services ceased. The inner city was the locus of some of the worse slums in Europe, and the slum poor went on a looting spree. Ward, *op. cit.*, p. 14.

33. The total number of martyrs was small compared to the daily casualties in the Great War, but for the Irish people it was as if they had watched a "stream of blood coming from beneath a closed door." As a result of the intercession by prominent Irish political figures, ninety-seven of the death sentences were commuted to penal servitude. O'Broin, *op. cit.*, p. 125.

34. Interview with Brother Mathias, August 8, 1984.

35. *Ibid.*

36. *Ibid.*

37. Brother Benignus Callan, O.H., "The Life of Outstanding Hospitaller Brothers of St. John of God" (unpublished manuscript, 1972), p. 183. ALBGS.

38. *Ibid.*

39. *Ibid.*, p. 185.

40. Brother Benignus Callan to author, June 12, 1986.

41. Brother Finbarr Murphy to author, June 12, 1986.

42. Callan, *op. cit.*, p. 187.

43. Interview with Brother Mathias, August 8, 1984.

44. Purcell, *op. cit.*, p. 37.

45. Interview with Brother Mathias, August 8, 1984.

46. *Ibid.*

47. *Ibid.*

48. *Ibid.*

49. As it turned out, the Irish-English delegation became a separate province in 1934. Purcell, *op. cit.*, pp. 54-55.

50. Interview with Brother Mathias, August 8, 1984.

51. *Ibid.*

Chapter Three

1. Interview with Brother Mathias, September 8, 1984.

2. Quoted in Jack A. Blyth, *The Canadian Social Inheritance* (Toronto: Copp Clark Publishing Co., 1972), p. 149.

3. *Ibid.*, p. 228. Ironically, at the same time in the U.S., Henry Ford was backing the Anti-Saloon League!

4. *Ibid.*, p. 159.

5. W.E. Mann, "The Social System of a Slum: The Lower Ward, Toronto," in S.D. Clark, ed., *Urbanism and the Changing Canadian Society* (Toronto: University of Toronto Press, 1961), p. 42.

6. McMahon, *Hospitaller Brothers of St. John of God*, p. 150.

7. *Ibid.* Brother Mathias says Oliver Asselin was also a stockbroker.

8. *Ibid.* The titular bishop of Montreal was still living, but negotiations were carried out principally by the coadjutor of the diocese.

9. Interview with Brother Mathias, July 28, 1985.

10. Robert Cortail to Arthur Gagnon, September 20, 1926. Archives, Hospitaller Order of St. John of God, Montreal. (From hereon, this reference will appear as ASJGM.)

11. King's Hospital in Louisbourg was built by the order in 1725. It was destroyed during the siege of Cape Breton in 1758. The Brothers were participants in the joint dedication in 1939 of three monuments to commemorate the heroic defenders during that siege. Brothers Aubert and Sylvius were present during a day of raw weather, August 10, 1939. The ruins of the hospital had fallen into the foundations. It had been an imposing structure and had once covered a whole city block, with accommodations for one hundred four beds in its main wards. Twelve Brothers perished or disappeared during the siege of Louisbourg. Standing on that windy site, Brother Aubert made a short speech in which he noted that "many more would be present, only the distance being an obstacle, but I know they are here in heart and spirit, especially our most Reverend Father General, who brings to you today his message of thanks, as also his delegate in Canada, Reverend Father Provincial Mathias, who for many years has worked ceaselessly to realize what we are accomplishing today." Albert Almon, *Rochefort Point: A Silent City in Louisbourg* (Glace Bay, Cape Breton, N.S.: MacDonald Printers, 1940), pp. 14, 15, 18, 23.

12. Interview with Brother Mathias, September 6, 1984. Brother Laurent would put little pieces of leather inside his shoes to make himself appear taller than he actually was.

13. Hermas Bastien, *L'Ordre Hospitalier de Saint-Juan-de-Dieu au Canada* (Montreal: Therien Frères Limitée, 1947), p. 89. Bastien tactfully avoids mentioning that no one was there to meet them.

14. Brothers Mathias, Laurent, and Hilary to the superior general, April 18, 1927. ASJGM.

15. McMahon, *op. cit.*

16. "The Flame of Charity," official organ of the Brothers of St. John of God, American province, Easter, 1949. ALBGS.

17. Minutes of the meeting of the administrative committee, April 24, 1927. ASJGM.

18. Bastien, *op. cit.*, p. 91.

19. *Ibid.*, p. 92.

20. *Ibid.*, p. 91.

21. *Ibid.*, p. 104.

22. *Ibid.*

23. Purcell, *op. cit.*, p. 67.

24. Interview with Brother Mathias, September 6, 1984.

25. *Ibid.*

26. Mann, *op. cit.*, p. 46.

27. Interview with Brother Mathias, September 8, 1984. He had other problems with Brother Laurent. Once, Mathias wrote to Bishop Kelly of Australia, "because he had an Irish name," and suggested that some Brothers could go to his diocese from Canada. Bishop Kelly wrote back, but Brother Laurent intercepted the letter. The second letter from the bishop contained $600 to finance travel expenses for the two expected Brothers. Laurent was irate. Mathias was told to return the money immediately and to apologize for his premature overtures to the Australian prelate.

28. Interview with Brother Mathias, September 8, 1984.

29. The municipal refuge had been established by a Norwegian named Muerling who left money to take care of men on the road. Interview with Brother Mathias, November 26, 1984.

30. *Ibid.* "I went to see the Superintendent and he was mad, not only because of me but because of the other complaints he had gotten. He asked me to take over a sandwich operation that was phasing out called the House of Ignace Bourget, after the first Archbishop of Montreal. So I wrote to the Vicar General and he gave me permission and I took it over. . . . Charity conquered!"

31. Bastien, *op. cit.*, p. 91.

32. *Ibid.*, p. 105.

33. *Ibid.*, p. 118.

34. McMahon, *op. cit.*, p. 158.

35. Interview with Brother Mathias, November 26, 1984.

36. *Ibid.*
37. Interview with Brother Mathias, September 21, 1984.
38. Bastien, *op. cit.*, p. 122.
39. *Ibid.*, p. 110. A benefactor gave the Brothers the use of his private beach for recreation, but their old truck broke down during renovation of the refuge and they had to confine themselves to walking the streets of the city. *Ibid.*, p. 127.
40. Interview with Brother Mathias, September 8, 1984. In 1930, other Irish Hospitallers were returning to Stillorgan, but not Brother Mathias. "Deep in conference with an enlarged Committee and Government officials, he was discussing not only a new hospital and novitiate, but also two new refuges to accommodate 600 men." Purcell, *op. cit.*, p. 68.
41. Interview with Brother Mathias, September 15, 1984.
42. Bastien, *op. cit.*, p. 104.
43. *Ibid.*, p. 105.
44. *Ibid.*, p. 118.
45. *Ibid.*
46. *Ibid.*, p. 131.
47. *Ibid.*, p. 161.
48. *Ibid.*, p. 148.
49. Interview with Brother Mathias, November 26, 1984.
50. Interview with Brother Mathias, September 8, 1984.
51. *Ibid.*
52. *Ibid.*
53. During the Spanish Civil War, excesses occurred on both sides of the struggle, but it was largely at the hands of the Republicans and their allies that members of the religious orders in Spain suffered. Brother Mathias and Father Trudeau composed a play in 1936 called "The Spanish March," which the juniors staged, and which was performed at several parish churches in Montreal before enthusiastic audiences. Briefly, the play concerns itself with one of the hospitals in Spain operated by the Brothers of St. John of God. One day, a man brings in his young son. On the same day, a young doctor comes to ask if he could join the order. The Brothers try to send the doctor to the Jesuits, but he persists, and so a Brother is instructed to show him around. He then sees the boy, whose father has by this time left him, and who is miserable. The doctor says, "He needs a transfusion, and I will give the blood." Ultimately, he is accepted into the order and takes first vows, but only after many hardships. His father dies and leaves him a fortune. His sister arrives to harangue him and to try to prevent him from making his final profession. She tells him he is "stupid," and that he could go to South America and become prominent. He continues to tend the sick who surround him. His final profession day arrives. He falls to his knees. The hymn "Come, Holy Ghost" is heard in the background. He becomes Brother John. The Civil War breaks out shortly thereafter, and the father of the little boy who had been brought to the hospital years earlier,

turns out to be the chief of the communists. Two other communists arrive at the hospital one morning and threaten the Brothers. The chief arrives and sees Brother John and the others who were so kind to him and his son. He tries to delay the shootings. In the chaos that ensues, shots are fired outside the window and they hit Brother John, who dies in the arms of the superior and of the communist father — the latter holding the Brother's head so it does not touch the floor. He asks God to pardon them. In reality, the order lost ninety-nine Brothers during the Civil War. As moving as this drama was, during one rehearsal, Brother Mathias, who was simulating the gunshots with a match and a hammer, struck too soon. The scene became a comedy. He apologized profusely but remembers that Father Trudeau "wanted to kill me." From an interview with Brother Mathias, September 15, 1984.

54. Address of Brother Mathias, March 20, 1935. ASJGM.
55. Interview with Brother Mathias, September 8, 1984.
56. Interview with Brother Mathias, October 15, 1984.
57. Brother Mathias to Fathers and Brothers, April 27, 1939. ASJGM.
58. In a letter he wrote to Archbishop Edwin Byrne of New Mexico, Brother Mathias gave his reason for leaving Montreal as being the fact that the "French Canadians wanted to have the Canadian Province that I established controlled by themselves." Letter from Brother Mathias to Archbishop Byrne, January 19, 1951. ALBGS.
59. Interview with Brother Mathias, September 8, 1984.
60. Bastien, *op. cit.*, p. 165.

Chapter Four

1. "Draft History of the American Province." Archives, Hospitaller Order of St. John of God, Ojai. (From hereon, this reference will appear as ASJGO.)
2. Brother Andrew Aucoin, "History." ASJGO.
3. *Ibid.*
4. Interview with Brother Hugo Stippler, March 25, 1986.
5. *Ibid.*
6. *Ibid.*
7. The Canadian Brothers did not speak English and there was little dialogue. This cleavage between the two groups was the main reason why Brother Mathias later wrote to the Irish province to get Irish Brothers to come to America.
8. Brother Andrew, "History." ASJGO.
9. John J. Barrett to Brother Mathias, December 27, 1940. ASJGO.
10. Interview with Cardinal Timothy Manning, March 26, 1986.
11. Bishop John Cantwell to Diego Palacios, September 22, 1930. Archives, Archdiocese of Los Angeles. (From hereon, this reference will appear as AALA.)
12. Bishop Cantwell's secretary to Diego Palacios, May 18, 1931. AALA.

13. Brother Mathias to Archbishop Cantwell, December 24, 1940. AALA.
14. *Ibid.*
15. Thomas J. O'Dwyer to Brother Mathias, January 4, 1941. ASJGO.
16. Archbishop Cantwell to Brother Mathias, January 21, 1941. ASJGO.
17. Interview with Brother Mathias, September 8, 1984.
18. Interview with James Barrett, March 22, 1986. His father, John Barrett, bought Brother Mathias a new pair of black shoes at Sears, Roebuck & Co., where he was employed, but within the week, Brother Mathias had given them away to "a poor feller who needed them more than I did."
19. Interview with Brother Mathias, September 8, 1984.
20. Interview with Cardinal Manning, March 26, 1986.
21. Interview with Brother Mathias, September 8, 1984.
22. *Ibid.*
23. *Ibid.*
24. *Ibid.*
25. *Ibid.*
26. Interview with Brother Andrew Aucoin, March 26, 1986.
27. Interview with Brother Mathias, September 8, 1984.
28. Brother Mathias to Auxiliary Bishop Joseph T. McGucken, February 19, 1943. AALA.
29. *The Tidings*, July 16, 1943, *Tidings* Archives.
30. *The Tidings*, July 2, 1943, *Tidings* Archives.
31. *The Tidings*, June 4, 1943, *Tidings* Archives.
32. Annual report, 1943, ASJGO.
33. Brother Andrew, "History." ASJGO.
34. *Ibid.*
35. Interview with Daniel Donohue, March 26, 1986.
36. *Ibid.*
37. *Ibid.*
38. Bishop McGucken to Raymond O'Flaherty, September 4, 1941. AALA.
39. Chancellory to Brother Mathias, June 29, 1943. Archbishop Cantwell signed the check on July 8, 1943. AALA.
40. Thomas O'Dwyer to Archbishop Cantwell, June 21, 1943. AALA.
41. Interview with Cardinal Manning, March 26, 1986.
42. Interview with Daniel Donohue, March 26, 1986.
43. Bishop McGucken to Brother Mathias, January 10, 1944, and Brother Mathias to Bishop McGucken, n.d. (March or April, 1944).
44. Brother Mathias to Archbishop Cantwell, August 10, 1943. AALA.
45. Archbishop Cantwell to Brother Mathias, April 27, 1942. AALA.
46. Robert Brennan to Brother Mathias, March 4, 1943. AALA.
47. Bishop McGucken to Brother Mathias, November 21, 1941. AALA.
48. *The Tidings*, July 9, 1943. *Tidings* Archives.
49. Earl J. Currivan in *St. Anthony's Messenger*, January 19, 1944.
50. *Ibid.*
51. Interview with Brother Mathias and Siobhan, Albuquerque, 1982. In the possession of Brother Thomas, B.G.S.

52. *Ibid.* When the man died, Brother Mathias sent a note to his New Jersey address. He received a reply from his daughter, who sent a photo of her five children, and asked that he not acknowledge her letter. She had told them her father had died five years before.
53. Brother Mathias to Bishop McGucken, April 19, 1944. AALA.
54. Brother Mathias to Bishop McGucken, May 14, 1944. AALA.
55. Brother Mathias to Bishop McGucken, August 12, 1944. AALA.
56. Bishop McGucken to Brother Mathias, March 1, 1945. AALA.
57. Brother Mathias to Archbishop Cantwell, March 4, 1945. AALA.
58. Interview with James Barrett, March 22, 1986.
59. Interview with Brother Patrick Corr, March 25, 1986.
60. "Program for the First Annual Garden Party." ASJGO.
61. *The Flame of Charity*, September, 1944, Vol. 1, No. 2.
62. Ed Sweeny to Brother Mathias, January 25, 1945.
63. Interview with Brother Mathias, October 14, 1984.
64. *Ibid.*
65. Archbishop Cantwell to Brother Mathias, August 18, 1945. AALA.
66. Purcell, *op. cit.*, p. 78.
67. Interview with Cardinal Manning, March 26, 1986.
68. Bishop McGucken to Brother Mathias, May 7, 1945. AALA.
69. Raymond O'Flaherty to Bishop McGucken, June 26, 1945. AALA.
70. Brother Mathias to Archbishop Cantwell, October 15, 1945. AALA.
71. Monsignor Manning to Brother Mathias, October 22, 1945, AALA.
72. Archbishop Cantwell to Brother Patrick Murphy, November 26, 1945. As fate would have it, the Brother Patrick who was sent to Los Angeles was not Brother Patrick Murphy, but Brother Patrick Corr, sent by the Irish provincial, Brother Norbert McMahon, in 1946.
73. Brother Mathias to Archbishop Cantwell, January 5, 1946. AALA.
74. Interview with Brother Mathias, April 12, 1986.
75. Interview with Brother Hugo Stippler, March 25, 1986.
76. Interview with Brother Andrew Aucoin, March 26, 1986.
77. Interview with Brother Oliver McGivern, March 26, 1986.
78. *Ibid.*
79. Interview with Brother Hugo Stippler, March 25, 1986.
80. Interview with Cardinal Manning, March 26, 1986.
81. Interview with Daniel Donohue, March 26, 1986.

·Chapter Five

1. Robert A. Woods, ed., *The City Wilderness: A Settlement Study by Residents and Associates of the South End House* (New York: Garrett Press, Inc., 1970; reprint of the 1898 edition), p. 201.
2. *Ibid.*, p. 213.
3. *Ibid.*, p. 211.
4. *Ibid.*, p. 217.
5. Carl Seaburg, *Boston Observed* (Boston: Beacon Press, 1971), p. 246.

6. George F. Weston, Jr., *Boston Ways*, updated by Charlotte Cecil Raymond (Boston: Beacon Press, 1972), p. 206.
7. *Ibid.*, pp. 46, 284.
8. *Ibid.*, p. 234.
9. *Ibid.*, p. 186. When the area for the Herald-Traveler Building was razed in 1954, six corpses were found in the abandoned buildings, "obviously derelicts." *Ibid.*, p. 275.
10. Henry Warner Bowden, "Richard James Cushing," *Dictionary of Religious Biography* (Westport, Conn.: Greenwood Press, 1977), p. 117.
11. Joseph Dever, *Cushing of Boston: A Candid Portrait* (Boston: Bruce Humphries, 1965), p. 107.
12. John H. Fenton, "Boston's Prince of the Church," in Howard M. Jones and Bessie Z. Jones, eds., *The Many Voices of Boston* (Boston: Little, Brown & Co., 1975), p. 431.
13. Dever, *op. cit.*, p. 97.
14. *Ibid.*, pp. 116-117, also 110.
15. *Ibid.*, p. 118.
16. John Fenton, *Salt of the Earth: An Informal Profile of Richard Cardinal Cushing* (New York: Coward, McCann, Inc., 1965), p. 54.
17. Dever, *op. cit.*, p. 96.
18. *Ibid.*, p. 97.
19. Letter of Brother Mathias to Most Reverend Richard Cushing, archbishop of Boston, March 3, 1945. Archives, Archdiocese of Boston. (From hereon, this reference will appear as AAB.)
20. *Ibid.*
21. Letter of Brother Mathias to Reverend John Wright, July 21, 1945. AAB.
22. Letter of Reverend John Wright to Brother Mathias, July 26, 1945. AAB.
23. *Ibid.*
24. *Ibid.*
25. Letter of Brother Mathias to Right Reverend John Wright, August 2, 1945. AAB.
26. Letter of Brother Mathias to Right Reverend Monsignor John Wright, August 9, 1945. AAB.
27. Letter of Brother Mathias to Right Reverend Monsignor John Wright, September 8, 1945. AAB.
28. *Boston Daily Globe*, February 5, 1952.
29. McMahon, *The Story of the Hospitallers of St. John of God*, p. 169.
30. Brother Vincent, "History of St. John of God" (unpublished manuscript), p. 4.
31. "The Flame of Charity." The first American to join the order in the United States was Daniel Donohue, who took the name of Brother Kevin. As of 1949, when Brother Mathias returned to Ireland, there were 53 Brothers of St. John of God in the United States. Of these, 11 had made solemn vows, 15 had made simple vows, 1 was an oblate, 17 were novices, and 9 were postulants.
32. Brother Vincent, *op. cit.*

33. Interview with Brother Mathias, September 8, 1984.
34. *Ibid.*
35. *Ibid.*
36. *Ibid.*
37. *Ibid.*
38. *Ibid.*
39. *The Pilot*, August 24, 1946.
40. Brother Vincent, *op. cit.*
41. *Ibid.*
42. *The Pilot*, December 28, 1946.
43. Interview with Brother Mathias, October 28, 1984.
44. Brother Vincent, *op. cit.*
45. Interview with Brother Mathias, October 28, 1984.
46. *Ibid.*
47. *The Pilot*, November 23, 1946. The article went on to inform readers, inaccurately, that Brother Mathias had been born in France!
48. Interview with Brother Mathias, October 28, 1984.
49. *The Pilot*, January 5, 1947.
50. *Ibid*; also issue of January 12, 1947. A new community center was also dedicated for the North End of Boston, called the Christopher Columbus Center.
51. *The Pilot*, March 1, 1947.
52. *Ibid.*
53. On January 28, 1947, the first indictment was handed down against an alleged communist in the State Department.
54. *The Pilot*, July 18 through August 8, 1947.
55. *Ibid.*, August 22, 1947.
56. *Ibid.*, September 19, 1947.
57. *Ibid.*, December 26, 1947. It was also called the Catholic Men's Home.
58. Interview with Brother Mathias, October 14, 1984.
59. *Ibid.*
60. *Ibid.*
61. Letter of Brother Mathias to Most Reverend Richard Cushing, February 7, 1948. AAB.
62. Letter of Brother Mathias to Most Reverend Richard J. Cushing, July 27, 1948. AAB.
63. *Ibid.*
64. *Ibid.*
65. McMahon, *op. cit.*, p. 171.
66. Purcell, *op. cit.*, p. 79.
67. Interview with Brother Mathias, April 13, 1986.
68. Brother Vincent, *op. cit.*, p. 4.
69. Interview with Brother Mathias, October 14, 1984.
70. Purcell, *op. cit.*
71. Interview with Brother Mathias, October 14, 1984.
72. *The Pilot*, March 5, 1949.

73. *Ibid.*, March 16, 1949.
74. *Ibid.*
75. *Ibid.*, July 9, 1949.
76. *Ibid.*, July 16, 1949.
77. The letter has survived. It reads, "In the name of holy obedience and in virtue of our authority, we order you to return as soon as possible to the province of the Immaculate Conception in Ireland, where you will . . . [remain] at the disposition of the Father Provincial of the Province. We ask God to bless and assist you." Ephrem Blandeau to Brother Mathias, June 27, 1949. ALBGS. The quote as it appears in the text is how Brother Mathias recalls it.
78. Letter from Archbishop Cushing to Brother Mathias, July 16, 1949. ALBGS. Unfortunately, the archival copy does not have Brother Norbert's letter attached to it.
79. Letter from Archbishop Cushing to Brother Mathias, September 2, 1949. ALBGS.
80. *The Pilot*, September 3, 1949.
81. *Ibid.*, September 10, 1949.
82. *Ibid.*
83. *Ibid.*, September 17, 1949.
84. *Ibid.*
85. *Ibid.*
86. Letter from Archbishop Cushing to Brother Mathias, February 12, 1951. ALBGS.
87. Letter from Archbishop Cushing to Brother Mathias, August 25, 1951. ALBGS.
88. Letter from Archbishop Cushing to Brother Mathias, April 3,1952. ALBGS.
89. Letter from Brother Mathias to Archbishop Cushing, September 1, 1967. ALBGS.
90. Letter from a Monsignor O'Brien to Brother Mathias, copy in ALBGS, n.d. This is attached to the preceding item.
91. *Ibid.*

(Author's note: Archbishop Cushing destroyed many of his papers before his death, according to a letter, August 21, 1985, from the current archivist, James M. O'Toole, to the author. What has been quoted here represents about everything that currently exists on the subject.)

Chapter Six

1. McMahon, *St. John of God*, p. 134.
2. Purcell, *op. cit.*, p. 79.
3. Interview with Brother Mathias, September 13, 1984.
4. *Ibid.*
5. Interview with Brother Mathias and Brother Raphael, n.d. ALBGS.

6. Interview with Brother Mathias not taped.
7. Letter of Brother Mathias to Monsignor Phaneuf, March 2, 1952. ALBGS. This remarkable letter, which is three pages long, is the most comprehensive account of the exile in Ireland from Brother Mathias's viewpoint.
8. Letter from Ephrem Blandeau to Brother Mathias, October 21, 1949. ALBGS.
9. *Ibid.*
10. Letter from Ephrem Blandeau to Brother Mathias, November 9, 1949. ALBGS.
11. Interview with Brother Mathias not taped.
12. Letter from Ephrem Blandeau to Brother Mathias, January 25, 1950. ALBGS.
13. Letter from Ephrem Blandeau to Brother Mathias, February 11, 1950. ALBGS.
14. Interview with Brother Mathias, September 13, 1984.
15. *Ibid.*
16. *Ibid.*
17. *Ibid.*
18. Letter from Ephrem Blandeau to Brother Mathias, June 24, 1950. ALBGS.
19. Interview with Brother Mathias, October 5, 1985.
20. Letter from Ephrem Blandeau to Brother Mathias, August 5, 1950. ALBGS.
21. Letter from Ephrem Blandeau to Brother Mathias, August 27, 1950. ALBGS.
22. Letter from Ephrem Blandeau to Brother Mathias, November 26, 1950. ALBGS.
23. Interview with Brother Mathias, October 14, 1984.
24. *Ibid.* It was a certain Father Williams who told him. Father Williams had come to Hammond Hall with only one lung, but he had a remarkable capacity in the remaining one. Brother Mathias claims that "if he'd had two, you could have heard him in Gibraltar!"
25. Interview with Brother Mathias, September 13, 1984.
26. Interview with Brother Mathias, September 15, 1985.
27. *Ibid.*

Chapter Seven

1. John Tracy Ellis, *American Catholicism* (Chicago: University of Chicago Press, 1969), p. 2.
2. Quoted in *ibid.*, p. 160.
3. *Ibid.*, p. 151.
4. *Ibid.*, p. 160.
5. Willa Cather, *Death Comes for the Archbishop* (New York: Vintage Books, 1927 and 1971), p. 5.

6. Aragón, de, Ray John, *Padre Martínez and Bishop Lamy* (Las Vegas: Pan-American Publishing Co., 1978), pp. 58, 70.
7. Chávez, Fray Angelico, *But Time and Chance: The Story of Padre Martínez of Taos, 1793-1867* (Santa Fe: Sunstone Press, 1981), p. 95.
8. George Sanchez, *Forgotten People* (Albuquerque: University of New Mexico Press, 1940), p. 7.
9. *Ibid.*, p. 11.
10. Ruth K. Barber and Edith J. Agnew, *Sowers Went Forth* (Menaul Historical Library of the Southwest, 1981).
11. T.D. Allen, *Not Ordered by Men* (Santa Fe: The Rydal Press, 1967), p. 5.
12. Henry Heitz, "Historical Notes on St. Vincent de Paul's Parish, 1874-1924" (Silver City, N.M.: Citizen Printers, 1924), p. 6.
13. *Ibid.*, p. 8.
14. *Ibid.*, p. 21.
15. "Seventh Synod of the Archdiocese of Santa Fe, celebrated on December 2, 1958 by His Excellency the Most Reverend Edwin Vincent Byrne D.D." (Albuquerque: Moulton Printers, 1958), p. 6.
16. *Ibid.*, p. 10.
17. *Ibid.*, p. 17.
18. *Ibid.*, p. 18.
19. *Ibid.*, p. 79.
20. Interview with Brother Mathias, September 15, 1985.
21. *Ibid.*
22. *Ibid.*
23. Interview with Brother Mathias, October 14, 1985.
24. *Ibid.*
25. *Ibid.*
26. Interview with Brother Mathias, September 13, 1984.
27. Interview with Brother Mathias, October 14, 1985.
28. *Ibid.*
29. *Ibid.*
30. Interview with Brother Mathias, September 14, 1985.
31. *Ibid.*
32. *Ibid.*
33. *Ibid.*
34. *Ibid.*
35. *Ibid.*
36. *Ibid.*
37. Interview with Brother Mathias, September 13, 1984.
38. Interview with Brother Mathias and Brother Thomas, 1974.
39. *Ibid.*
40. Brother Mathias to Archbishop Byrne, December 22, 1950. ALBGS.
41. *Ibid.*
42. *Ibid.*
43. *Ibid.*

44. Brother Michael Carlyle, B.G.S., has noted that Brother Mathias finds it difficult to "have someone over him." Interview with Brother Michael Carlyle, June 19, 1985.
45. Archbishop Byrne to Rev. Matthew Locks, assistant chancellor of Honolulu, quoted in Brother Michael Carlyle, "Soldiers of Charity," p. 6., n.d. ALBGS.
46. Brother Michael Carlyle, *op. cit.*
47. Interview with Brother Mathias, September 13, 1984.
48. Brother Michael Carlyle, *op. cit.*
49. Archbishop Byrne to Brother Mathias, July 7, 1951.
50. Interview with Brother Mathias, October 14, 1985.
51. Brother Mathias to Archbishop Byrne, January 4, 1951.
52. Archbishop Byrne to Brother Mathias, January 11, 1951. ALBGS.
53. *Albuquerque Journal*, January 19, 1951.
54. Interview with Brother Mathias, October 14, 1985.
55. Brother Mathias to Archbishop Byrne, February 8, 1951. ALBGS.
56. Interview with Brother Mathias and Brother Thomas, 1974.
57. Interview with Brother Mathias, September 13, 1984.
58. *Ibid.*
59. Brother Mathias to Archbishop Byrne, April 4, 1951. ALBGS.
60. Archbishop Byrne to Brother Mathias, March 20, 1951. ALBGS.
61. Brother Mathias to Mother Theodora, March 20, 1951. ALBGS.
62. Brother Mathias to Archbishop Byrne, February 8,1951. ALBGS.
63. *Ibid.*
64. Archbishop Byrne to Brother Mathias, February 20, 1951. ALBGS.
65. Archbishop Byrne to Brother Mathias, April 30, 1951. ALBGS.
66. *Ibid.*
67. Archbishop Byrne to Brother Mathias, May 19, 1951. ALBGS.
68. Brother Mathias to Archbishop Byrne, February 18, 1951. ALBGS.
69. Brother Mathias to Archbishop Byrne, April 29, 1951. ALBGS.
70. *Ibid.*
71. Brother Mathias to Archbishop Byrne, April 9, 1951. ALBGS.
72. Brother Mathias to Archbishop Byrne, September 25, 1951. ALBGS.
73. Brother Mathias to Archbishop Byrne, August 30, 1951. ALBGS.
74. *Ibid.*
75. Brother Mathias to Archbishop Byrne, July 15, 1951. ALBGS.
76. Brother Mathias to Archbishop Byrne, May 18, 1951. ALBGS.
77. Interview with Brother Mathias, September 15, 1985.
78. Brother Mathias to Archbishop Byrne, May 23, 1951. ALBGS.
79. Archbishop Byrne to Brother Mathias, September 5, 1951. ALBGS.
80. Brother Mathias to Archbishop Byrne, September 6, 1951. ALBGS.
81. Brother Mathias to Archbishop Byrne, August 18, 1951. ALBGS.
82. Brother Joseph Duffy to Archbishop Byrne, August 23, 1951. ALBGS.
83. Brother Mathias to Archbishop Byrne, June 14, 1951. ALBGS.
84. Archbishop Byrne to Brother Mathias, June 15, 1951. ALBGS.
85. Brother Mathias to Archbishop Byrne, July 15, 1951. ALBGS.

86. Archbishop Byrne to Brother Mathias, September 21, 1951. ALBGS.

87. *Ibid.*

88. Interview with Brother Mathias, September 13, 1984.

89. *Ibid.*

90. *Ibid.*

91. *Ibid.*

92. Neil Addington, "Brothers of the Good Shepherd," *The Shepherd's Call*, Vol. 1, No. 2, December, 1951.

93. *Ibid.*

94. *Ibid.*

95. *Ibid.*

96. Interview with Aldo Vaio, January 25, 1986.

97. *Ibid.*

98. *Ibid.*

99. *Ibid.*

100. *Ibid.*

101. *Ibid.*

102. Brother Mathias to Archbishop Byrne, January 11, 1952. Archives, Archdiocese of Santa Fe. (From hereon, this reference will appear as AASF.)

103. Brother Mathias to Archbishop Byrne, January 14, 1952. AASF.

104. *Albuquerque Journal*, February 4, 1952.

105. *The Shepherd's Call*, Vol. 1, No. 2, December, 1951.

106. *Ibid.*

107. *Ibid.*

108. Archbishop Byrne to Brother Mathias, February 11, 1952. AASF.

Chapter Eight

1. Interview with Brother Mathias, September 30, 1984.

2. *Ibid.*

3. *Albuquerque Journal*, May 12, 1952.

4. *Ibid.*

5. Brother Mathias to Archbishop Byrne, February 19, 1952. ALBGS.

6. Brother Mathias to Archbishop Byrne, February 27, 1952. ALBGS.

7. Archbishop Byrne to Brother Mathias, March 1, 1952. ALBGS. Brother Mathias wrote back on March 5, 1952, that "the Helpers of the Holy Souls do not teach." ALBGS.

8. *Albuquerque Journal*, July 20, 1952.

9. *Ibid.*

10. *Albuquerque Journal*, September 10, 1952.

11. *Ibid.* There was a testimonial dinner at the Hilton Hotel on September 28 for all those who had participated.

12. Archbishop Byrne to Brother Mathias, March 13, 1952. ALBGS.

13. Archbishop Byrne to Brother Mathias, March 5, 1952. ALBGS.

14. Brother Mathias to Archbishop Byrne, March 9, 1952. ALBGS.

15. Brother Mathias to Archbishop Byrne, June 10, 1952. ALBGS.
16. Brother Mathias to Archbishop Byrne, July 11, 1952. AASF.
17. Brother Mathias to Archbishop Byrne, August 4, 1952. AASF.
18. *Ibid.*
19. Archbishop Byrne to Brother Mathias, October 8, 1952. AASF.
20. Brother Mathias to Archbishop Byrne, October 7, 1952. AASF.
21. *Ibid.*
22. Brother Mathias to Archbishop Byrne, November 28, 1952. AASF.
23. Registration book — June 22, 1952, to March 20, 1953. ALBGS.
24. Interview with Brother Mathias, September 30, 1984.
25. *Ibid.*
26. *Ibid.*
27. *Ibid.*
28. *Ibid.*
29. *Ibid.*
30. *Ibid.*
31. Brother Mathias to Archbishop Byrne, March 13, 1953. AASF.
32. Brother Mathias to Archbishop Byrne, July 10, 1953. AASF.
33. Brother Mathias to Archbishop Byrne, August 27, 1953. AASF.
34. Brother Mathias to Archbishop Byrne, May 31, 1953. AASF.
35. Brother Mathias to Archbishop Byrne, March 7, 1954. AASF.
36. Archbishop Byrne to Brother Mathias, March 17, 1954. AASF.
37. Brother Mathias to Archbishop Byrne, March 14, 1954. AASF.
38. Brother Patrick to Archbishop Byrne, July 6, 1954. AASF.
39. Brother Mathias to Archbishop Byrne, March 26, 1954. AASF.
40. *Ibid.* Father Hebert had been giving "Weekend with God" retreats at Villa Maria in Alameda where the weekend lasted three days, during which meditation, spiritual reading, and study of the liturgy were pursued "in complete silence."
41. Brother Mathias to Archbishop Byrne, July 16, 1954. AASF.
42. Brother Mathias to Archbishop Byrne, August 27, 1953. AASF.
43. Father Pochily to Archbishop Byrne, December 18, 1954. AASF.
44. *Ibid.*
45. Brother Mathias to Archbishop Byrne, January 20, 1955. AASF.
46. *Ibid.*
47. *The Shepherd's Call*, November, 1953. ALBGS.
48. Brother Mathias to Archbishop Byrne, May 14, 1954. AASF.
49. Annual Report of the Little Brothers of the Good Shepherd, 1954. ALBGS.
50. Brother Mathias to Archbishop Byrne, June 12, 1955. AASF.
51. *Ibid.*
52. Archbishop Byrne to Brother Mathias, July 21, 1955. AASF.
53. The subject of the secular institute and the other forms of organization that the Little Brothers used is treated in a separate chapter.
54. Archbishop Byrne to Brother Mathias, March 17, 1954. AASF.
55. *Ibid.*

56. *Ibid.*

57. Archbishop Byrne to Brother Mathias, June 6, 1955. AASF.

58. Archbishop Byrne to Brother Mathias, October 18, 1955. AASF.

59. *The Shepherd's Call*, January, 1955. ALBGS.

60. *Ibid.*

61. *Ibid.*

62. *Ibid.*

63. *The Shepherd's Call*, Vol. 1, No. 3, n.d. ALBGS.

64. *Ibid.*

65. *The Shepherd's Call*, June, 1956. ALBGS.

66. Father Gerald Fitzgerald to Archbishop Byrne, January 4, 1956. AASF.

67. *Ibid.*

68. Archbishop Byrne to Brother Mathias, December 17, 1955. AASF.

69. Brother Mathias to Archbishop Byrne, January 4, 1956. AASF.

70. Louise Waagon Masters to Brother Mathias, February 28, 1956. AASF.

71. Interview with Brother Mathias, September 21, 1984.

72. *Ibid.*

73. *Ibid.*

74. *Ibid.*

75. Daniel Donohue, Jr., to Archbishop Byrne, January 8, 1956. AASF.

76. Brother Mathias to Archbishop Byrne, April 2, 1956. AASF.

77. Brother Mathias to Archbishop Byrne, May 7, 1956. AASF.

78. Archbishop Byrne to Brother Mathias, August 7, 1956. AASF.

79. Brother Mathias to Archbishop Byrne, October 24, 1956. AASF.

80. Brother Mathias to Archbishop Byrne, December 21, 1956. AASF.

81. Archbishop Byrne to Brother Mathias, December 24, 1956. AASF.

82. Brother Mathias to Archbishop Byrne, October 3, 1956. AASF.

83. Brother Mathias to Archbishop Byrne, November 15, 1956. AASF.

84. Brother Mathias to Archbishop Byrne, December 4, 1956. AASF.

85. Brother Mathias to Archbishop Byrne, June 2, 1957, and June 6, 1957. AASF.

86. Brother Mathias to Archbishop Byrne, June 20, 1957. AASF.

87. Brother Mathias to Archbishop Byrne, January 24, 1957. AASF.

88. Brother Mathias to Archbishop Byrne, March 19, 1957. AASF.

89. Archbishop Byrne to Brother Mathias, March 15, 1957. AASF.

90. Brother Mathias to Archbishop Byrne, April 23, 1957. AASF.

91. Archbishop Byrne to Brother Mathias, April 30, 1957. AASF.

92. Brother Mathias to Archbishop Byrne, May 7, 1957. AASF.

93. Archbishop Byrne to Brother Mathias, May 13, 1957. AASF.

94. Brother Mathias to Archbishop Byrne, August 18, 1957, and September 9, 1957. AASF.

95. Archbishop Byrne to Brother Mathias, September 13, 1957. AASF.

96. Brother Mathias to Archbishop Byrne, January 15, 1958. AASF.

97. *Albuquerque Tribune*, May 19, 1958. AASF.

98. Brother Mathias to Archbishop Byrne, May 22, 1958. AASF.

99. Brother Mathias to Archbishop Byrne, July 19, 1958. AASF.

100. Archbishop Byrne to Brother Mathias, July 21, 1958. AASF.
101. Brother Mathias to Archbishop Byrne, August 16, 1958. AASF.
102. Archbishop Byrne to Brother Mathias, August 18, 1958. AASF.
103. Brother Mathias to Archbishop Byrne, September 7, 1958. AASF.
104. Brother Mathias to Archbishop Byrne, December 27, 1958. AASF.
105. Edward Heston to Archbishop Byrne, September 24, 1958. AASF.
106. Brother Mathias to Edward Heston, October 3, 1958. AASF.

Chapter Nine

1. Interview with Brother Mathias, December 17, 1984.
2. "Purpose of the Brother Martin Home," p. 3. ALBGS.
3. *Ibid.*
4. Interview with Brother Kevin Carr, June 17, 1986.
5. *Ibid.*
6. *Ibid.*
7. Interview with Brother Mathias, December 17, 1984.
8. *Ibid.*
9. Interview with Brother Kevin Carr, June 17, 1986.
10. *Ibid.*
11. Letters from Brother Kevin to Brother Mathias, 1955.
12. Brother Kevin to Brother Mathias, November 7, 1955. ALBGS.
13. Brother Kevin to Brother Mathias, November 10, 1955. ALBGS.
14. Brother Kevin to Brother Mathias, February 26, 1956. ALBGS.
15. Brother Kevin to Brother Mathias, February 5, 1956. ALBGS.
16. *Ibid.*
17. Brother Kevin to Brother Mathias, February 8, 1956. ALBGS.
18. William Mitchell, M.D., to Brother Mathias, February 2, 1956. ALBGS.
19. *Ibid.*
20. Interview with Brother Mathias, December 17, 1984.
21. Brother Mathias to William Mitchell, M.D., February 12, 1956. ALBGS.
22. *Ibid.*
23. Bishop Michael J. Ready to Brother Mathias, April 19, 1956. ALBGS.
24. Interview with Brother Mathias, December 17, 1984.
25. *Ibid.*
26. *Ibid.*
27. Brother Camillus Harbinson to Brother Mathias, May 24, 1957. ALBGS.
28. *Ibid.*
29. Brother Kevin to Brother Mathias, March 18, 1956. ALBGS.
30. Brother Camillus to Brother Mathias, June 16, 1958. ALBGS.
31. "St. Martin's Chatter," Vol. 1, No. 1 (October, 1961). ALBGS.
32. Wilbur L. Shull to Brother Laurence, August 28, 1964. ALBGS.
33. *Columbus Dispatch*, October 9, 1973.
34. Interview with Brother Mathias, December 17, 1984.
35. *Ibid.*
36. *Ibid.*

37. *The Shepherd's Call*, Vol. 5, No. 2 (March-April, 1964). ALBGS. The bishop also loaned $100,000 for remodeling and an additional $100,000 came from a federal grant through the Accelerated Public Works Program.
38. Interview with Brother Mathias, December 17, 1984.
39. *Ibid.*
40. *The Shepherd's Call*, August, 1969. ALBGS.
41. Brother Camillus to Brother Mathias, June 5, 1967. ALBGS.
42. *Ibid.*
43. Interview with Brother Mathias, December 17, 1984.
44. *Ibid.*
45. Brother Mathias to Archbishop Byrne, Febuary 11, 1955. ALBGS.
46. Brother Kevin to Brother Mathias, April 24, 1955. ALBGS.
47. Interview with Brother Mathias, December 17, 1984.
48. *Ibid.*
49. Brother Mathias to Archbishop Byrne, April 8, 1955. ALBGS.
50. "Five Year Report." ALBGS.
51. Mayor deLesseps Morrison to Brother John, April 2, 1960, in "Ozanam Inn: A Report of Five Years of Service." ALBGS.
52. Interview with Brother Mathias, May 8, 1986.
53. *Ibid.*
54. *Ibid.*
55. *Ibid.*
56. *Boston Sunday Globe*, April 30, 1961. The article was one in a series on "Mission Opportunities."
57. *Ibid.*
58. *Ibid.*
59. *The Miami Voice*, February 3, 1961.
60. *Ibid.*
61. *The Miami Voice*, August 16, 1963.
62. *The Shepherd's Call*, Vol. 4, No. 5 (September/October, 1963). ALBGS.
63. Brother Mathias to Archbishop Byrne, May 6, 1963. ALBGS.
64. *Catholic Standard and Times*, August 30, 1963.
65. *Ibid.*
66. *The Shepherd's Call*, Vol. 4, No. 5 (September/October, 1963), ALBGS.
67. *The Shepherd's Call*, Philadelphia, Special Edition (1964).
68. *Ibid.*
69. *Philadelphia Daily News*, June 15, 1974.
70. *Philadelphia Inquirer*, November 22, 1974.
71. *Philadelphia Daily News*, November 21, 1979.
72. *Ibid.*
73. *Philadelphia Sunday Bulletin*, August 5, 1973.
74. *Ibid.*
75. *Ibid.*

76. A.L. Huber to Brother Mathias, December 1, 1965. ALBGS.
77. *Ibid.*
78. Brother Mathias to David J. O'Connor, March 13, 1966. ALBGS.
79. *Ibid.*
80. Brother Mathias to Most Reverend Charles Helmsing, July 29, 1966. ALBGS.
81. Interview with Brother Mathias, December 23, 1984.
82. *Ibid.*
83. *Ibid.*
84. Brother Mathias to Archbishop Davis, January 24, 1967. ALBGS.
85. Most Rev. Charles Helmsing to Brother Mathias, February 7, 1967. ALBGS. Mention is made in this letter to Archbishop Davis's approval.
86. *The Shepherd's Call*, April, 1969.
87. "Good Shepherd Manor Guild Membership Roster," 1971-1972. ALBGS.
88. "Rod and Staff," Good Shepherd Manor, Kansas City, Vol. 5, No. 4 (July/August, 1978).

Chapter Ten

1. Interview with Brother Michael Carlyle, June 18, 1985.
2. George Bane to Archbishop Byrne, April 28, 1951. ALBGS.
3. *Ibid.*
4. Interview with Brother Kevin Carr, June 19, 1985.
5. *Ibid.*
6. *Ibid.*
7. Brother Kevin to Brother Mathias, May 13, 1957. ALBGS.
8. *Ibid.*
9. "Tribute to Brother James," pamphlet. ALBGS.
10. *Ibid.*
11. Interview with Brother Camillus, June 17, 1985.
12. *Ibid.*
13. Brother Camillus to Brother Mathias, June 7, 1958. ALBGS.
14. "Brother Mathias Had His 1,000th Customer Last Week." *Time*, Vol. LVIII, No. 2 (July 9, 1951), p. 41. The article included a candid photograph of Brother Mathias standing in the New Mexico sun, wearing an old T-shirt and suspenders.
15. Interview with Brother Mathias, September 21, 1984.
16. *The Shepherd's Call*, April, 1969.
17. Interview with Brother Michael Carlyle, June 17, 1985. Among his song titles are "Bicylculum pro duos" (Bicycle built for two), and "Domus in prater" (Home on the range).
18. "Head Shepherd at Camillus House Was Business Tycoon," *Miami Voice*, February 7, 1975. ALBGS.
19. *Ibid.*
20. Interview with Brother Jerome McCarthy, June 2, 1985.
21. *Ibid.*

22. *Ibid.*
23. *The Shepherd's Call*, Summer, 1954.
24. "Membership Directory," p. 33.
25. *Ibid.*
26. Interview with Brother Mathias not taped.
27. Lillian O'Brien, "Year of the Flame" (unpublished manuscript), 1976. ALBGS.
28. *Ibid.*, pp. 32, 39.
29. Interview with Brother Mathias, September 21, 1984.
30. O'Brien, *op. cit.*, p. 43.
31. "The Brothers of the Good Shepherd," *The Shepherd's Call*, October, 1961, p. 3.
32. Ralph Looney, "Derelicts at the Door," *Catholic Digest*, September, 1962, p. 147.
33. Brother John to Brother Mathias, December 30, 1965. ALBGS.
34. *Ibid.*
35. Brother Mathias to Brother John, January 1, 1967. ALBGS.
36. *Ibid.*
37. Brother Mathias to Brother John, January 1, 1968. ALBGS.
38. Letter to Brother Mathias, December 11, 1967. ALBGS.
39. *Ibid.*
40. Letter to Brother Mathias, November 27, 1967. ALBGS.
41. Brother Mathias to Brother Leonard, June 25, 1967. ALBGS.
42. Brother John to Brother Mathias, March 28, 1967. ALBGS.
43. *Ibid.*
44. *Ibid.*
45. Brother Mathias to Brother John, March 7, 1967. ALBGS.
46. Brother Mathias to Brother Michael, March 6, 1967. ALBGS.
47. Brother Mathias to Brother Damian, May 15, 1968. ALBGS.
48. *Ibid.*
49. Brother Mathias to Brother Joseph, January 29, 1967. ALBGS.
50. Brother Mathias to "My Dear Little Brother," July 14, 1968. ALBGS.
51. *Ibid.*
52. *Ibid.*
53. Brother Mathias to Brother Joseph, October 8, 1968. ALBGS.
54. *Ibid.*
55. Brother Mathias to Brother Paul, June 11, 1968. ALBGS.
56. *Ibid.*
57. Brother Mathias to Brother Damian, July 11, 1968. ALBGS.
58. *The Shepherd's Call*, August, 1969. The award included a grant of $250.
59. Thomas A. Horken, Jr., to brother Mathias, July 12, 1968. ALBGS.
60. Joseph M. Fitzgerald to the president of the United States, July 23, 1968. ALBGS.
61. Interview with Brother Mathias, September 15, 1985.
62. Ron Kovic, *Born on the Fourth of July* (New York: McGraw-Hill, 1976), p. 146.

63. *Ibid.*
64. *The Shepherd's Call*, September, 1969.
65. *The Shepherd's Call*, August, 1969.
66. Brother Joseph Dooley to Brother Mathias, November 18, 1969. ALBGS.
67. Report on Discussion and Recommendations, November 19, 1969, ALBGS.
68. Brother Joseph Dooley to All Brothers in Wilmington, Hamilton, Toronto, Philadelphia, and Montreal, November 23, 1969. ALBGS.
69. Questionnaire, March 23, 1970, from the Eastern Regional Centre to All Brothers in the Eastern Region. Among some of the responses were the following: (1) Fifteen out of twenty-two Brothers meditated daily for ten to thirty minutes. (2) In answer to the question "Do you ever use our manual of prayers?" four said yes and seventeen said no. (3) "Poverty" was described as "using gifts wisely" and as "simplicity" and "sharing," as well as the more traditional understanding of "giving up" and "owning nothing." (4) "Chastity" was described as "personal integrity" and "restraint," as well as the more traditional "celibacy." (5) "Obedience" was understood by the Brothers answering the questionnaire as a precept to "accept direction" and to "accept God's will through lawful authority."
70. Memo to All Regional Directors from Brother Mathias, February 11, 1970. ALBGS.
71. *Ibid.*

Chapter Eleven

1. Brother Michael W. Carlyle, "Soldiers of Charity: The Life Story of the Little Brothers of the Good Shepherd" (unpublished manuscript), p. 11. ALBGS. This history covers the period of the foundation of the community in 1951-1952.
2. *Ibid.*
3. *Ibid.*, p. 12.
4. *The Shepherd's Call*, September/October, 1963, p. 2. ALBGS.
5. *Ibid.*
6. Sisters of St. Dominic, Congregation of the Most Holy Rosary, *The Rule of St. Augustine* (Adrian, Mich.: 1973), p.1, privately printed. (Author's note: I have changed the gender of the pronouns to accord with conventional use by an order of Brothers.)
7. *Ibid.*, p. 6.
8. *Ibid.*, p. 16.
9. *Ibid.*, p. 38.
10. *Ibid.*, p. 42.
11. The Hospitaller Order of St. John of God appointed a study commission to research the vow of hospitality. The report ran to thirty-five pages and is titled "Characteristics of Hospitality." It contains a history of the subject in the early Christian community, in monastic communities,

and in the order itself. Sources of doctrine are covered, as are offenses against the vow. The Brothers of St. John of God are required by the vow to "promise to follow the Good Samaritan who tenderly healed the wounds of suffering humanity doing good wherever he passed" (p. 11). However, the Brother is not obliged by the vow to tend to the spiritual welfare of the sick, only to their temporal, corporal welfare, with the exception of women and those with a contagious disease, unless the person afflicted is another Brother (p. 22). There are five degrees of hospitality, depending on the difficulty of the patient's temperament, the repugnance of the disease, and the degree of sacrifice demanded of the Brother (pp. 27-28). The report has no date. ALBGS.

12. "Suggested Outline of Constitutions of the Little Brothers of the Good Shepherd," 1951, p. 4. ALBGS.
13. *Ibid.*, p. 16.
14. "Rule of the Novitiate," Good Shepherd Novitiate, June 27, 1961. Mimeographed booklet. ALBGS.
15. *Ibid.*
16. *Ibid.*
17. Archbishop Edwin Byrne to Brother Mathias, March 3, 1961. ALBGS. The letter appears in the bound copy of the society's constitutions.
18. *Constitutions of the Secular Institute of the Little Brothers of the Good Shepherd* (Patterson, N.J.: St. Anthony Guild Press, n.d.), p. 4. ALBGS.
19. *Ibid.*, pp. 6-7.
20. *Ibid.*
21. *Ibid.*, p. 14.
22. *Ibid.*, p. 19.
23. *Ibid.*, p. 26.
24. *Ibid.*, p. 27.
25. *Ibid.*, p. 35.
26. *Ibid.*, pp. 64-65.
27. James P. Davis, archbishop of Santa Fe, to Brother Mathias, October 14, 1966. ALBGS. The letter appears at the front of the constitutions of the society.
28. *Ibid.*
29. Brother Mathias to Brothers, December 27, 1960. ALBGS.
30. Brother Mathias to Brothers, October 24, 1961. ALBGS.
31. *Ibid.*
32. Brother Mathias to Brothers, April 16, 1962. ALBGS.
33. Brother Mathias to Brothers, July 1, 1962. ALBGS.
34. *Ibid.*
35. *Ibid.*
36. Brother Mathias to Brothers, September 24, 1962. ALBGS.
37. *Ibid.*
38. *Ibid.*
39. Brother Mathias to Brothers, February 20, 1963. ALGBS.

40. *Ibid.*
41. Brother Mathias to Brothers, June 28, 1963. ALBGS.
42. *Ibid.*
43. *Ibid.*
44. Brother Benignus Callan, "The Life of Outstanding Hospitaller Brothers of St. John of God," p. 186. ALBGS.
45. Brother Mathias to Brothers, July 21, 1964. ALBGS.
46. Brother Mathias to Brothers, October 26, 1965. ALBGS.
47. *Ibid.*
48. *Ibid.*
49. Brother Mathias to Brothers, October 24, 1965. ALBGS.
50. Brother Mathias to Brothers, July 21, 1966. ALBGS.
51. *Ibid.*
52. Brother Mathias to Brothers, March 14, 1967. ALBGS.
53. Brother Mathias to Brothers, September 8, 1967. ALBGS.
54. *Ibid.*
55. Brother Mathias to Brothers, September 19, 1967. ALBGS.
56. Brother Mathias to Brothers, May 5, 1968. ALBGS. All the various houses of the community were asked to contribute to the expenses of the novitiate and the motherhouse. Unless there was an extraordinary expense, the amount requested was $100 per month per Brother. That this amount was not always forthcoming is suggested by Brother Mathias's reminders of the obligation.
57. *Ibid.*
58. Brother Mathias to Brothers, January 19, 1969. ALBGS.

Chapter Twelve

1. Archbishop Byrne to Brother Mathias, January 21, 1960. AASF.
2. D.A. Warme to Brother Mathias, February 23, 1960. AASF.
3. Brother Mathias to D.A. Warme, March 1, 1960. AASF.
4. Archbishop Byrne to Brother Mathias, April 25, 1960. ALBGS.
5. Brother Mathias to Archbishop Byrne, May 21, 1960. ALBGS.
6. Archbishop Byrne to Brother Mathias, February 14, 1961. ALBGS.
7. *The Shepherd's Call*, Tenth Anniversary Edition, January, 1961. ALBGS.
8. *Ibid.*
9. Brother Mathias to Archbishop Byrne, October 27, 1961. ALBGS.
10. Archbishop Byrne to Brother Mathias, October 19, 1961. ALBGS.
11. Brother Mathias to Archbishop Byrne, January 28, 1962. AASF.
12. Brother Mathias to Archbishop Byrne, August 16, 1962. AASF.
13. Daniel Donohue to Archbishop Byrne, August 20, 1962. AASF.
14. Brother Mathias to Archbishop Davis, December 18, 1965. AASF.
15. *Ibid.*
16. Interview with Brother Mathias not taped.
17. *The Shepherd's Call*, January/February, 1963. ALBGS.
18. *Ibid.*

19. *Ibid.*
20. "The Story of the Good Shepherd Refuge — Toronto," n.d. ALBGS.
21. Brother Mathias to Archbishop Byrne, June 20, 1963. ALBGS.
22. *Ibid.*
23. *The Shepherd's Call*, July/August, 1963. ALBGS.
24. *Ibid.*
25. Brother Mathias to Archbishop Davis, March 20, 1964. AASF.
26. Rev. Lucien C. Hendren to Brother Mathias, March 23, 1964. AASF.
27. Brother Mathias to Archbishop Davis, May 13, 1964. AASF.
28. Archbishop Davis to Brother Mathias, May 11, 1964. ALBGS.
29. Interview with Brother Mathias, June 14, 1986.
30. Brother Mathias to Archbishop Davis, June 8, 1964. AASF.
31. *Albuquerque Journal*, January 30, 1965.
32. *Ibid.*
33. Brother Mathias to Archbishop Davis, June 19, 1965. AASF.
34. Brother Mathias to Daniel Donohue, April 17, 1966. AASF.
35. Brother Mathias to Nigel Hey, April 8, 1966. AASF.
36. Daniel Donohue to Brother Mathias, April 13, 1966. AASF.
37. *Albuquerque Journal*, April 18, 1966.
38. *The Shepherd's Call*, March/April, 1966. ALBGS.
39. Archbishop Davis to Brother Mathias, February 23, 1966. ALBGS.
40. Brother Mathias to Archbishop Davis, February 25, 1966. ALBGS.
41. *Ibid.*
42. Interview with Brother Mathias, June 14, 1986.
43. Brother Mathias to Archbishop Byrne, May 31, 1966. AASF.
44. *The Shepherd's Call*, Summer, 1966. ALBGS.
45. Daniel Donohue to Brother Mathias, August 18, 1966. ALBGS.
46. Monsignor Francis O'Byrne to Brother Mathias, October 14, 1966. ALBGS.
47. Archbishop Davis to Brother Mathias, November 3, 1966. ALBGS.
48. *Albuquerque Journal*, January 14, 1967.
49. Brother Mathias to Cardinal Cushing, February 21, 1967. ALBGS.
50. Brother Mathias to Senator Joseph Montoya, July 8, 1967. ALBGS.
51. Brother Mathias to Helen Raveling, November 13, 1967. ALBGS.
52. Brother Mathias to Mother Mary Luke Tobin, November 15, 1967. ALBGS.
53. Brother Mathias to Judge James Maloney, November 26, 1967. ALBGS.
54. Brother Mathias to Archbishop Davis, November 26, 1967. ALBGS.
55. Brother Mathias to Senator Joseph Montoya, January 16, 1968. ALBGS.
56. Interview with Brother Mathias, June 14, 1986.
57. Brother Mathias to Archbishop Davis, January 26, 1968. AASF.
58. Brother Mathias to Brother Paul, April 6, 1968. ALBGS.
59. Brother Mathias to Brother Isadore, April 6, 1968. ALBGS.
60. Hilda Raveling to Brother Mathias, June 17, 1968. ALBGS.
61. *The Shepherd's Call*, April, 1969. ALBGS.
62. *The Shepherd's Call*, Autumn, 1973. ALBGS.
63. Brother Mathias to Richard Krannawitter, October 23, 1967. ALBGS.

64. *Ibid.*
65. Archbishop Davis to Brother Mathias, May 17, 1968. AASF.
66. Archbishop Davis to Brother Mathias, February 8, 1968. AASF.
67. Brother Mathias to Archbishop Davis, June 7, 1968. ALBGS. The Brothers appointed were: Francis Abraham, Kevin Carr, Camillus Harbinson, Lawrence Dillmuth, Joseph Dooley, and Vincent de Paul Woodhouse.
68. Brother Mathias to Brother Kevin, April 2, 1968. ALBGS.
69. Richard Krannawitter to Brother Mathias, April 4, 1968. ALBGS.
70. Brother Mathias to Archbishop Davis, April 5, 1968. ALBGS.
71. Archbishop Davis to Brother Mathias, April 10, 1968. ALBGS.
72. Brother Mathias to Archbishop Davis, April 3, 1968. ALBGS.
73. Brother Mathias to Daniel Donohue, May 13, 1968. ALBGS.
74. Brother Mathias to All Brothers, June 24, 1968. ALBGS.
75. *Ibid.*
76. Brother Mathias to Archbishop Davis, July 2, 1968. AASF.

Chapter Thirteen

1. Robert Coles, *A Spectacle Unto the World, the Catholic Worker Movement*, (New York: Viking Press, 1973), p. 14.
2. *Ibid.*, p. 35.
3. William D. Miller, *A Harsh and Dreadful Love: Dorothy Day and the Catholic Worker Movement* (New York: Liveright Publishing Corp., 1973). p. 23.
4. Interview with Judge Thomas Mescall, May 2, 1986.
5. Gerald Suttles, *The Social Order of the Slum: Ethnicity and Territory in the Inner City* (Chicago: University of Chicago Press, 1968), p. 5.
6. Donald J. Bogue, *Skid Row in American Cities* (Chicago: University of Chicago Press, 1963), p. 106.
7. *Ibid.*, p. 111.
8. *Ibid.*, p. 169.
9. Interview with Brother Mathias, February 24, 1985.
10. *Ibid.*
11. Brother Mathias to All Brothers, January 4, 1970. ALBGS.
12. *Ibid.*
13. Brother Mathias to Archbishop Davis, January 4, 1970. AASF.
14. Brother Mathias to Archbishop Davis, January 13, 1971. AASF.
15. *Catholic News Register*, January 15, 1971.
16. *Albuquerque Journal*, January 20, 1971.
17. Brother Justin to Brother Mathias, January 20, 1971. ALBGS.
18. Brother Mathias to Archbishop Davis, February 7, 1971. AASF.
19. Brother Mathias to Archbishop Davis, March 7, 1971. AASF.
20. Archbishop Davis to Brother Mathias, March 9, 1971. AASF.
21. Archbishop Davis to Monsignor Ralph Kuehner, March 30, 1971. AASF.
22. Archbishop Davis to Brother Mathias, March 30, 1971. AASF.

23. Brother Mathias to All Brothers, April 15, 1971. ALBGS.
24. Brother Mathias to Archbishop Davis, April 18, 1971. AASF.
25. *Ibid.*
26. Brother Camillus to Brother Joseph, April 23, 1971. AASF.
27. Brother Mathias to Rev. David Temple, May, 1971. AASF.
28. Archbishop Davis to Rev. David Temple, May 24, 1971. AASF.
29. Archbishop Davis to Monsignor Ralph Kuehner, May 17, 1971. AASF.
30. Brothers Aloysius and Eugene Francis to Archbishop Davis, May 30, 1971. AASF.
31. Brother Joseph to Brother Mathias, June 6, 1971. AASF.
32. Brother Mathias to Brother Joseph, June 15, 1971. AASF.
33. Sam Hartnett *et. al.* to Archbishop Davis, July 2, 1971. AASF.
34. Archbishop Davis to Brother Mathias, July 6, 1971. AASF.
35. Archbishop Davis to Brother Mathias, Brother Jerome, and board of directors of Good Shepherd Manor, July 12, 1971. AASF.
36. *Ibid.*
37. Archbishop Davis to Brother Mathias, July 12, 1971. AASF.
38. Interview with Brother Jerome, June 11, 1986.
39. Archbishop Davis to Sam Hartnett, August 16, 1971. AASF.
40. Archbishop Davis to Rev. David Temple, August 16, 1971. AASF.
41. Brother Vincent de Paul to All Brothers, August 18, 1971. AASF. Emphasis his.
42. *Ibid.*
43. Archbishop Davis to Rev. David Temple, September 1, 1971. AASF.
44. *Ibid.*
45. Archbishop Davis to Arthur J. O'Neill, bishop of Rockford, September 7, 1971. AASF.
46. Richard Krannawitter to Archbishop Davis, n.d. AASF.
47. *Ibid.*
48. Brother Mathias to Rev. David Temple, October 14, 1971. AASF.
49. Archbishop Davis to Rev. David Temple, December 9, 1971. AASF.
50. Brother Mathias to to All Brothers, July 7, 1972. AASF.
51. *Ibid.*
52. Brother Mathias to Archbishop Davis, August 21, 1972. AASF.
53. Brother Mathias to Archbishop Davis, October 8, 1972. AASF.
54. Interview with former Brother Thomas Driber, June 14, 1986.
55. Brother Mathias to Archbishop Davis, December 19, 1972. AASF.
56. Brother Mathias to Archbishop Davis, January 21, 1973. AASF.
57. Brother Mathias to Archbishop Davis, October 21, 1973. AASF.
58. *The Shepherd's Call*, Winter, 1973.
59. *Ibid.*
60. "The Episcopal Ordination and Installation of Robert Fortune Sanchez as Tenth Archbishop of Santa Fe, July 25, 1974." AASF.
61. Brother Mathias to Archbishop Robert Sanchez, December 4, 1974, AASF.
62. *Our Sunday Visitor*, January 20, 1974.

63. *The Shepherd's Call*, Memorial Edition, 1974.
64. *The Shepherd's Call*, Spring, 1974.
65. Brother Mathias to Archbishop Robert Sanchez, July 6, 1975. AASF.
66. Archbishop Sanchez to Bishop Floyd L. Begin, June 4, 1975 (draft). AASF.
67. Archbishop Sanchez to Brother Mathias, November 7, 1975. AASF.
68. Interview with Brother Mathias, June 14, 1986.

Chapter Fourteen

1. Archbishop Sanchez to ladies' auxiliary, January 17, 1976. AASF.
2. "25 Years of Devoted Services to the Poor and Afflicted," pamphlet. ALBGS.
3. *Ibid.*
4. *Ibid.*
5. *Ibid.*
6. Interview with Celina Raff, July 21, 1986.
7. *Albuquerque Tribune*, March 28, 1962.
8. *The Shepherd's Call*, March/April, 1962.
9. The first figure is for 1962, the second for 1968. Summary statements for all years. ALBGS.
10. Interview with Noel Martin, June 25, 1986.
11. *Albuquerque Journal*, March 11, 1982.
12. *Albuquerque Journal*, March 14, 1983.
13. Interview with Brother Mathias, June 14, 1986.
14. *Ibid.*
15. *Ibid.*
16. *Ibid.*
17. Interview with Brother Camillus, June 17, 1985.
18. Interview with Daniel Donohue, March 26, 1986.
19. Brother Camillus to the author, July 1, 1986. ALBGS.
20. Noel Martin, "Brother Mathias: a True Servant," *National Hibernian Digest*, September/October, 1983.
21. *The Shepherd's Call*, July, 1980.
22. *The Shepherd's Call*, Summer, 1981.
23. Interview with Thomas Mescall, May 1, 1986.
24. *Ibid.*
25. *Ibid.*
26. Expense statement, "August 16, 1983." ALBGS.
27. *Ibid.*
28. Brother Mathias to J.H. Hottenroth, November 25, 1983. AASF.
29. *Ibid.*
30. *Ibid.*
31. Brother Camillus to Archbishop Sanchez, November 28, 1983. AASF.
32. Brother Mathias to Archbishop Sanchez, May 31, 1984. AASF.
33. Interview with Brother Mathias, June 14, 1986.

34. *Albuquerque Journal*, March 5, 1984.
35. *Albuquerque Journal*, December 21, 1982.
36. "Meeting of Archbishop Sanchez with Local Directors, Brothers of the Good Shepherd," October 3, 1984. AASF.
37. *Ibid.*
38. Interview with Noel Martin, June 25, 1986.
39. *Belfast Morning Star*, January 19, 1984.
40. *Kilkenny People*, January 20, 1984.
41. *Ibid.*
42. Program of Award, in possession of Brother Thomas Byrne.
43. Tape of ceremony. ALBGS.
44. *Ibid.*
45. *Ibid.*
46. *Ibid.*
47. Interview with Noel Martin, June 25, 1986.
48. *Albuquerque Journal*, March 15, 1984.
49. Patricia O'Connell, "Brother Mathias," *Albuquerque Living Magazine*, Vol. 2., No. 12 (December, 1984), p. 46.
50. 37th Legislature, First Session Memorial, n.d.
51. Pam Bauer, "The Irish Brother Who Turns No One Away," *Our Sunday Visitor*, Vol. 74, No. 7 (June 16, 1985), p. 10ff.
52. Interview with Brother Jerome, June 18, 1986.
53. Interview with Archbishop Robert Sanchez, July 18, 1986.
54. Tape of ceremony. ALBGS.
55. *Ibid.*
56. *Ibid.*
57. *Ibid.*
58. Interview with Don and Barbara Brennan, July 25, 1986.
59. *Albuquerque Journal*, August 5, 1985.
60. Interview with Don and Barbara Brennan, July 25, 1986.
61. Program for St. Patrick's Day dinner, March 17, 1986.
62. Interview with Brother Mathias, September 21, 1985.
63. Interview with Brother Mathias, June 14, 1986.
64. Author's notes.
65. *Ibid.*
66. *Ibid.*
67. *Ibid.*
68. *Ibid.*
69. Interview with Noel Martin, June 25, 1986.
70. Joanmarie McLaughlin Wermes, "Mathias: 'I'm Tired Now and Want to get on Home to Heaven,'" *Irish American News*, Vol. 10, No. 3 (May, 1986).
71. Interview with Eurath Lucas, July 28, 1986.
72. Interview with Virginia Reva, July 29, 1986.
73. Interview with Frances Hardwick, July 30, 1986.
74. Interview with Noel Martin, June 25, 1986.